Professional Wrestling

by Bryan Alvarez
Award-winning author and professional wrestler

Gene Selassie
Award-winning comics writer, sports journalist, and novelist

for dummies®
A Wiley Brand

Professional Wrestling For Dummies®

Published by: **John Wiley & Sons, Inc.,** 111 River Street, Hoboken, NJ 07030-5774, www.wiley.com

For general information on our other products and services, please contact our Customer Care Department within the U.S. at 877-762-2974, outside the U.S. at 317-572-3993, or fax 317-572-4002. For technical support, please visit https://hub.wiley.com/community/support/dummies.

Wiley publishes in a variety of print and electronic formats and by print-on-demand. Some material included with standard print versions of this book may not be included in e-books or in print-on-demand. If this book refers to media that is not included in the version you purchased, you may download this material at http://booksupport.wiley.com. For more information about Wiley products, visit www.wiley.com.

Library of Congress Control Number is available from the publisher.

ISBN 978-1-394-41730-8 (pbk); ISBN 978-1-394-41731-5 (ebk); ISBN 978-1-394-41732-2 (ebk)
SKY10168079_090926

Contents at a Glance

Table of Contents

Introduction

Wrestling has been around since before history was even written down. From the Ancient Olympics (and before!) to sportsman's clubs in the 19th century and beyond, wrestling has been a fixture in cultures around the world. The last 200 years have brought forth an evolution of professional wrestling, combining entertainment with athleticism. The many styles, numerous platforms, and variety of superstars have made the sport an enduring one that still pulls in millions of viewers to this day — with the authors of this book being two of those viewers.

Co-author Gene Selassie has watched matches from various promotions since he was a child — seeing the British Bulldogs versus the Hart Foundation at Madison Square Garden, the Flair/Steamboat trilogy of matches that made Ron Simmons become the first Black World Championship Wrestling (WCW) World Heavyweight Champion, "The Franchise" Shane Douglas throwing away the old National Wrestling Alliance (NWA) Eastern Championship Wrestling title belt, or Kazuchika Okada and Kenny Omega redefining what makes a main event match.

Co-author Bryan Alvarez's first experience with pro wrestling was a Hulk Hogan poster that his sister hung in her bedroom, which he hated. When his grandmother Francesca moved up from Mexico, she'd sit on the couch in the living room and mutter, "*Lucha . . . lucha!*" His father told him: "She wants to watch wrestling." Although he didn't want to do it because of his hatred of the aforementioned Hulk Hogan poster, 12-year-old Bryan switched on the only wrestling he knew of — World Wrestling Federation (WWF) *Prime Time Wrestling*. It certainly wasn't the *lucha* Francesca was looking for, but she tolerated it, and after a few weeks of also tolerating it, Bryan suddenly realized, "Hey, this is cool." And that's why he ended up writing this book.

About This Book

Bryan and Gene had the unenviable job of trying to take the entire history of professional wrestling and condense it into an easy-to-digest guide. It's even more difficult than it sounds on the surface because, unlike almost any other subject on Earth, pro wrestling liberally mixes fantasy with reality. The history of pro wrestling that you can read in various places on the internet often offers the pro wrestling version of history, meaning often and sometimes wildly inaccurate. We aim to not only to tell the history of this sport from the very beginning, but also to treat pro wrestling with respect by providing the actual history.

What *Professional Wrestling For Dummies* does focus on is the following:

- An introduction to pro wrestling, which includes the terminology, tools, and the talent that have made the business into what it is.
- A look at the earliest days of the sport and how it has evolved over a century and a half.
- An explanation about the major promotions focusing on the most popular period in the history of the business.
- The lowdown on how the sport recovered after burning out after its hottest period (the late 1990s), branching off into different styles of presentation.
- In-depth breakdowns of professional wrestling from various parts of the world, such as Japan, Mexico, and the United Kingdom.
- A glimpse of the prominent figures, from wrestlers to managers, and even promoters.

Because of the size and scope of this project and a finite amount of space, your favorite wrestler's name might never appear. We apologize in advance. We invariably skip names and events for purposes of space, but that certainly doesn't mean those people or those events didn't have a huge impact on professional wrestling.

Foolish Assumptions

Like most *For Dummies* books, we make certain assumptions about you and why you're reading this book:

- You've never seen one minute of professional wrestling and are intrigued about the characters and action; you want to have a primer for who's who.
- You've been a casual fan of professional wrestling for years, occasionally watching big events when you're flipping through the channels (probably at the height of the sport's popularity in the late 1990s), but you don't understand what goes on behind the scenes.
- You have a family member or friend who's a fanatic about professional wrestling and who has been trying to get you to like it for years.
- You're a diehard fan of professional wrestling and want to gain a better understanding of it.

Icons Used in This Book

Throughout this book, icons in the margins highlight certain types of information. Here are the ones we use:

REMEMBER

These icons flag important bits of info that are worth storing away in your brain.

TECHNICAL STUFF

These icons point out bits of a wrestler's background, behind-the-scenes info about wrestling promotions, or important historical info that's interesting, but not essential.

TIP

These icons highlight information that can help you better understand the how and why of pro wrestling.

WARNING

These icons point out places where we discuss the darker side of wrestling — how and where things can go wrong.

Beyond the Book

This book is loaded with details and information about professional wrestling. For even more useful tidbits, go to www.dummies.com and search for "Professional Wrestling For Dummies Cheat Sheet."

If you're a professional wrestling fan and you're looking for everything you could possibly want to know about the sport, check out the following:

- **Podcasts at www.wrestlingobserver.com:** Co-author Bryan Alvarez has produced more than a dozen professional wrestling podcasts per week every week since www.wrestlingobserver.com launched in 2005. Many of the biggest stars in wrestling history that you read about in this book have been interviewed (everyone from John Cena to Ric Flair to Bruno Sammartino!), and all of the podcasts are archived and searchable on the website. You can choose to download more than 16,000 podcasts! You can also subscribe to the podcasts by searching "Wrestling Observer" on Apple Podcasts, Spotify, and YouTube!

» ***Wrestling Observer Live* daily on Sports Byline USA radio:** Co-author Bryan Alvarez and a variety of hosts present *Wrestling Observer Live* on the Sports Byline Broadcasting Network every day at 3 p.m. ET, free on Sports Byline terrestrial radio affiliates, YouTube, and Twitch (just search "Wrestling Observer Live"). No matter where you are in the world, you can listen to an hour of pro wrestling talk every day of the week — for free!

» **The "Wrestling Observer Newsletter" at `www.wrestlingobserver.com`:** The weekly bible of professional wrestling, Dave Meltzer's "Wrestling Observer Newsletter" comes out every week and features 40,000 words on everything that happened in the business over the past seven days: all the insider news, history pieces and more. Plus, website subscribers get access to every issue of the "Wrestling Observer Newsletter" written since 1991 (prior to that, Dave typed the issues by hand on a typewriter!), all available and searchable instantly!

» **Books:** Co-author Bryan Alvarez has written two other books on professional wrestling, *The Death of WCW* and *100 Things WWE Fans Should Know and Do Before They Die,* available at your favorite online retailer and at brick-and-mortar bookstores everywhere!

Where to Go from Here

Like all *For Dummies* books, *Professional Wrestling For Dummies* is modular, meaning you don't need to read the book from front to back cover to understand what we're discussing. If you want to discover the basics about professional wrestling, start at Chapter 1. Or you can look through the Index or the Table of Contents to find a topic that particularly interests you or addresses questions that you're now pondering. Flip to that chapter or section and start reading.

For instance, if you're brand new to the world of professional wrestling, start with Part 1. If you're already a fan, head to Part 3 to find out more about major pro wrestling promotions. If you're interested in international pro wrestling, go to Part 4.

No matter where you start, we're confident that you'll find lots of information about professional wrestling that you didn't know.

1

Getting Started with Professional Wrestling

IN THIS PART . . .

Gain an overview of professional wrestling.

Find out the basics of professional wrestling so that you have a general idea what's going on inside the ring.

Discover the items and elements used in pro wrestling.

IN THIS CHAPTER

» Defining the elements of professional wrestling

» Appreciating the themes that draw a pro wrestling audience

» Seeing the whole array of people behind a pro wrestling event

Chapter 1
The Lowdown on Professional Wrestling

Although humans have wrestled for thousands of years, what you'd recognize as "professional wrestling" began in the early 19th century and evolved into what you see today. Fans around the world can be fanatical about what goes on both inside and outside the ring.

This chapter serves as an entry point to this book and explains what professional wrestling is — what it is, what's real, what's not, who's involved, and more. This chapter also explores why professional wrestling has been and continues to be so popular with its vocal fans all over the world.

Understanding What Professional Wrestling Is at Its Core

Professional wrestling is an athletic theatrical art form. It has existed in the United States for around 200 years and worldwide for at least that long — and for all we know, some form of it has existed as long as human beings have walked the Earth.

Looking at what defines pro wrestling

Professional wrestling has many dimensions to what makes it what it is. The following bullets help paint a picture of the sport:

- **It's not real, but it's not fake.** Someone decides who wins and loses and the wrestlers work together to put on a physical performance. But the wrestling ring isn't a trampoline, the falls are real, and wrestlers sometimes get hurt, and even killed.
- **It's not legitimate competition, although legitimate competition exists.** Pro wrestling has been *worked,* meaning it's not been a legitimate competition of skill, pretty much since the sport's early days. Wrestlers aren't all paid equally, and a more successful wrestler does make more money. Therefore, wrestlers compete in different ways to become bigger stars, whether it be through their physique, their talking ability, their charisma, and so on.
- **It's not choreographed, except when it is.** There's no one way to perform a professional wrestling match. Some wrestlers plan out a match move-for-move, start to finish. Other wrestlers improvise the entire match. Often, a match is a mix of improv and choreography.
- **It's one of the most fascinating art forms to ever have existed on the planet.** Professional wrestling is a pseudo-sport that's also a form of improvisational entertainment. With the death of Roller Derby (an old sport that was very much like professional wrestling with pre-planned winners and losers, although modern-day Roller Derby is legitimate), no other form of sports or entertainment on Earth is exactly like it.

Most chapters in this book look at the history of professional wrestling in the United States, as well as other countries, during different eras. In the 1800s, what historians can confirm suggests that matches were often legitimate. And around the 1920s, they morphed into the purely theatrical professional wrestling known today.

REMEMBER

Although far more legitimate matches happened in the 19th century than in the 20th, for reasons we examine in Chapter 4, the reality is that professional wrestling always had a worked element to it likely from day one. And contrary to popular belief, newspapers in the early 1800s didn't shy away from the fact that many wrestling matches weren't on the level.

Respecting the physical work

Pro wrestling isn't a legitimate athletic contest in the same way that amateur wrestling is. But although pro wrestlers predetermine matches and their results, the physical aspects of the match itself are very real.

TIP

Consider a bodyslam, a very basic pro wrestling move that everyone has heard of. You lift your opponent up and slam them onto their back on the mat. This sounds like taxing physical work:

TIP

- Lifting another human being, turning them upside-down, and then holding them aloft for a moment requires a lot of physical strength and coordination.
- And even if you can bodyslam an unwilling opponent, that effort burns a lot of energy that you need to continue wrestling for another 15 to 20 minutes (on average).

For these reasons, pro wrestlers finesse their bodyslams, working together to make them easier on them both. The slammer and the *slammee* (we made that word up) work together on the lift:

1. **The slammer grabs the slammee.**
2. **The slammee *goes up* (adds to the slammer's momentum so it takes less effort for them to lift the slammee).**

   The slammee jumps a little, pushes off the slammer's body a little, whatever can help make the lift easier. Think of two people working together to do a lift in cheerleading.
3. **The slammee comes down.**

   The fall is real and the impact is real.
4. **The slammee tries to do a *flat back bump*.**

   Like a fall in martial arts, the slammee attempts to spread out the impact of the *bump* (the fall) by landing flat and dispersing their weight over a large area. A good flat back bump, if done properly, shouldn't hurt at all.

   If they don't succeed, they can get injured for real.

WARNING

Injuries, both minor and major, happen on pretty much every show on any given day all over the world. Wrestlers are taught how to fall. And although some wrestlers claim that every *bump* (fall) feels like getting into a minor car wreck, as a former wrestler, co-author Bryan Alvarez can tell you that this claim just isn't true. The vast majority of bumps that a wrestler takes are perfectly comfortable. However, any bump can also go wrong, and the damage caused by a career of bumps takes its toll over the years. Wrestlers have broken their backs and their necks, they have ended up paralyzed, and some have died. Most end up in pain in their later years from the chronic physical stress of a life in professional wrestling.

What's real

Many aspects of professional wrestling are completely real:

REMEMBER

- **Physicality:** The physical aspects of professional wrestling are definitely real, even if the moves and results are predetermined (think of a professional dancer who knows their moves before the show starts — they still have to execute those moves and accept the effects to their body — with the main difference that dancers don't fall on purpose).
- **Tools:** The props for a pro wrestling match — items such as steel chairs, tables, and thumbtacks — are all real (although a few types of tools are *gimmicked* (fake); we talk about all the bits and pieces in Chapter 3).
- **Blood:** More often than not, you see real blood, which the wrestler often draws themselves with a razor blade (see Chapter 3), although very occasionally a wrestler might use a Halloween-style blood capsule.
- **The ring:** Despite what you might have heard, the ring doesn't bounce like a trampoline; it's a very firm (some might saying unforgiving) surface. Check out Chapter 3 for more about what makes up a pro wrestling ring.

Suffice it to say, to call pro wrestling as a whole fake does the art form and the participants a great disservice.

What's fake

You can call pro wrestling fake to the extent that, before the match begins, both wrestlers know who's going to win and how, a decision made by the person in charge of the show. It's not a legitimate contest of abilities. Sometimes a *shoot* occurs (when the staged performance turns into a legitimate competition), which we talk about in Chapter 4 and elsewhere. But those situations happen so infrequently nowadays that you probably won't actually see one happen.

We discuss how wrestlers put matches together in Chapter 2. But the degree of planning varies:

- Completely choreographed from start to finish
- Completely improvised from start to finish
- Half choreographed and half improvised, or any mix of the two

The same variation occurs in those bombastic interviews (called *promos*). Sometimes a writer scripts the whole thing and the wrestler memorizes that script. Sometimes the wrestler gets a live mic and improvises an unplanned soliloquy. Sometimes, the promo is a mix of both scripted points and improvisation.

REMEMBER

When it comes to pro wrestling, both in the ring and out, you don't have a one-size-fits-all pattern or approach. But, in virtually every case, you know that you're watching a performance.

EXAMINING AMATEUR WRESTLING'S CONNECTION TO PRO WRESTLING

Amateur wrestling is a legitimate sport that pits two individuals against each other in a bona fide sporting contest. Schools and colleges all over the world have wrestling programs, and it has been an Olympic sport dating back to the original Olympic Games in Ancient Greece. Realistically, other than running, it's probably the oldest sport on Earth.

In the United States, professional wrestling actually predates amateur wrestling. In fact, if you or a family member happens to be an amateur wrestler, the sport in its modern form dates back to the turn of the century and is the legacy of a man named Frank A. Gotch, who was, in fact, one of the greatest professional wrestlers of all time. (Chapter 4 discusses Gotch and his contributions in greater detail.)

In the past, and to a smaller extent today, some amateur wrestlers looked down on professional wrestling because it was fake. Nowadays, with the inner workings of pro wrestling more out in the open than ever before, many amateur wrestlers respect the hard work, dedication, and physical skills necessary to become a pro wrestler. Some of the biggest stars in pro wrestling history came from the Olympic and National Collegiate Athletic Association (NCAA) ranks of amateur wrestlers, including Kurt Angle (1996 Olympic Gold Medalist, multi-time NCAA Division I All-American), Brock Lesnar (multi-time NCAA All-American), Dan Gable (1972 Olympic Gold Medalist and multi-time NCAA National Champion), Danny Hodge (1956 Olympic Silver Medalist, multi-time NCAA Champion, and the man the amateur wrestling Hodge Trophy was named after), Verne Gagne (multi-time NCAA Champion and 1948 Olympic alternate), Jack Brisco (two-time NCAA All-American and a Division I Champion), Bob Backlund (NCAA Division II Champion), and "Mad Dog" Vachon (1948 Olympian).

Figuring Out Pro Wrestling's Popularity

Because pro wrestling is predetermined, the people who put pro wrestling shows together can write stories that make you really like certain wrestlers and really dislike others, and then they can give you a reason to want to see them fight. At its core, that's all it is. And although pro wrestling worldwide always has its ups and downs and its times of great success and times of failure, we can't imagine any period where humans wouldn't be interested in the core concepts behind professional wrestling.

Pro wrestling as a form of entertainment offers the audience just what they want:

TIP

- **Having an escape, and a way to relax and unwind:** Pro wrestling is like most other sports or forms of entertainment. After a hard day of work, you can sit back, watch it, and follow along with what's happening. Pro wrestling fans are just as passionate as any other group of fanatics.
- **Becoming invested:** Because of its predetermined nature, and the fact that it runs before a live audience weekly without any sort of off-season, the people in charge can control wins and losses, and storylines, to better satisfy their audience. Sure, your favorite wrestler can't always win every match, but when the time is right, unlike with any other sporting event, the fan favorite can win the championship at a time when it means the most to their fans.
- **Controlling the action:** Because wrestling airs weekly to a live audience, in some ways the fans can dictate the course of action, unlike with sports, film, or other entertainment choices. On many occasions, pro wrestlers whom the promoters at first didn't push hard to stardom ended up becoming gigantic superstars because the audience demanded it.

  World Wrestling Entertainment (WWE) head Vince McMahon considered Daniel Bryan, one of the most talented wrestlers of the 2000s, too small and "plain-looking" (he was called "Goat Face" on TV) to become a tippy-top star. But the fans demanded it and refused to relent, until McMahon finally gave Bryan the big *WrestleMania* main event win that the fans wanted to see.

Getting vicarious thrills and satisfaction

Pro wrestling allows fans to live vicariously through the performers. The audience might see a wrestler as surrogate for their personal situation. Or they may feel that the wrestler represents the best parts of their culture.

Sticking it to the man

The wrestler "Stone Cold" Steve Austin became the biggest pro wrestling star of the 1990s through his feud with Vince McMahon. At its core, the storyline was simple:

- **The regular guy:** Austin, in his jean shorts and T-shirt, portrayed the beer-drinking common man.
- **The slick schemer:** McMahon portrayed, well, himself as the evil owner of the World Wrestling Federation (WWF) and Austin's boss.

TIP

After a hard day's work at a job that perhaps they hated (or maybe they liked the job but hated their boss), fans could turn on the TV and watch, almost on a weekly basis, Austin beating up McMahon, getting some sense of satisfaction by watching him triumph.

It was like a *Looney Tunes* Wile E. Coyote cartoon. Every week, the evil boss McMahon (as Wile E. Coyote) would come up with some diabolical plan to screw Austin; and although some of these plans would succeed briefly, in the end, Austin (the Roadrunner) would overcome the odds and leave the boss lying flat on his back on the mat. Even though it happened virtually every single week, fans couldn't get enough of it, and millions tuned in for years. (Flip to Chapter 6 for more about Austin.)

Taking pride in your country's people

The biggest star in the history of Japanese pro wrestling, Rikidōzan, rose to fame in the aftermath of Japan's defeat in World War II (and the rise of television in that country). Rikidōzan came to represent Japan (which was ironic because he was secretly part Korean, a fact that was hidden from the public at the time). Promoters flew in big, tough American (and sometimes Canadian) wrestlers to lose to him.

REMEMBER

His victories over white wrestlers became such a massive symbolic part of Japanese cultural history that millions and millions of fans bought televisions for the first time in the mid-1950s and early 1960s just to watch his matches. To this day, Japanese and Korean elementary school textbooks relate the story of Rikidōzan.

Appreciating the drama

Ultimately, pro wrestling is popular because of human nature. You can always find an audience when two people are fighting to settle their differences, particularly two people that the observer knows something about.

If you go to a basketball game and a fight breaks out, you stop watching the game to watch the fight. If you're at the movies and two people in front of you get into a disagreement, then one of them hits the other with a box of popcorn and a brawl erupts, you stop watching the movie to watch the brawl. And if you go to a family reunion where a fight breaks out between Gramma Gladys and Uncle Terry, you're going to watch that fight even more intently because of all you know about the relationship between the two.

Recognizing Who's Involved in Professional Wrestling

A lot of different people make up a professional wrestling match. From the competitors in the ring, to the promoters and the announcers, to the behind-the-scenes personnel, a lot of moving parts work together. These sections walk you through some of them.

Considering the competitors

Professional wrestlers are the heart and soul of professional wrestling. They're the "competitors" who square off to determine who's the best. They represent humanity in all its facets — big, small, male, female, and everything in between, from cultures all over the world. You can read about different wrestlers in every chapter of this book.

Refereeing the matches

The referee is the hidden participant in the match (or at least, they're supposed to be; you should never notice a great referee). In storyline, they officiate the action and enforce the rules. In real life, they communicate with backstage during the matches, they relay information from one wrestler to another, and they often even work to put the ring together and take it down after the show. We discuss them more in Chapter 3.

Hearing the announcers

Announcers, who often broadcast the event on TV or radio, are the voice of the action. And some of them have become bona-fide legends to fans who grew up listening to and watching them over the decades. Chapter 12 discusses what makes a great announcer and identifies some of the greatest announcers of all time.

WHAT ABOUT WARDROBE AND MAKEUP?

Only the biggest professional wrestling organizations employ full-time makeup and wardrobe specialists. For the most part, wrestlers do their own makeup, and they either make themselves or have someone else make their ring gear and costumes. Much of what a wrestler needs, from trunks and tights to boots, can be ordered from companies on the internet.

Ring announcers are different; they're the people who introduce the wrestlers to the crowd before the matches begin. Chapter 12 looks at them in greater detail.

Focusing on managers

Pro wrestling managers are actually on-screen characters who supposedly manage the affairs of their wrestlers. They do everything from create characters to generate *heat* (get the audience angry and create tension in the ring). Refer to Chapter 12 for more information about managers.

IN THIS CHAPTER

» Translating wrestling lingo

» Understanding wrestling storylines

» Seeing how matches get put together

» Getting into the biz

Chapter 2
Tackling the Basics of Professional Wrestling

Professional wrestling is a form of entertainment that's been around for more than 100 years — and potentially has existed in some form for thousands of years. It's essentially theatrical combat, where two or more competitors work together to perform a wrestling match that has a predetermined ending. Fans watch the action unfold either on television or at live events, and the storylines are designed to compel viewers ultimately to pay for the right to watch the big climactic matches. Professional wrestling today is a multibillion-dollar touring entertainment and television/streaming business, and the various wrestling promotions have millions of fans tuning in weekly.

Professional wrestlers are incredible athletes who perform remarkable feats of athleticism, but they don't really compete against each other to determine who's the best grappler. They work together to create grudges designed to sell tickets to fans, who watch so that they can boo and cheer, hoping that their favorite comes out victorious. A person called a *booker* determines the match results, but wrestlers can suffer a physical toll in the performance.

This chapter answers questions related to professional wrestling, including how storylines and matches are put together and who decides who wins or loses, and why.

Mastering Key Jargon Related to Professional Wrestling

Before you can fully understand professional wrestling, you need to be able to recognize some important terms used in the business. Because pro wrestling is unlike any other form of sport or entertainment, you can't fully understand it without first examining some of its exclusive terminology.

REMEMBER

Some professional wrestling promoters and wrestlers worked very hard to preserve authenticity through probably the late 1990s, hoping to leave doubt in the minds of fans and allowing those fans to suspend disbelief when watching. In other words, those promoters and wrestlers believed that their audiences thought professional wrestling was real, thinking that even if fans strongly doubted its authenticity, they didn't know 100 percent for sure. In reality though, most fans over the age of 12 knew professional wrestling was predetermined dating back to the 1800s.

Speaking in a secret language

Professional wrestling promoters and stars went to great lengths to protect the business, including utilizing their own secret language to communicate inside and outside the ring. The language itself, called *carny,* was first used in the touring carnivals of the late 1800s and early 1900s (which often featured wrestling matches as a sideshow act). Carnival workers were often called *carnies,* and many pro wrestling terms you hear nowadays came directly from the carnivals. Essentially, to speak carny, you add a *z* or *iz* before every vowel sound of a word. Here's an example:

- **Carny:** Sizo thizis sizentizence wizould rizead lizike thizis.
- **English:** So this sentence would read like this.

If the wrestlers in the ring communicated to each other in carny about which move they planned next, a fan at ringside who happened to hear them communicating wouldn't have any idea what they were saying. This secret language helped to keep the *worked* (preplanned or scripted) nature of wrestling under wraps before the current generation. Nowadays, professional wrestlers simply whisper (or sometimes scream) *spots* (planned series of moves) in plain English during televised matches.

Understanding kayfabe

The carny language was a part of a larger concept called *kayfabe*, which was the idea of keeping the inner workings of wrestling secret. The word *kayfabe* actually has multiple meanings:

- **Not authentic:** If someone appears to get injured on a wrestling show, you can question whether they suffered a legitimate injury or a kayfabe injury.
- **Keeping quiet:** In the old days, if two wrestlers were talking and a fan walked near, one would say, "Kayfabe" to alert the other to stop talking about any inside workings of the business.
- **Trick someone:** You can use it as a term to indicate a plan to fool the fans in some way or another — "I'm going to kayfabe them."

A *mark* is a derogatory term for anyone that a carny is attempting to fool, utilizing some con to swindle the gullible mark out of their money. You want to knock down the three milk jugs with the baseball? Go for it, mark. They gimmicked one of the milk jugs to make it impossible to knock down. (See the following section for the lowdown on gimmick.)

Getting a gimmick

The term *gimmick* has two meanings:

- Any sort of device that the user rigged so that it doesn't behave as expected. For example
  - A gimmicked coin (yes, magic also uses carny terms) might have two heads.
  - A gimmicked game is rigged to make it almost impossible to win.
  - A gimmicked chair in professional wrestling might have a shaved-down seat so that it wraps around a person's head while also protecting them from a full-on blow.

    REMEMBER

    Using a gimmicked chair is extremely rare in pro wrestling — same with gimmicked tables.
  - Oddly, legitimate weapons in pro wrestling, real brass knuckles, or kendo sticks, are also referred to as gimmicks.
- A wrestler's *persona* (the character they play)

Describing types of wrestlers

Wrestling has particular terms for good guys, bad guys, and so on. Here are the main terms:

- **Heels:** Bad guys who use unfair tactics and gimmicks.
- **Babyfaces:** Good guys who abide by the rules and do what's right.
- **Tweeners:** Wrestlers who fall somewhere between the heels and the babyfaces. Contrary to popular belief, not many real tweeners appear in pro wrestling (see the nearby sidebar for details).
- **Authority figures:** The person who is in charge of the show in storyline and makes decisions about future matches and business. Called variously the *General Manager, Commissioner, Director of Authority,* and so on. Usually just an actor playing a role, although sometimes a real-life owner or boss will play the role on TV as well.

TIP

"Stone Cold" Steve Austin, who often hit his Stone Cold Stunner finishing move on babyfaces after a match, did so as part of his anti-hero gimmick (meaning his persona; see the preceding section). His character always said, "Never trust anybody!", and so anyone, babyface or heel, could fall victim to the Stone Cold Stunner at any time. Fans loved Austin and they loved the Stunner, so they always cheered no matter who he attacked. But he was 100 percent a babyface and his top feuds were always with the big heels. He was a babyface with an edge, a gimmick that fans historically love. Chapter 6 discusses Austin in greater detail.

Explaining action terms

Pro wrestling has specific terms covering the action in the ring:

- **Finisher:** A specific move that a wrestler uses often to win a match. For example, Shawn Michaels used a finisher called the *Superkick,* which was a martial arts side kick. Dwayne "The Rock" Johnson used the *Rock Bottom,* a variation of a judo throw called the *Uranage.*
- **Bump:** Any fall in wrestling. When a wrestler hits you with a finisher, you often take a bump. When you bump, you can fall flat on your back, flat on your face, or on top of your head (a bad idea).

- **Submission:** A grappling hold designed to force your opponent to give up. The only decisive finish in which a wrestler doesn't take a bump.
- **Tapping out:** Striking the mat or your opponent to signal that you give up. Wrestling took this concept from the sport of judo, and it became popularized in the mid-1990s by the Ultimate Fighting Championship (UFC), a legitimate mixed martial arts organization.

Getting a handle on terms of legitimacy

Professional wrestling isn't a legitimate contest of opponents' skills. It's a show. The pro wrestling world has terminology that describes the scripted and unscripted aspects of the sport:

- **Work:** Anything in wrestling that isn't real. A preplanned wrestling match that has a predetermined winner and loser is a *worked match.* A fake injury is a *worked injury.* If something isn't real, it's a *work.*
- **Shoot:** When action (inside or outside the ring) becomes legitimate. UFC bouts are *shoots.* A wrestler can shoot if they go off script in an interview or promo. A real-life injury is a *shoot injury.*

  WARNING

  In real life, shoots in the ring and on the microphone happen incredibly rarely. A preplanned or scripted promo that references real life isn't a shoot, even if it's designed to make fans think it is. Probably 99 percent of famous promos touted as shoots, such as CM Punk's famous pipe bomb promo (which you can read about in Chapter 15), weren't shoots at all.
- **Promo:** The talking done on wrestling shows, either solo or during interview segments. Ideally, the idea behind a promo is, in fact, to promote upcoming matches and storylines, address things that happened in angles, and so on.
- **Angle:** A point in a story where an event occurs that moves it in another direction. Perhaps a babyface attacks their friend during a promo segment and turns heel. Perhaps a heel does something diabolical, and the authority figure gives them a storyline suspension.
- **Enhancement match:** A match in which a superstar beats a low-level wrestler (called a *jobber*) whose job, as it were, mostly involves losing and making the superstars look, well, like superstars. Enhancement matches are usually short, the jobber gets little to no offense in, and the superstar hits all of their big moves and their finisher to win.

Enhancement matches are much rarer today than they were in the 1980s and early 1990s, where they took up the bulk of television programs. During that period, virtually all of the biggest matches took place either on pay-per-view (PPV) television or at live, untelevised events where you had to buy a ticket to see the special matches.

- **Jobber:** A low-level wrestler whose job mostly involves losing to and making a superstar look good.

TECHNICAL STUFF

Prior to the 1990s when television featured mostly enhancement matches, angles happened very rarely, usually only to set up matches on quarterly PPV events. When the World Wrestling Federation (WWF) shot an angle where voodoo master Papa Shango put a curse on the Ultimate Warrior and forced him to barf up green slime and have black goo ooze out of his forehead in 1992 (you don't have to ask — of course this really happened), television stations replayed that angle every single week for six weeks leading up to big blow-off matches at live events. Nowadays, where fans have access to dozens of hours of first-run programming from promotions all over the world, you often see several angles on every television show, many of which never get replayed at all.

Rounding out the wrestling terms

This section gives you a few other terms that we use in this book (but you can find hundreds of others — check out Wikipedia to expand your vocab):

- **Blading:** Also called a *blade job.* When a wrestler makes a very small cut (usually to the forehead, although wrestlers will bleed from anywhere) by using a small piece of a razor blade in order to draw blood, which then mixes with perspiration to look very dramatic.
- **Blood capsule:** A blood capsule is a capsule filled with red powder that you put in your mouth to turn your saliva red, mimicking real blood. Wrestlers don't often use blood capsules — the blood that you see is more often than not real. (And no, nobody ever uses ketchup.)
- **Book/booking:** The storylines told in wrestling events, as well as the act of assigning wrestlers to storylines.
- **Booker:** Traditionally, the person who creates all the storylines for a promotion. The owner of a promotion may be the booker, or they may hire someone else as the booker. In many places even today on the independent scene, the booker just happens to also be the perennial champion!

- **Botch:** When someone screws up something in a match, such as a spot, a finish, or a line in a promo. *Botch* actually isn't an insider wrestling term, but rather a term used by fans. The insider term involves the F-word, so for the purposes of this book, we shall use *botch.*
- **Finish:** The end of a match.
- **Finisher:** A wrestler's move that they use to win most of their matches, such as Hulk Hogan's *Legdrop of Doom* (which was as it sounds, he jumped in the air and dropped his leg on his opponent's face). For reasons unknown, wrestlers always refer to their finishers as *patented* or *trademarked,* as if the wrestlers filed applications on professional wrestling moves with the U.S. Patent and Trademark Office.

  TECHNICAL STUFF

  On the other hand, either the promotions or the wrestlers themselves almost always actually do trademark their ring names.
- **Hardway:** When a wrestler bleeds because of an accidental cut, and not through the usage of a blade or blood capsule.
- **Heat:** This term has several meanings in the wrestling world:
  - A negative reaction from the crowd to something that's happening in the show. It can take the form of loud booing or even throwing objects at the ring.
  - The portion of the match where the heel is beating down the babyface.
  - A genuine dislike between two wrestlers.
- **House show:** A non-televised wrestling show, played for just the audience at that venue (or *house*) that night. Angles and title changes almost never happen at house shows, although occasionally something noteworthy occurs to convince fans that if a house show comes to their town, they should attend because something big might happen there, as well.
- **Light:** Conducting a wrestling performance to make it look as realistic as possible while only softly touching your opponent, or very smoothly working together to do a spot as safely as possible.
- **Pop:** An intense positive reaction from the crowd, such as loud cheering.
- **Push:** When the booker or promoter decides to move a wrestler into a higher-profile role, usually by providing them with a series of victories.
- **Rib:** A practical joke. (Also, a bone in your body.)
- **Schmozz:** An unsatisfying finish usually featuring multiple people getting involved and no decisive conclusion. A schmozz usually results in a disqualification or no-contest (no winner) ruling.

- **Screwjob:** This word has a dual meaning:
  - A *worked* (preplanned) unfair finish. Screwjobs happen all the time in worked professional wrestling matches, usually multiple times per show.
  - A talent legitimately being double-crossed. Once or twice in a lifetime a real-life legitimate screwjob occurs, such as the 1997 Montreal Screwjob that involved wrestler Bret Hart, which we discuss in Chapter 6.

WARNING

- **Selling:** The reaction or body language that tells the story of what just happened in a match. If you punch me, I can sell it by falling down or grabbing my face in pain. If I hit you with a move but you pop right back up unfazed, I can sell my shock through body language that conveys my astonishment and fear.

  You can also *no-sell,* meaning you don't react at all, or *oversell* by overreacting to the interaction (for example, if you touch me with one finger and I respond by doing a full flip, falling out of the ring, and then running headfirst into the ring post).

REMEMBER

- **Spot:** Short for *highspot.* Traditionally, a series of maneuvers in sequence designed to garner a crowd reaction. Can sometimes just refer to a single move, reversal, and so on. Nowadays, people often use the full term *highspot* to describe a more spectacular-looking singular maneuver, such as a *450 splash* (which is a flip off the top where you land on your opponent — it's not really a 450-degree flip because that would deposit the wrestler on their head).
- **Squash:** When one wrestler completely destroys another in a match, and the loser doesn't get to put up any sort of offense. Jobbers (whom we talk about in the preceding section) are usually squashed by a star.
- **Stiff:** This term has two meanings in the wrestling world:
  - Grabbing, holding, or hitting too hard in the course of a wrestling performance.
  - A comment that strikes a little too close to the truth or makes the other wrestler uncomfortable.
- **Snug:** In between light and stiff. Most wrestlers today work snug.
- **Swerve:** When an angle goes a direction that the audience didn't expect. Often, swerves make no sense, and bookers do them to surprise the audience with something completely out of left field. The best swerves are unexpected but actually make sense in the overall story.
- **Turn:** To go from babyface to heel or vice versa.

Examining the Different Storylines

The fact that professional wrestling isn't legitimate has never really been much of a secret. Newspapers dating all the way back to the earliest days of the sport in the United States — the early 1800s — openly discussed wrestling matches being fixed. Of course, even up until today, some fans (usually kids 12 and younger) still believe pro wrestling is legitimate, but the general adult public has known it isn't legit (or at the very least deeply suspected it wasn't) since Day One. Even in the early 1970s, at best some fans believed the main event World Title matches were likely real, but all the other matches on the card were fake.

TIP

Storylines are what allows pro wrestling to capture the imagination of fans week in and week out. Pro wrestling has no off-season; it runs year-round. The biggest promotions in the world, World Wrestling Entertainment (WWE) and All Elite Wrestling (AEW), both run multiple televised shows every week, plus monthly PPV or *Premium Live Event* (PLE) specials. All in, in the United States alone, between WWE, AEW, and *Total Nonstop Action* (TNA), more than 70 hours of first-run programming is broadcast every month, the majority of which is live. (Check out Chapter 8 for details.)

Investing in people

If you put two random people in a pro wrestling match, you can't hold an audience's attention past the first week or two. They don't feel invested in the fight in any way.

Before we go any further, keep in mind that when we discuss 70 hours of first-run wrestling programming every month, each of those programs probably features an average of 6 to 7 matches — so more than 400 matches per month.

Now, if you live in a city where, in an average month, 400 fights break out around you, as long as you don't get personally affected, you probably don't take long to not care one bit about pretty much any of them.

On the other hand, say you run into your two best friends, John and Paul. You grew up with John since you were both 5 years old — you used to bike to each other's houses, you played music together, in high school you made student films together, and he was the best man at your wedding. Paul, you met a few years ago. He used to be 400 pounds, but he started jiu-jitsu with you and lost over 100 pounds. His daughter and your daughters are best friends, and you all swim together every weekend at the pool in his apartment complex. Two great guys.

When you run into them, John and Paul are arguing. John made some political comment that Paul didn't agree with, and things got heated. John told Paul that even though he lost 100 pounds he was still fat. Paul told John that he lost more weight than John could bench with two spotters. John eventually got so mad that he hit Paul with a dead Alaskan wild salmon, at which point, Paul took John down with a *double-leg* (an amateur wrestling takedown) right there on the cement and was fixing to snap his skinny arm.

No matter how numb you feel when you see 400 fights around town over the course of the last month, you care a lot about Paul beating the stuff out of John. Why? Because you know them. You know their stories and their personalities. You feel some way about them, either positive or negative. And you understand why each guy was upset with the other and what they each said and did to cause this fight to break out.

In other words, you understood the story of this fight.

Creating compelling characters

Pro wrestling as a business focuses on creating characters that fans can relate to and then creating reasons for those characters to wrestle each other. The reasons can be simple or complex:

- **The underdog:** WWE wrestlers Sami Zayn and Drew McIntyre have wrestled 12 times, and McIntyre beat Zayn all 12 times. So, Zayn stands as an underdog in their next matchup and wants to win the World Title for the first time in his career.
- **A pet snake:** Jake "The Snake" Roberts had a pet snake that he always carried to the ring in a bag. In one storyline, Earthquake, a gigantic former sumo wrestler, got hold of the bag, put it in the ring, and then did a *running sit-down splash* (when you jump and sit right on your opponent) onto the bag, supposedly killing the snake. Roberts, mourning the loss of his beloved serpent, vowed revenge. (Of course, the snake — Damian — wasn't actually in the bag and wasn't killed.)

  In another storyline, Roberts was feuding with "Macho Man" Randy Savage, and the snake bit Savage's arm after Roberts tied Savage to the ring ropes. Although the bite was part of the storyline, the snake legitimately gnawed on Savage's arm, drawing a good amount of blood. (Snakes don't follow storyline direction very well.)

Crafting the story

Traditionally, one person, the booker, does most of the storytelling, often with some input from the bigger stars. Many promotions today still create their storylines this way. Since the early 2000s, some promotions (most notably, WWE) have a head booker, but also a full writing team that scripts promos, creates formats for the TV show or PPV, and so on.

Generally, to create a storyline, you follow these steps:

1. **Pick an end date for the storyline.**

   Say you choose *WrestleMania.*

2. **Come up with a proposed lineup for all the big matches on the show.**

   Maybe you decide that *WrestleMania's* main event will be Dwayne "The Rock" Johnson versus "Stone Cold" Steve Austin, with Austin dethroning the current champion "The Rock."

3. **Go back and determine who wins and loses in the events leading up to the end date.**

   For "The Rock" versus Austin, you go back to the preceding show that features Austin (*the Royal Rumble*). Austin, of course, wins that match. But you can have a show preceding *the Royal Rumble* in which Triple H beats Austin. Therefore, after Austin wins the title from "The Rock," he has a built-in challenger waiting in line, Triple H.

WARNING

Of course, because pro wrestling runs live every single week, a lot of things can happen. Perhaps Austin legitimately suffers a neck injury at an event and may not be able to do the match at *WrestleMania* after all. Well, all the plans are out the window, and the storytellers have to come up with a new narrative.

Sometimes, a wrestler whom the storyline didn't focus on happens to organically get a big following among the fans, for whatever reason. A good booker can listen to the fans and shift gears, placing more emphasis on this new star. The best bookers have long-term plans, sometimes even years in advance, but can adapt and shift when opportunities arise.

Putting Together Matches

Many fans believe that all pro wrestling matches are "scripted" move-for-move. Some are, some aren't. Wrestlers put their matches together in all sorts of ways. These sections take a closer look at those different ways.

Using a script

Wrestlers script some matches from start to finish. By *script*, we don't mean that someone gets a piece of paper and writes down every move from start to finish — although that does happen sometimes. One of the most famous examples, and also one of the greatest matches of the 1980s, featured "Macho Man" Randy Savage versus Ricky Steamboat in *WrestleMania III:*

- In the months leading up to *WrestleMania,* Savage wrote down the entire match, move for move, and then numbered every move in order.
- Savage gave the script to Steamboat and told him to memorize it.
- In the weeks leading up to the match, Savage quizzed Steamboat. "Fifty-two!" Savage exclaimed. "Arm drag!" Steamboat responded. (Steamboat had a great *arm drag,* which involves whipping the opponent to the mat by their arm.)
- By the time the match took place, both had it memorized from start-to-finish. They hit every move exactly as planned, and fans called it one of the greatest matches in *WrestleMania* history.

Wrestlers choreograph some matches basically from start to finish, particularly:

- TV matches that have a relatively short time limit (which the booker decides as part of *timing out* (meaning determining how long each segment can last) the entire show; typically TV shows last two hours, whereas PPV lasts four to five hours.
- Matches that feature new talent.

Whether a match is completely scripted or not often depends on experience:

- **Practice, practice, practice.** Newer talent in WWE's NXT developmental league usually spend a week or so practicing their match move-for-move at WWE's Performance Center in Florida before performing it at a show.
- **Put it together at the last minute.** More experienced wrestlers can create a match largely move-for-move backstage in the hours before a show, pantomime it between themselves in the locker room, and then perform it before the crowd.

Calling it in the ring

Often basically pre-1990s, wrestlers *called it in the ring,* meaning they went to the ring with little to nothing planned. Perhaps they planned one spot to set up the *heat* (the sequence where the bad guy seems to best the good guy) and a short sequence leading to the *finish* (the end of the match).

TECHNICAL STUFF

On rare occasions, usually involving a veteran wrestler and a green rookie, the wrestlers went to the ring with nothing planned at all. These matches were improvisational performances. The veteran *called the match* (essentially whispering every spot or sequence to the opponent), and the rookie's job was to shut up and listen — and do everything that the veteran told them to do. The veteran decided when to call the finish when they felt the time was right. Wrestlers respected other wrestlers who could go to the ring with nothing planned and call excellent matches on the fly with anyone.

Mixing choreography and improv

Nowadays, even among experienced wrestlers, most matches include a mix of preplanned choreography and a spattering of improvisation. Because wrestlers perform most matches live on TV, they have to strictly adhere to time limits. Therefore, wrestlers usually choreograph the following:

- A *shine* sequence (one that makes the babyface look like the more impressive wrestler early)
- Some *spot* to set up the *heat* (where the heel beats up the babyface)
- Some spot to set up the *comeback* (where the babyface finally fights back)
- A choreographed finishing sequence to end the match

Depending on the experience level of the performers, the rest of the match can feature varying amounts of choreography and improvisation.

Understanding Who Shapes Matches

Wrestlers generally can't just decide, "Hey, I'll slam you through the announcer's table tonight!" They have to clear those decisions with the producer and booker. Obviously, if the main event's wrestlers plan to break a table, you don't want an *undercard* (someone not in the main event) wrestler performing in a preliminary match to break the table first.

Who decides what happens within the matches? The wrestlers, the bookers, or someone else? Here we take a look at the supporting characters.

Working with producers

Major promotions usually have *producers* (formerly called *agents*) who coordinate with the booker (discussed in the following section) about:

- What they want to see in the match
- The story going into and coming out of the match
- Who is going to win and how
- How much time the wrestlers have in the ring

With this information, the producer helps the wrestlers put the match together. How much input they have often depends on the experience level of the wrestlers involved:

REMEMBER

- **Offering guidance:** Sometimes, if an experienced producer is working with rookie wrestlers, they actually help the wrestlers figure out match choreography.
- **Staying more hands-off:** When the match involves experienced wrestlers, the wrestlers largely come up with all the ideas for the match on their own. Sometimes, the producer gives some input, other times they don't.

Turning to bookers

The *booker*, who creates the promotion's storylines, can tell the producer (whom we talk about in the preceding section), and thus the wrestlers, what the wrestlers can do in a match and what they can't. Some bookers are stricter, and there are pros and cons to both strict and lenient bookers:

- **Strict:** Dictate the details of the match, not giving the wrestlers much room to make their own decisions. A strict booker might say, for example, "The main event has blood; therefore, nobody else can bleed in the show."
- **Lenient:** Give the wrestlers more leeway in terms of what they want to do, which wrestlers love. But if every match in the show includes blood and broken tables, after two hours of carnage, fans get numb to it and may not get excited about the main event when it rolls around.

Recognizing the Types of Matches

You can find all types of matches in professional wrestling. You can broadly group those matches into straight and gimmick matches, which we talk about here.

Wrestling in straight matches

Straight matches are almost exclusively *one-fall matches* (meaning once somebody gets a win (a *fall*), it's over).

Ending a match

Here are the basic rules dealing with how a match can end:

- **Pinfall/Pin:** A referee hits the mat three times with their hand after one wrestler puts the other wrestler's shoulders on the mat.
- **Submission:** One wrestler gives up.
- **Disqualification:** The referee ends the match because someone breaks the rules.
- **Countout:** One or more wrestlers go outside the ring for a certain period of time — either a 10-count or 20-count, depending on the promotion.

Playing fair

According to the generally-accepted pro wrestling rules (being a performance art, there are no legitimate rules that must legitimately be followed), wrestlers can't do anything considered unfair, such as:

- Pulling hair
- Biting
- Poking eyes
- Hitting their opponent with a weapon
- Pulling tights
- Striking someone in the groin

REMEMBER

In pro wrestling matches of any sort, referees almost never enforce these fair-play rules.

A WEIRD RULE OF DISQUALIFICATION

WARNING

One pro wrestling rule has evolved over the years so that it makes absolutely zero sense to a rational person. In short, to get disqualified, something has to happen. That may sound like a meaningless statement, but allow us to explain: In a straight wrestling match (which we talk about in the section "Wrestling in straight matches" in this chapter), nobody can interfere with the wrestlers in the match. But for the referee to recognize someone as interfering, that person has to physically assault a player:

- **Allowed to get in the way.** For example, if a manager gets inside the ring, that manager's wrestler isn't disqualified unless the manager then proceeds to hit someone. So, if a heel manager gets in the ring and the babyface wrestler punches them, the manager's wrestler isn't disqualified because the manager didn't hit the babyface (and the babyface can hit the manager because the manager isn't an active participant in the match itself). And if, while hitting the manager, the heel then pins the babyface, the rules consider that fair game.
- **Deadly weapons get a pass.** Say a manager gets in the ring carrying a baseball bat wrapped in barbed wire (a weapon actually used in pro wrestling). Even though a human being not involved in the match has entered the ring wielding what any rational human would consider a deadly weapon, pro wrestling doesn't consider it a disqualification unless the manager hits someone with the deadly weapon.

Imagine watching a football game, and in the middle of the game, one of the coaches races onto the field carrying a machine gun, and the refs decide that the game can continue unless the coach actually starts shooting people. This rule is stupid. But in pro wrestling, many fans not only accept the rules after a lifetime of fandom but also defend them vigorously in debates.

Regulating multi-person matches

Straight matches can include any variation of a multi-person match, including:

- **Tag matches:** Two wrestlers versus two wrestlers.
- **Six-man or Trios matches:** Three wrestlers versus three wrestlers.
- **Elimination matches:** If an individual wrestler in a match gets pinned or *submitted* (gives up), they leave the match; and the match continues until one entire team or all other participants have been eliminated, leaving a single person or a team the winner.
- **Mixed tag matches:** A team consists of both men and women.

TECHNICAL STUFF

You can also find some obscure rules about multi-person matches. For example, in WWE tag team matches, a wrestler can *make a save* (contact the wrestler involved in the pinfall, causing the referee to stop counting) once. WWE has never acknowledged that rule publicly, but the wrestlers are required to follow it (and most fans are completely unaware of it).

Adding stipulations

Straight matches can have stipulations attached to them, such as:

- **Iron Man:** Whoever wins the most falls in a predetermined amount of time — say, 30 minutes or 60 minutes — is the winner.
- **Flag:** Winner has to capture the opponent's flag, which hangs above one of the ring posts.
- **Hair-versus-Hair:** The loser gets their head shaved.
- **Mask-versus-Mask:** The loser must unmask.
- **Mask-versus-Hair:** The loser either unmasks or gets their head shaved, depending on whether they wore a mask or had hair going into the match.
- **Submission:** Also called an "I Quit" match. The match can end only when one wrestler gives up.

Getting crazy in gimmick matches

Gimmick matches, though advertised on television as stipulation matches (which we talk about in the preceding section), always involve some sort of gimmick. (See the section "Getting a gimmick" earlier in this chapter for an explanation of this pro wrestling term).

REMEMBER

Although you can find literally hundreds of different types of gimmick matches, for the most part, they often come down to basically one concept: Anything goes.

You want to bring that barbed wire baseball bat into the ring? Go for it! That machine gun? Well, it's anything goes, so technically you can. (Pro wrestling almost never uses guns, but they have appeared in storylines in the past. Fans almost always violently hate these angles because it's impossible to suspend your disbelief.)

A gimmick by any other name

Most gimmick matches have exotic names, such as the following, but have the same basic anything-goes concept:

- Street fight
- No disqualifications (DQ)
- Hardcore
- Unsanctioned
- Donnybrook (U.K. term for wild brawl)
- Death Match
- Anarchy in the Arena

TIP

Sometimes, you even see a feud where two wrestlers have an anything-goes match, then rematch in a street fight, and then blow off the rivalry in a no DQ match. In fact, they're all the same type of match.

Tweaking a gimmick

Promotions have many variations of the anything-goes gimmick match where the only difference is how you win:

- **Ladder match:** You win by climbing a ladder and grabbing something (a belt, a contract, whatever) hanging from the ceiling. However, because a ladder match is a gimmick match (so anything goes), wrestlers can use whatever weapons they'd like prior to climbing.
- **TLC match:** Tables, Ladders, and Chairs; exactly the same as a ladder match, just with a fancier name. In a TLC match, the rules state that you can use all three gimmicks — tables, ladders and chairs.
- **Cage match:** A gimmick match where you can often win by being the first to leave the *cage* (a big chain link cage) and put both your feet on the floor. In other cage matches the idea is you aren't supposed to leave; two wrestlers are locked inside and have to win by pinfall or submission.
- **Falls count anywhere match:** You can pin someone anywhere you want, inside or outside the ring (or building!).

Other matches take place in specific locations. For example, a Boiler Room Brawl is a gimmick match that takes place in a boiler room.

At this point, after more than 140 years of professional wrestling all over the world, if you can imagine a stipulation for a gimmick match, it's probably been done somewhere. Can you say piranha death match? In 1996, Big Japan Wrestling promoted a match between Kendo Nagasaki and Mitsuhiro Matsunaga that for the purposes of history was titled "The Amazon River Piranha and Barbed Wire Board

Death Match." The goal was to put your opponent into a tank filled with real piranhas for ten seconds. Nagasaki won, throwing Matsunaga into the fish tank and covering it with a barbed wire board, and Matsunaga legitimately got a small hole gnawed in his chest by the fish. To this day it's one of the most famous matches in Japanese Death Match history.

Having a battle royal

Many gimmick matches are variations of a *battle royal,* which involves multiple wrestlers all inside the ring at the same time. You get eliminated if someone throws you over the top rope and both your feet touch the floor. You very rarely see a disqualification or count-out in a battle royal, and wrestlers often do use weapons.

Variations include matches such as the *Royal Rumble,* where two wrestlers start the battle royal, and then a new wrestler enters at timed intervals (say, every two minutes) until all the wrestlers have entered. The last person left in the ring wins.

Wrestling Under the Bright Lights

If you're paid to wrestle, you're a professional wrestler! However, how successful you are and how much money you make depends on many different factors, including where and how often you work, your position on the card, and more.

Independent pro wrestling

Unless you're a high-level athlete — for example, an Olympic freestyle wrestling gold medalist, such as Kurt Angle, who had a brilliant career with WWE and TNA — if you want to become a professional wrestler, you probably start your career on the independent circuit.

Finding independent promotions

Independent promotions are usually wrestling companies that:

- Run in a local area
- Don't have an affiliation to any major organization
- Don't have any major television or large-scale streaming deals

Despite (or because of) their small size, they can have rabidly loyal followings. Although independent promotions can vary greatly in terms of professionalism and financial backing, the majority of independent promotions nowadays:

- Book independent wrestlers from around the world.
- Promote and run shows on a regular schedule (usually monthly).
- Sell tickets, merchandise, and concessions.
- Often stream their events, either on YouTube or through some independent pro wrestling streaming service.

TIP

Sometimes, the wrestlers are almost entirely local talent from around the area, usually students training at the promotion's wrestling school. Often, a promotion will fly in one or more bigger-name independent talents to wrestle on a show. Often, these bigger names also put together a training seminar for the local wrestlers before the event.

Making a living as an independent wrestler

What independent wrestlers get paid varies wildly based on their level of experience:

- **Wrestling students:** Small, local promotions that use wrestling school students for their shows often don't pay the wrestlers at all. The students work the shows to gain experience.
- **Rookie wrestlers:** Wrestlers who have limited experience (meaning relatively few matches, often none outside their local area) can make as little as $25 to $50 per show.
- **Known wrestlers:** Wrestlers who have more well-known names can make anywhere from $100 to $1,000 or more per show, depending on their level of star-power, such as whether they have experience on television for a major promotion such as WWE or All Elite Wrestling AEW.
- **Famous wrestlers:** Sometimes, a genuine Hall of Fame–level superstar will agree to work a show (and not even necessarily wrestle!). They can make as much as five figures for one appearance.

Many former big-name wrestlers can make good money on the independent scene if they can hustle. Some have legitimately made more money while working independent shows than they did working for major TV promotions. Besides having a big name, it takes a lot of hard work to make that kind of money. You must:

» Network in such a way that you can work two to three times every weekend.
» Oversee production and sales of your own merchandise (such as T-shirts and 8-by-10-inch photos).

WARNING

Sometimes, when wrestlers leave a big-time promotion such as WWE or AEW, they enjoy returning to the more Wild West life of an independent professional wrestler. But, after a year or two, the constant hard work begins to take its toll, and they invariably start to feel the desire to return to a major league promotion. In other cases when a wrestler is released from a major promotion, their mindset is the big-time or bust, and they retire.

Finding a niche — Minis wrestling

Nowadays, you see old-school niche wrestling concepts mostly in indie shows.

Little people (those who have dwarfism) who do professional wrestling call themselves *minis*. In the old days, promotions called them midget wrestlers, an outdated and derogatory term. Interestingly, many mini wrestlers themselves have publicly voiced displeasure about the disappearance of the term midget because they say the change takes away their livelihood in certain forms of entertainment.

You almost never see minis wrestling in any major promotion worldwide, except for *Consejo Mundial de Lucha Libre* (CMLL) and *Asistencia, Asesoría y Administración de Espectáculos* (AAA) in Mexico.

REMEMBER

Mini wrestlers, because of their small size, have some distinct qualities:

» They can do some of the most incredible acrobatics.
» Because they're so small and almost always wear costumes and masks, little children see them as relatable superheroes and absolutely love to watch their matches.

TECHNICAL STUFF

In CMLL and AAA, the cut-off height for the minis division is 5 feet 2 inches tall, although they don't have really hard and fast rules. One of the greatest *luchadores* (Mexican wrestlers) of all time, Rey Mysterio, was, in fact, 5 feet 2 inches tall — he almost ended up in the minis division, which would have changed his career immeasurably.

Televised pro wrestling

In the late 1940s, television exploded in the United States, and with it came televised professional wrestling. From that time all the way through the late 1990s, television itself wasn't all that lucrative. In fact, for decades, nearly all wrestling promotions that aired on television had made barter deals with the TV stations to get their programming on the air.

The promotions saw television as merely an advertising vehicle to expose the promotion and its stars to a large local audience, to whom they would sell tickets to live events. Some promotions did such incredible local ratings that the television stations paid the promotion for the content — but this relationship was incredibly rare.

All of that changed in the late 1990s when the WWF's *Monday Night RAW* became a huge hit, and so valuable that the USA Network began paying bigger rights fees to retain the programming. Today, WWE's broadcast deals are worth more than one billion dollars per year.

Working in the wrestling territories

In the 1980s, the United States featured dozens of pro wrestling territories, all promoting locally in their own specific area, including Dallas and Amarillo, Texas; New York; Georgia; and Florida. (See Chapter 5 for more discussion about the territory system.) The WWF took a sledgehammer to the territory structure, which you can read about in Chapter 6.

Making TV money

The WWF exploded in popularity in the mid-1980s, and by the end of the decade, it was actually beginning to make some money through television rights fees. By the late 1990s, television was no longer simply a vehicle to sell tickets to house shows and generate PPV buys; it was becoming a strong revenue generator on its own.

At the time of writing, television stations and streaming platforms pay upwards of $100 million per year for the rights to air pro wrestling programming. In 2025, WWE signed a 10-year deal with Netflix valued at $5 billion for *Monday Night RAW*. And WWE has separate deals with other networks, such as the USA Network for *WWE SmackDown*, the CW for *NXT*, and ESPN for *Premium Live Events* (PLEs).

TIP

Broadcasting rights are, by far, the single most lucrative revenue generator for pro wrestling promotions, to the point that virtually no promotion in the United States regularly runs untelevised live events anymore.

Paying to watch

At the time of writing, the biggest wrestling events are broadcast on PPV television for promotions such as AEW and TNA. WWE got out of the PPV business after transitioning to their own PLE streaming network in the early 2010s; they have a streaming deal with ESPN at the time we write.

REMEMBER

With linear television collapsing, you can almost always find a streaming option available for any big promotion.

Both PPV and PLE events bring in plenty of money:

- **PPV:** Companies such as AEW and TNA make big money on PPV. Most AEW PPVs average around 140,000 buys at $50 a pop (that's about $7 million in revenue), of which the company keeps about half (the rest goes to the PPV providers).
- **PLE:** WWE's deals with streaming services basically just pay the promotion a flat fee for a certain number of PLEs per year, so WWE makes no additional money based on how many viewers any individual show gets. Despite that, WWE pushes PLEs as the biggest events in a calendar month, with rare exceptions, because, well, that's how they've always done it.

TIP

Arguably the most important pay-to-view event (technically, the first *WrestleMania* didn't air on PPV, only on closed-circuit) in wrestling history is the first *WrestleMania*, which took place on March 31, 1985, at Madison Square Garden in New York City. This event included Hulk Hogan and Mr. T wrestling against Paul Orndorff & Roddy Piper with Muhammad Ali featured as one of two special guest referees. The same event included Wendi Richter facing Leilani Kai for the WWF Women's Title with singer Cyndi Lauper in Richter's corner. Refer to Chapter 16 for more details about these matchups.

The double-whammy of Mr. T and Cyndi Lauper, and the accompanying explosion of press in the days leading up to the show, helped *WrestleMania* draw 19,121 fans to the show and over a million closed-circuit buyers, at that point in history the all-time record.

In the late '90s *WrestleMania* went from being an annual wrestling PPV to an *event*, *the* big WWF show of the year. Today, it's by far the biggest wrestling show worldwide every year, spanning two days and often drawing more than 100,000 live fans. Cities now engage in bidding wars. So not only does WWE make big money through hugely expensive ticket sales (as much as $40,000 for front row seats on the secondary market), but the WWE also makes millions in on-site fees just bringing the show to a town. The 2027 two-day *WrestleMania* in Saudi Arabia, between site fees and ticket sales, will almost surely gross more than $250 million dollars over that weekend.

Making a living in wrestling

The biggest wrestling stars on TV make millions of dollars per year. The champion of your local independent promotion almost certainly has a real job to pay the bills. Professional wrestling, like all forms of entertainment, has a vast pay structure depending on who you are, where you work, and your overall star-power.

Getting paid per match

Believe it or not, in the 1980s, the WWF offered wrestlers only a flat fee of $50 to wrestle a television match. At that time, wrestlers made the bulk of their money working hundreds of untelevised events annually (at one point in the 1980s, WWF ran three different tours at the same time all over the United States). At that time, Vince McMahon felt that wrestling on television before millions of eyeballs upped your worth as a performer, so a wrestler should have no problem doing a television performance for next to nothing.

Wrestlers in the 1980s got paid by the match, meaning they didn't have salary contracts. For that reason, many wrestlers then got hooked on steroids to maintain their muscular physique, which McMahon treasured in his performers. Many also became addicted to pain pills and alcohol so that they could work through the pain and continue to make money. (If you got hurt and didn't wrestle so that you could recover, you didn't get paid.)

Signing contracts

With the rise of the WCW in the 1990s, the industry slowly shifted to offering guaranteed money contracts because guaranteed money meant that if you got hurt and had to take a year off, you got paid the entire time:

- **WCW:** Offered flat-fee guaranteed contracts — say, $750,000 per year, regardless of how often or how little you worked.
- **WWF:** Offered contracts that included *downside guarantees,* meaning you were guaranteed a small amount of income, but you got paid extra for all your *house show matches* (matches that occurred in front of a live audience without being televised), PPV matches, and so on.

At the time of writing, all wrestlers have guaranteed deals, and wrestlers can make more money today than ever before. Here are the pay breakdowns:

- **Big star wrestlers:** Often $5 million per year or more.
- **Main-event wrestlers:** Often $1 million per year or more.

- **Middle of the pack:** *Mid-card* wrestlers (not regular main-eventers) can make anywhere from $250,000 to $750,000 per year.
- **Bottom of the barrel:** Beginning television star contracts start at around $100,000.

Working as an independent contractor

Wrestlers in all major television promotions are classified and paid as *independent contractors* (a very controversial designation amongst both fans and those in the wrestling business.) Long story short, wrestlers are treated like employees (told when and where they can and can't work, who they can and can't give interviews to, and so on), while being paid as independent contractors. Many wrestlers and fans believe that WWE in particular, with their very restrictive demands, is misclassifying the wrestlers, but the matter has never successfully been challenged in court.

Life as an independent contractor varies depending upon where you work:

REMEMBER

- **Getting hurt on the job:** The major league television promotions do pay for treating any injuries (including surgery and physical therapy, if needed) that wrestlers suffer on the job. Wrestlers have to pay for their own health insurance, but if they break their leg on the job, the company handles all medical bills related to that injury. How that happens varies, based on the promotion. For example, WWE and AEW take different approaches that have their own positives and negatives (but in the end, the promotion pays for everything):
  - *WWE:* The company takes care of everything, but you have to go to whatever medical facilities and healthcare providers they deem appropriate.
  - *AEW:* If you break your leg, you have to find a doctor and pay for all the treatment, rehab, and so on; but then you use an app to get reimbursed for everything.
- **Travel and accommodation:** Wrestlers may have to pay their own travel and accommodation expenses, depending on the promotion and the wrestler's status. AEW (and, interestingly, many much smaller independent promotions) pay for transportation and hotels.

  In WWE, the talent often must pay for their own. Obviously, the biggest WWE stars get to fly to events in the company jet. Some wrestlers purchase their own tour buses to get around. Big stars sometimes request a tour bus during contract negotiations.

NOT ALL GIMMICKS WORK: WRESTLING BEARS

Mostly in the 1960s and 1970s, some promotions made wrestling bears a thing. Even then, it was a niche of a niche. Bears don't follow storylines or understand gimmicks. The matches sucked. But if you wanted to, you could pay money to see a wrestler take on a trained bear.

IN THIS CHAPTER

» Putting together the proper venue for a pro wrestling match

» Exploring all those crazy weapons — and whether they're real

» Going for blood in the ring

Chapter 3

Identifying the In-the-Ring Essentials

Professional wrestling involves much more than two or more people pretending to fight. It takes place somewhere, and the location adds to the experience; the wrestling promoters have to spice the fight up to keep viewer engagement high, week after week, month after month, year after year; and it involves dozens — sometimes hundreds — of supporting players, from announcers to managers, without which you can't have a show. This chapter looks at what wrestlers and promoters use to create a pro wrestling spectacle inside the ring. Chapter 12 focuses on the people outside the ring who make professional wrestling what it is.

Setting the Stage for a Professional Wrestling Match

Although professional wrestling isn't a legitimate sport, the idea is to pretend it is. Therefore, it needs a playing surface (the ring) and rules that everyone involved is expected to follow (but often don't), which the following sections explore.

The ring: Where the action happens

The pro wrestling *ring* is a raised surface covered in canvas and surrounded by ring ropes where all the action typically takes place. Although sometimes fans and people in the business give it a fancy (and maybe a little silly) name, such as The Squared Circle, most everyone just calls the ring what it is — a ring.

But if you think every wrestling ring is the same, think again. You often hear the phrase "they come in all shapes and sizes" when talking about all kinds of things, and in the case of wrestling rings, that's literally true. Some rings are taller, some are shorter, some are bigger, some are smaller, some aren't even square — and in most of them, the ropes aren't even made of rope (see the section "The ropes: Keeping the action in the ring" later in this chapter, for rope talk).

REMEMBER

Even though every ring is slightly different, most wrestlers say that it usually doesn't take much time to adjust to whatever ring they end up working in.

Obviously, you can't go to a big box store and buy a professional wrestling ring. But you can, believe it or not, buy a pro wrestling ring via mail order. In general, companies that plan to hold pro wrestling events hire professional construction teams to build their wrestling rings, and the promotion gets to decide how they want those rings built.

These sections look at the parts of the ring and how they can differ, depending on the promotion.

The floor: Where everyone takes bumps

Pro wrestling doesn't have universal equipment standards or requirements in the way that many other sports do. Although no governing body mandates a ring must be a certain size, the promotion World Wrestling Entertainment (WWE) uses rings that are 20-by-20 feet — basically the largest ring you'll see in the biz.

The floor of the ring usually consists of:

- **Apron frame:** A steel frame that helps hold everything together.
- **Apron:** A sheet that hangs down so you can't see underneath the ring, that varies mostly based on what material it's made of (sometimes, promoters use a real cloth apron, similar to a bed skirt; other promotions use an LED board).
- **Ring posts:** The gigantic, heavy steel or iron corner posts that also help hold everything together. The hardest part of the ring, despite what announcers say about the apron frame.

» **Metal beams:** Contrary to popular belief, most rings don't have a gigantic spring underneath to make them bouncy. Instead, metal beams usually run from one side of the ring apron frame to the other, and then a second set of beams crisscrosses to make two layers.

TECHNICAL STUFF

In the middle of those beams, you can find some give. On TV, they often claim that the ring apron is the "hardest part of the ring." What they mean is that the middle of the ring has the most give (it's the bounciest part), and the outer part by the ring apron has the least amount of give.

» **Wooden boards:** Laid over the apron frame. Sometimes the construction uses long planks, sometimes larger sheets of plywood.

» **Padding:** The boards are covered with 1- to 2-inch foam padding.

» **Canvas:** The padding is covered with a canvas. Often, the ring floor is covered with several layered canvases that the staff can peel off one by one in the middle of a show if the top canvas ends up covered in blood or other debris.

TIP

Contrary to popular belief, most rings don't have a gigantic spring underneath to make them bouncy. But both the promotions World Wrestling Federation (WWF; later renamed WWE) and American Wrestling Association (AWA) did at one point decades ago have springs underneath their rings. The WWF ring was poorly engineered, and the spring offered almost no give at all. But the properly engineered AWA spring did actually give some bounce, which wrestlers obviously preferred because *bumps* (falls) hurt less.

In many places in Mexico, the wrestling rings are actually boxing rings. A boxing ring is different from a dedicated wrestling ring because its construction gives you a significantly harder mat surface with much less give. Therefore, lucha libre (Mexican wrestling) traditionally has fewer high-impact flat-back *bumps* (falls), and more rolling-style acrobatic bumps to prevent the wrestlers from suffering injuries from falling repeatedly on such a hard surface.

Many wrestling rings on the independent circuit are relatively small, usually 18 by 18 feet and sometimes even 16 by 16 feet. The promotion World Championship Wrestling (WCW) always used smaller 18-by-18-foot rings, which helped make their cruiserweight matches always feel fast and state-of-the-art. Visually, because of the difference in playing-field size, if you do the exact same high-speed match in a 20-by-20-foot ring and an 18-by-18-foot ring, the match in the smaller ring appears faster and more dynamic. So when faster, high-flying WCW wrestlers jumped to WWF in the late 1990s, their matches never looked quite as dynamic as they did in WCW.

WARNING

NO GIVE TO THIS RING

I, Bryan Alvarez, was once a wrestler, and one of the promotions I worked for hired a guy to build the wrestling ring who didn't have experience building wrestling rings — he built bridges. The ring he built, like a bridge, was exceedingly durable. But if you had to choose one place you don't want to be taking bumps, it's on a bridge. This ring was hard as a rock. He also installed a gigantic — and I mean gigantic (probably two feet in diameter) — spring underneath the ring floor, presumably with the idea that if you want to make a ring bouncy, you should put a spring in it.

Well, this spring was so gigantic that the only way you could make it bounce was by dropping a 400- or 500-pound person on it — and even then, it didn't spring much. For the smaller wrestlers, such as myself (I was 145 pounds at the time), this spring offered no give at all. This ring sucked to wrestle on: Every part of the ring was the hardest part of the ring.

The ropes: Keeping the action in the ring

Even though WWE, as a pro wrestling organization, tends to lie about a lot of things, they actually use legitimate ropes for their rings. They string three ropes around the ring using turnbuckles connected to the four ring posts. They then secure the posts and the entire ring together by using heavy gauge cables underneath the ring.

In the old days, the ring posts were just that — big, heavy metal posts. Nowadays, promotions sometimes cover the posts in LED boards that light up to make everything look a little fancier.

TIP

Outside of WWE, most promotions don't use actual rope for ropes. Instead, they use steel cables, usually encased in a garden hose or rubber tube, and then wrapped completely in tape. Steel cables, in general, don't have as much give as actual ropes, which makes it easier for wrestlers to perform high-flying moves off the ropes. However, if you really cinch WWE ropes tight, you can't really tell the two apart when you perform on them. The differences arise while the show goes on because the real ropes start to loosen up and sag. Saggy ropes make *springboard maneuvers* (jumping off the ropes) such a disaster because saggy ropes offer no spring.

ROLLING THE SIX-SIDED RING

Probably the biggest departure from the traditional square ring is the six-sided ring. First used in Mexico in the promotion *Asistencia, Asesoría y Administración de Espectáculos* (AAA), the six-sided ring later became a trademark of the promotion Total Nonstop Action (TNA). It's essentially the same as any other ring except (obviously) it has six sides instead of four.

Almost universally, the wrestlers think the six-sided ring sucks. A few kind of like the idea that it's unique, that you have two extra corners to work with, and that sort of thing. But most of those wrestlers do agree that, other than those few positives, it sucks.

It sucks because of those two extra sides. When you add two sides, you're engineering a more complicated shape and essentially creating a significantly larger area in which the floor has no give. Therefore, unless you're bumping exactly in the middle of the ring, you most likely land on a very hard part of the ring floor.

TNA wrestlers in the mid-2000s constantly complained about the six-sided ring because, during that time, they not only had to do normal wrestling matches, but also all sorts of high-risk *gimmick matches* (matches with different rules), such as Ultimate X, which required them to fall from great heights all over the ring. It's a wonder that more people didn't suffer significant injuries.

MAKING THE RING COMFY FOR THE BOSS

In big-time television promotions, the *ring crew,* those responsible for putting up the ring and tearing it down, are often the referees assigned to work on the show. When *Monday Night RAW* ends, your favorite referee is hauling boards into the ring truck and preparing to drive to the next town. On independent shows, the *green* (new) wrestlers usually do the construction — overseen, obviously, by someone who knows what they're doing.

Until about the mid-1990s, everyone knew that WWF ring floors were very stiff and no fun to take bumps on. In the 1980s, wrestlers worked significantly more dates than they do nowadays, often more than 125 shows per year (which is more than ten shows per month). Those wrestlers worked a lot of shows in really hard rings. As a result, the WWF wrestling style during that period was very slow-paced and had far fewer big-time bumps than you see nowadays.

So, what changed? Well, in the mid-1990s, the owner of the company, Vince McMahon, Jr., became a wrestler. Suddenly, he was in the ring night after night taking bodyslams, suplexes, and rock bottoms. (Chapter 2 defines these moves and more.) Very shortly thereafter, WWF redesigned all the rings to make taking bumps more comfortable.

Putting them in cages

Everyone, wrestling fan or not, has heard of steel cage matches: It's a term in the mainstream lexicon, and it comes from professional wrestling.

A *steel cage* is exactly what it sounds like: a giant cage placed around the ring, so that, supposedly, when two people are wrestling inside, nobody can get in to interfere and nobody can escape. The feud must be settled fair and square.

REMEMBER

Of course, when a modern wrestling promotion announces a cage match, you know someone is getting inside that cage, one way or another, because, well, that happens in every match now. In the very first WWF *Hell in a Cell* event, the wrestler Kane just ripped the cage's door off its hinges and went inside.

Identifying the types of steel cages

The first steel cages were all made of standard chain link fencing (although the actual first-ever cage used in a match was made out of chicken wire in the 1930s). The steel cages today are made of the same type of chain link, but they have a much more solid frame construction.

In the 1980s, McMahon thought that the audience couldn't easily see the action through a chain link fence, so he had these giant blue cages constructed that contained large openings between the bars, more like an enormous Connect Four game. The larger openings in these blue cages allowed huge wrestlers such as Hulk Hogan and Big Bossman to climb the sides of the cage like a ladder.

But, by the mid-1990s, WWF phased out those blue cages in favor of chain link again: WWF began a *hardcore era* (more violence) in the 1990s, and McMahon thought that old-school galvanized-steel chain link looked more hardcore than the pretty blue cages.

The promotion Total Nonstop Action (TNA) uses the same style of wide-barred cage that WWF used in the 1980s, but they paint their cages black, not blue.

Putting together steel cages

Originally, the ring crew quickly constructed a steel cage right before the match began, setting it up on the apron so that it contained only the ring. But in the mid-1980s, cages started getting bigger and more elaborate:

» ***Thunder Dome:*** Promotion National Wrestling Alliance (NWA) constructed much bigger cages that not only covered the ring but also left an area at ringside where the wrestlers could brawl or get weapons from underneath the ring.

» ***War Games:*** NWA also created gigantic cages that were big enough to cover two rings side by side for this event.

» ***Hell in a Cell:*** WWF made their cage for this event much larger and much taller than your average cage and included a roof on top — allegedly to make sure nobody could get inside. (Before the cage had a roof, wrestlers from outside the cage would just run down during the match and climb over the top.) Of course, in that very first *Hell in a Cell* is when Kane ripped the door off its hinges.

» ***Doomsday:*** Both World Class Championship Wrestling (WCCW) and NWA created very expensive and elaborate three-story cages (yes, three cages stacked on top of one another). WCW's version resulted in one of the worst matches in wrestling history at the *WCW Uncensored* PPV in 1996, a sloppy, ugly mess of bad "wrestling".

REMEMBER

Years later, when the movie *Ready to Rumble* used a similar three-tiered cage (a horrible film aimed at wrestling fans, but that featured characters that made wrestling fans look completely stupid), WCW brought the concept back for two largely terrible matches. It was a movie tie-in to the point that the star of the film, 160-pound comedy actor David Arquette, not only wrestled in one of the matches, but shortly thereafter actually won the WCW World Heavyweight Title in a moment largely universally reviled by WCW fans.

Most of the blood in cage matches is real, usually the result of the wrestlers *gigging* (cutting themselves with a small piece of a razor blade to draw blood). But because the cage is made of real galvanized steel, running into it in the wrong way sometimes results in *hardway juice* (meaning accidental cuts). We discuss blood in greater detail in the section "Getting Gory — Blood in the Ring" later in this chapter.

Choosing a Weapon

So much of professional wrestling isn't real. But in the case of one of the more dangerous types of wrestling, matches that involve weapons, more often than not, the weapons used are all real (though some of them are *gimmicked* [fake]). We talk about the most common weapons in the following sections.

Chairs

The most famous weapon used in a wrestling match is probably the steel chair. Even non-fans know that pro wrestlers hit each other with chairs.

The steel chairs used in pro wrestling, despite what you might read in certain places online, are for the most part legitimate steel chairs. They're the same 18-gauge steel folding chairs that you can buy at a big box store or online. Sometimes, at smaller independent events, they use cheaper plastic chairs, but for the most part, on televised big-time wrestling shows, a steel chair is a legitimate steel chair.

The wrestlers don't fake the *chairshots*, as they call these hits with a chair; they simply rely on physics (distribution of impact for the back hits, chair design for the modern-day headshots). Here are the types of chairshots often used in professional wrestling:

- **Across the back:** In the early days of using steel chairs as weapons in wrestling (which started in the late 1930s or early 1940s), for the most part, wrestlers hit each other across the back with them. When you take a wide, flat area of a person's body (their back) and you hit it with the wide, flat area of the chair (the seat), the impact makes a really loud noise but is spread out, so it really doesn't hurt that bad at all.
- **In the gut:** Wrestlers can fold the chair up, hold it sideways, and ram the top edge of the seatback into someone's gut. The wrestler *works* (fakes) this type of attack in the sense that they don't really ram it as hard as they can into their opponent's gut, they *pull* it, like you do a punch — instead of following through with your shot, like you would if you wanted to break a board in karate, you pull back right before impact. And it's your opponent's job to *sell* it, making it seem like you really hit them hard.
- **To the head:** Chairshots to the head became the norm throughout professional wrestling during the late 1990s and early 2000s. The concept started in Japan before it came to the States. In Japan, the chairs have seats riveted into the frames. Those seats consist of just a thin piece of wood covered with padding and vinyl. The wrestlers originally put a hand up to protect their head from the blow. But someone figured out that if the chair hit you in the head, the seat just popped off. It was a cool visual, largely safe, and the fans went crazy for it.

  Pro wrestlers in the United States actually misunderstood what Japanese wrestlers were doing. When they watched Japanese pro wrestling tapes and saw this move, they determined that real tough-guy wrestlers shouldn't put their hands up to block chairshots. The problem was, U.S. chairs at wrestling events were heavy, hard steel chairs, and the seats didn't pop off. Fans still went crazy for hard unprotected chairshots to the head, and it caught on, first in Extreme Championship Wrestling (ECW) in the mid-1990s and spreading throughout WCW and WWF, which later was renamed World Wrestling Entertainment (WWE).

WARNING

The problem with headshots involve the concussions that they can cause, which can lead to serious brain damage. (See the sidebar "Recognizing the tragic effect of headshots" in this chapter for details about this trauma and a tragic example of what can happen.) When wrestlers do go for chair headshots today, the storyline almost always does it with the idea that fans get legitimately outraged when they see an unprotected chairshot to the head.

Tables and doors

Probably the second most-popular weapon used in wrestling, after the chair (see the preceding section), is the table. Rare is the pro wrestling show where someone doesn't get slammed through a table. Fans love table bumps so much that they often chant "We want tables!" at least once during any given wrestling show. Even in an ultra-hardcore match where the wrestlers are attacking each other with barbed wire, glass, and who knows what else, the fans can inexplicably decide that they really want to see someone go through a wooden table.

TIP

Tables offer wrestlers a great *gimmick* because, for the most part, going through a table gives you a fun bump. Fans often think the promotion gimmicked the tables so that they break more easily, but in fact, a wrestler doesn't want the table to break too easily: A solid table can break their fall on the way to the ground. The ideal table, your typical big box store table made of wood that has metal legs, gets broken by a 220-pound human, but that human doesn't go straight through it like a knife through hot butter, so the fall is cushioned. And the table makes a tremendous crashing sound, and even sometimes sends pieces of wood flying. Fans love it, wrestlers love it: Everyone wins.

But not all tables are made the same. In Japan, for example, the tables used in pro wrestling are smaller than the typical tables used in U.S. pro wrestling. They appear to be (but aren't actually) made of oak and titanium. But regardless of what they're made of, they don't cooperate with a wrestler's bump most of the time. In the best circumstance, a wrestler's rear end smashes through the middle of the table, and they get their butt stuck in the unbroken frame — a position that's no fun for anyone.

WARNING

RECOGNIZING THE TRAGIC EFFECTS OF HEADSHOTS

In June of 2007, WWE star Chris Benoit murdered his wife Nancy and his young son Daniel, then hanged himself by using a workout machine. In the aftermath, neurosurgeons discovered that Benoit suffered from *chronic traumatic encephalopathy* (CTE) — in other words, severe brain damage almost certainly brought on by multiple concussions suffered during his wrestling career.

The fact is, everyone has known concussions have negative effects, dating back almost 100 years. In the 1920s, the prestigious *Journal of the American Medical Association (JAMA)* published articles that described *punch-drunk syndrome,* essentially retired boxers suffering from neuropathological issues stemming from getting hit in the head and concussed repeatedly during their careers. By the 1930s, it got a more official Latin name, *dementia pugilistica* (which translates to *boxer's dementia*).

Did people know about the abnormal protein tangles in the brain that manifest as CTE during that period? No. But did they know concussions and strikes to the head were bad news? Absolutely. From the earliest days of weapons in pro wrestling, everyone knew that you needed to take care of your opponent's head. When chairshots to the head first appeared in wrestling, either the hitter used incredibly weak shots or the person taking the hit put their hand up to protect their own head.

Wrestling even used concussions in storylines throughout the years, where supposedly concussed wrestlers were hospitalized or reported that they suffered from post-concussion syndrome (PCS) after an attack.

But in the 1990s, wrestlers started taking full-force, massively hard chairshots to the head, maybe because they felt invincible (drugs and alcohol can do that) or they felt they needed to gain respect. And this practice stuck around for a solid decade or so. Famously, Bret Hart suffered multiple legitimate concussions over a very short period of weeks in 2000 and had to retire early because of it — seven years before Benoit murdered his family.

Pro wrestling pulled back hard from unprotected chairshots to the head when the effects of blows to the head came to the public consciousness. Nowadays, almost nobody does them, and in the very rare times that you see it, the performers use gimmicked chairs that have the seat shaved down significantly to the thickness of maybe a pie pan.

REMEMBER

Sometimes, a promotion may find tables in short supply (this was a real issue during the COVID-19 pandemic), and wrestlers have to use doors instead. You can use a door in a similar way to how you use a table, but they're inconsistent: Some may be hard to break, and some break too easily.

Ladders

In *ladder matches*, something (such as a title belt or a contract for a title match) is hung from the ceiling, and the wrestlers must try to climb a ladder to grab it. Of course, the ladders also end up being used as weapons. These matches rose to popularity in the 1990s.

More often than not, these matches use real ladders. Occasionally, a match uses a gimmick ladder designed to break easily, but that's the exception. Taking a bump on a ladder ranges from easy to painful, depending on how you set up:

WARNING

- **Bouncing:** If you lean a ladder against the bouncy ring ropes and take a flat back bump onto it, you probably don't have a problem.
- **Hitting a corner:** If you mistime something and take a bump on the corner of a ladder that's laying on the mat, that sucks and can hurt.
- **Falling:** Falling off a ladder is falling off a ladder. You need to know how to take a good bump; otherwise, you can get seriously injured.

HOW PROFESSIONAL WRESTLING TOOK A LIKING TO KENDO STICKS

In 1993, an American teenager living in Singapore named Michael Fay was arrested and accused of vandalism and stealing road signs. He pleaded guilty and was sentenced to six lashes with a cane. Fay later claimed that although he did steal street signs, he didn't do any of the vandalism he was accused of, and that the only reason he pled guilty was because the authorities led him to believe that if he did plead guilty, he wouldn't be caned.

Because he was an American citizen, the incident received worldwide coverage and briefly led to strained relations between the United States and Singapore. Ultimately, allegedly out of respect for then-President Bill Clinton, the Singapore government did reduce his sentence from six lashes to four. At the time, being sentenced to caning was a routine punishment in Singapore (it was not done with a kendo stick, by the way; they used a far more brutal rattan cane).

Assorted other weapons

The weapons used in pro wrestling are as varied as a wrestler's imagination:

- **Thumbtacks:** Contrary to popular belief (and what you may have read online), the thumbtacks used in professional wrestling are legitimate sharp, pointy thumbtacks, for the most part. When you see a wrestler lifted high into the air and dropped onto a pile of thumbtacks, what you see is what you get. Yes, getting thrown legitimately into a pile of real thumbtacks sucks for them. But many wrestlers have noted that it doesn't hurt as much as the average viewer might think — at least, the initial (usually back-first) *bump* (fall) into them. What hurts more than the bump itself is after the match, when you have to pick them all out of your skin (or have someone else do it).
- **Kendo sticks:** A *kendo stick* is technically a *shinai,* which is a Japanese sword made from bamboo that's used to practice martial arts. The worldwide news coverage in 1993 of an American teenager convicted of vandalism and stealing, and being sentenced to a caning as punishment in Singapore (see the nearby sidebar in this chapter) brought the cane as a weapon to U.S. consciousness and led to the widespread usage of canes as weapons in professional wrestling. At the time, those in wrestling referred to them as *Singapore canes,* although nowadays people almost universally refer to them as simply kendo sticks.

  WARNING

  Although I (co-author Bryan Alvarez) as a wrestler haven't engaged in every kind of hardcore shenanigan that you see nowadays in wrestling, I have gone through tables, been thrown into steel cages and hit with chairs, and fallen off ladders. I've also been hit by kendo sticks. By far — and it's not even close — the single most painful thing that has ever happened to me as a pro wrestler involved being hit hard with a kendo stick.
- **Trash cans:** Pro wrestling uses real trash cans as weapons. They're made from galvanized steel, but because the cans are large and the steel walls of the can are thin, they make a really loud, dramatic noise, but also dent really easily and thus don't do much damage to the target, if any. Trash can lids have the same effect.
- **Light tubes:** Sometimes wrestlers hit their opponent with *light tubes* (glass fluorescent lightbulbs that come in the shape of a tube). Don't try this at home. Besides the fact that you risk cutting yourself with broken glass, smashed light tubes release mercury vapor, a neurotoxin. You can get a new knee or hip replacement (many wrestlers do at the end of their careers). You can't get a new brain.

» **Fire:** Wrestlers sometimes use fire in the form of throwing a fireball at another person. They create the fireball by using old-school magician's flash paper treated with sulfuric acid and nitric acid, so that when it's lit, it instantly ignites into the supposed victim's face. If the opponent effectively sells the fireball (reacts), the fire looks devastating but is quite safe.

  Of course, people always must raise the bar. Since the 1990s, pro wrestling has seen a rise of flaming tables. Essentially, someone pours lighter fluid all over a wooden table, lights it, and then slams their opponent through it. Because lighter fluid is fast-burning and will quickly extinguish, the spot looks spectacular but isn't particularly dangerous.

  WARNING

  Fire is an elemental force and doesn't like to cooperate. Therefore, matches always have someone standing nearby with a fire extinguisher. And often, the performer who's going to go through the table wears some sort of fire retardant on their gear. Even with all precautions taken, some wrestlers have been burned badly when stunts have gone awry.

TECHNICAL STUFF

» **Bed of nails:** Yes, you read that right. However, a bed of nails is actually an illusion first used by carnies and magicians. It's also physics. If you lay down a piece of wood and you stick one single nail straight up in the air, don't lie on that board. However, if you take a board and stick 5,000 nails straight up all over that board, your weight distributes over the large area such that you can lay upon the nails without a single nail puncturing you.

Considering commonly gimmicked weapons

Some weapons in wrestling are sometimes gimmicked; and if we're honest, they're not gimmicked enough. Here are some that tend to get gimmicked:

» **Barbed wire:** In fact, many wrestlers engage in barbed wire matches that use actual sharp, pokey barbed wire. You can tell the barbed wire is real if you see it sticking to clothes and skin.

  TIP

  Some wrestlers use gimmicked barbed wire, and some have a little bit of real barbed wire mixed in with gimmicked pieces of barbed wire. By using a bit of real barbed wire, when something gets caught up or stuck in the real barbed wire, fans may think that all the barbed wire in the match is real.

- **Breakaway glass:** Sometimes called *Hollywood glass.* An easily broken material, such as sugar or brittle plastic, that looks like glass. But, of course, some wrestlers don't like going halfway and hit each other or take bumps with real glass. If someone takes a bump into broken glass and their back is all sliced up and bleeding, they almost certainly didn't use Hollywood glass.
- **Guitars:** Wrestlers who have singer gimmicks (for example, Honky Tonk Man, who did an Elvis impersonator gimmick and sang his own entrance music and Jeff Jarrett, who never sang or played an instrument a day in his life) use their instruments as a common weapon. They usually use real guitars, but the wrestlers gimmick most (although not all) the guitars by removing the internal support beam so that they break much more easily over a person's head. If no one removes that support beam, however, you don't want to be hit over the head with a guitar (it could easily concuss you or injure your neck, both of which have happened in wrestling).

TECHNICAL STUFF

In years past, particularly in the mid-1990s, for reasons unknown (but likely just for the visual excitement of it), the wrestler placed white powder in the guitar so that when it exploded, powder went flying everywhere like a bomb went off. These gimmicked guitars often contained baby powder — but the ECW guys took a lot of drugs, so who knows.

- **Striking implements:** Cover the gamut from crowbars, hammers, brass knucks, *shillelaghs* (an Irish club), baseball bats, and so on. Sometimes the wrestlers use real versions, sometimes gimmicked. If a wrestler can believably use a real baseball bat and safely *pull a shot* (not impact hard) to their opponent's gut, for example, they may use a real one. If a moment requires a wrestler to use a weapon on an opponent's head or any part of the body where the margin of error is small, they might use a plastic or rubber version of the weapon.
- **Guns and knives:** Historically, wrestlers have used these weapons very sparingly in angles; and at the time of writing, basically no one uses them anywhere. In one of the most notorious angles in history, "Stone Cold" Steve Austin (supposedly) broke into Brian Pillman's house on the November 4, 1996, edition of *Monday Night RAW.* Pillman pulled a gun on him, and the screen cut to static (it was back in the day, when analog TVs showed static when they lost signal). Fans were supposed to believe that Pillman might have shot Austin. Of course, he didn't, but the USA Network almost shot *RAW* off their programming lineup because the angle went against their decency standards and many viewers complained.

Getting Gory — Blood in the Ring

For years, one of the biggest misconceptions about wrestling was that the blood was fake. People thought it was stage blood, ketchup, blood capsules, or whatever. In fact, in almost all cases, when you see blood in a pro wrestling match, it's real.

TIP

That being said, wrestlers do sometimes use fake blood. If the storyline has a wrestler suffer an internal injury that requires them to spit up blood, they usually use a *blood capsule* (the same kind you can get around Halloween). Very rarely, a brawl spills backstage, where a wrestler gets made up by using Hollywood stage blood before returning.

The following sections take a closer look at the basics of blood in professional wrestling.

Using a blade to cause the bleeding

Originally, wrestlers bled by using a *blade*, which is exactly what it sounds like — a small piece of razor blade usually concealed in a piece of tape on the wrestler's finger. They used the blade to make a small puncture wound, usually in the forehead. The blood mixed with sweat, creating the famous *crimson mask* (what announcer Gordon Solie and others called a wrestler's face covered in a red mix of blood and sweat). Sometimes, wrestlers took aspirin before a match to thin the blood and make the bleeding look more dramatic.

You may be aghast at this seemingly barbaric practice, but the cut that the wrestler makes with a blade is normally (but not always!) very small, so the bleeding looks significantly worse than the injury really is, and the cut often naturally closes up before the match even ends. Some people can *gig* (cut themselves) many times over their lifetime, and you can't tell from casually looking at their foreheads.

REMEMBER

Other wrestlers — the most famous of which was the aptly named Abdullah The Butcher — deliberately made long, deep cuts in their heads, which then scarred up, leaving their foreheads looking like an old-school road map. The massively scarred-up forehead (see the nearby sidebar) became part of their persona, and they used it to make tons of money.

BLEEDING INCOGNITO

On an independent pro wrestling show in the early 2000s, I (co-author Bryan Alvarez) wrestled *Los Villanos* (The Villains) IV and V, a Hall of Fame–level act in lucha libre (Mexican wrestling). (At this point in their career, these two were past their prime and working smaller events.) If there was one thing that all Los Villanos liked to do, it was bleed.

While we prepared for the match, I had to try very hard not to stare at their foreheads, which were scarred almost beyond description from years of blading. Villano V said to me, "Did you know, I am a dentist!" He then explained to me that wearing a mask as one of the legendary Los Villanos was a great benefit. He said to me, while I fought to the death not to look at his forehead (which looked like it would leave grill marks if I cooked a hot dog on it): "Nobody knows I'm a wrestler!"

Hiding the blade

More appalling than the act of blading itself (see the preceding section) is where the blade goes before and after the act. Here are some of the places that wrestlers hide the blade:

- **On their body:** A wrestler tapes the blade to their fingers or hides it in their wrist tape.
- **In their trunks:** Less so today, but often in the past (pre-2000s), they stored the blade in their own *wrestling trunks!* They then pulled it out, cut themselves, and then returned it to their trunks.
- **In their mouth:** They actually have the blade in their mouth, either before or after cutting themselves.
- **With the ref:** Nowadays, wrestlers usually get the blade from the referee and then hand it back discretely after the deed is done.

Banning the blade

At one point, WWE banned the blade because McMahon wanted the world to know that he didn't support this barbaric practice. But, of course, McMahon sometimes arranged an angle that would be much more dramatic if blood was involved. His supposedly civilized solution was anything but.

WARNING

In a very famous incident at *SummerSlam 2016* in Brooklyn, New York, Brock Lesnar was booked to beat Randy Orton in the main event by referee stoppage after a savage, mixed martial arts-style beating. But because McMahon banned the blade, he had Lesnar, a former heavyweight champion in the real-as-real-can-be Ultimate Fighting Championship (UFC), strike Orton's head repeatedly with the point of his elbow, smashing up Orton's skull, drawing blood, and basically knocking him silly. Very civilized.

Strapping on the Championship Belt

Professional wrestling championship awards largely consist of belts (although you can find a number of other prizes, as well). Here we delve into what you need to know about the championship belt.

What they're made of — belt materials

In real life — and we were devastated to learn this fact when we got older — big gold belts aren't, in fact, made of solid gold. Here's the materials used to make a modern-day pro wrestling championship belt:

- **Plates:** Usually made of a zinc alloy and then plated with 24 karat gold.
- **Strap:** If you go to, for example, the online WWE Shop (`https://shop.wwe.com`), you can buy a very nice replica of any of their titles for several hundred dollars, which usually have polyurethane (*pleather*) straps.

Most big-time wrestling companies have road belts and show belts:

- **Show belts:** Exceedingly fancy, sometimes hand-engraved and mounted on legitimate leather straps and can exceed five figures in cost.
- **Road belts:** Get tossed around and smashed up and are more like the belts you can buy from the promotion's merchandise store.

To your casual observer, a mass-produced belt looks almost identical to a hand-engraved version (but *don't* say this to a collector, unless you want them to hit you over the head with a hand-engraved vintage WWF Winged Eagle belt).

Reggie Parks and Dave Millican are two of the most famous old-school belt creators, and their original ring-worn belts can sell for as much as $15,000.

THE EVOLUTION OF THE BELT

Pro wrestling belts, particularly the World Championship, are the top prize in any wrestling promotion, yet fans often take their history for granted. Here's a brief overview of how they came to be:

- The first verifiable professional wrestling belts date from the mid-1800s. In 2024, an English pro wrestling belt went to auction, dating to 1862. It was essentially a thick leather belt that had a simple metal buckle on it and a few fancy-looking side plates. It looked identical to the belt that Santa Claus wears in traditional images.

  Based on books of the era, champion wrestlers received primitive belts like this one dating back to the late 1700s and early 1800s in Europe.

- Championship belts nowadays are quite extravagant, usually big and gold, covered in engravings and paint, and attached to leather straps. In recent years, promotions add special side plates customized for the current champion.

Who gets the belt

Where the belt stays after a wrestler wins it has changed over the years:

- **A prize to keep:** In the Pioneer Era (19th century) of pro wrestling, if you won a championship match, the belt was basically your prize to keep. In your next title fight, you fought for the championship, but not the actual belt. If you won, you got a new belt and retained your championship status. Therefore, if you defended your title eight times before losing, you had nine belts sitting on your mantle.
- **A prize to defend:** Since the early 20th century in pro wrestling, if you're the champion, you get the championship belt, which you then have to defend. If someone beats you, you have to hand over the belt, and the new champion now has the one championship belt.

2

Appreciating the History of Pro Wrestling

IN THIS PART . . .

Find out where professional wrestling started and how it evolved.

Examine what the territories were and how they operated.

See the surge in popularity when wrestling went national.

IN THIS CHAPTER

- Seeing where wrestling all began
- Following the different eras of professional wrestling
- Relating world events to changes in professional wrestling

Chapter 4

Looking Beyond the Ring: Wrestling's Origin Stories

Professional wrestling has existed in some form for at least several hundred years. Most likely, it dates back even further (although no one has found any records of earlier pro wrestling). In this chapter, we look at professional wrestling from the beginning (we mean *way* back!) through its first television boom period in the late 1940s and early 1950s.

Examining the Roots of Wrestling in the Ancient World

A person can argue that wrestling is one of the oldest sports in the world. Humans have surely wrestled dating back hundreds of thousands of years. Cave art from the south of France depicts humans wrestling as far back as 20,000 years ago. You can find images of people wrestling in the art of ancient Mesopotamia, Iraq, Mongolia, Egypt, China, Greece, and Europe.

A mural found in the burial chamber of Ancient Egyptian official Baqet III from 2000 B.C. depicts numerous holds and throws that would be classified as *freestyle wrestling* (today's amateur wrestling), judo, or *jiu-jitsu* (the latter two both Japanese grappling arts) techniques today, including what appear to be arm drags, single-leg takedowns, a collar-and-elbow tie-up, a Karelin lift (clearly not invented or popularized by Alexander Karelin, but someone else can tell him that), and even what appears to be a set up for a piledriver and a back body drop. (We discuss some different moves in Chapter 2.) The following sections look at wrestling in the ancient world.

TECHNICAL STUFF

What separates modern big-time professional wrestling from amateur wrestling is obviously the fact that amateur wrestling is a legitimate sporting event and professional wrestling is a performance that has pre-determined winners and losers. We doubt anyone will ever answer the question as to when professional wrestling first became *worked* (not legitimate), but if you're looking at it from the perspective of a match that wasn't *on the level* (legitimate), with two people cooperating to put on a show with a pre-determined outcome, most likely bouts like this occurred dating back to prehistoric times for one reason or another.

Wrestling in the original Olympics

Wrestling was a sport in the original Olympic Games at least as far back as 704 B.C. By this point, it had evolved to include *pinfalls* (putting an opponent's shoulders on the ground) as a method of victory and bouts that went best-of-three-falls. The Games eventually featured three combat sports — boxing, wrestling, and *pankration*. Boxing and wrestling were similar to the sports as you know them today, and *pankration* was essentially similar to today's mixed martial arts (MMA), a bare-knuckle sport that involved striking, grappling, and submission holds.

Because the human body hasn't evolved much at all over the past 3,000 years or more, if humans were wrestling and applying submission holds dating back to at least the early Olympic Games, they very likely used similar wrestling maneuvers and applied the same submission holds that you see in the 21st century.

Grappling in 1300s England

Records note what became known as *Lancashire wrestling* as early as 1330 in Manchester, England. The wrestling tradition in this area remains strong through today, with surrounding areas acting as a hotbed for catch wrestling in the mid-20th century. (See Chapter 11 for more talk about catch wrestling.) Obviously, no one reinvented wrestling in Bolton, but it was here that immigrants from France, Germany, and elsewhere blended their styles with the local style to create a brand new style known under various names, including Lancashire up-and-down fighting and the Bolton Method.

It was a loose style of grappling that allowed punching, kicking, wrestling, and choking. Matches basically ended via submission. The loser either:

- Was throttled unconscious by their opponent
- Submitted, giving up either verbally or by raising a hand (no *tap-outs* — where you tap to signal defeat — yet).

This style continued to be practiced for centuries around Europe and elsewhere.

Identifying some notable ancient-world wrestlers

Here are some notable wrestlers of long ago (some real, some fictional):

- **Jacob:** In the Book of Genesis in the Bible, Jacob has a wrestling match with an angel all through the night, after which the angel blesses him and gives him the name *Israel* (which means *he struggles with God*). Whoever this angel was, he was a bad dude because he dislocated Jacob's hip in the match, so Jacob walked with a limp the rest of his life.
- **Gilgamesh:** Wrestled the wild man Enkidu in *The Epic of Gilgamesh,* the oldest surviving epic poem. Although Gilgamesh wins, he's so impressed with Enkidu's prowess that the two become close friends. (This storyline has appeared countless times in modern professional wrestling.)
- **Odysseus:** A legendary ancient Greek king whose tale Homer presents in his epic poems *The Iliad* and *The Odyssey.* In *The Iliad,* Odysseus wrestles Ajax during the funeral games for Trojan War hero Patroclus.
- **Bhima and Jarasandha:** In the Sanskrit epic *Mahabharata,* these characters had what can only be described as an MMA fight. They grapple, punch, and kick at each other "like two mad elephants."
- **Plato:** An ancient Greek philosopher who allegedly competed in the Isthmian Games, which were held the year before and the year after the Olympic Games.
- **Ptolemy II and Ptolemy III:** Macedonian rulers of Ancient Egypt from 284 B.C. to 222 B.C. who have been depicted in art as great wrestlers.

Entering the Pioneer Era — Where Pro Wrestling Began

In the *Pioneer Era* — the time from the late 1700s through the early 1900s — professional wrestling evolved into a form similar to modern professional wrestling. But realistically, it probably dates back much further. (Historical documents suggest that wrestling continued to be a popular sport throughout the world following the fall of the Roman Empire in about 476 A.D.)

However, in Europe, you can find the roots of modern professional wrestling. From the earliest days of the Pioneer Era of professional wrestling, many bouts were *worked* (not legitimate).

In the following sections, we delve into the beginning of professional wrestling as it's known today, as well as some of the most noteworthy wrestlers.

Catch-as-catch-can wrestling takes off

By the early 1820s, many people had been badly injured or killed over the years while wrestling by using the Bolton method (see the section "Grappling in 1300s England" earlier in this chapter), so local authorities essentially outlawed that wrestling style. Those who made money off prizefighting were none too pleased. And soon a new, safer style came into vogue, variously called catch-as-catch-can or Lancashire wrestling. Chapter 11 discusses the ins and outs of catch-as-catch-can wrestling.

When the first European settlers came to North America in the 15th century, they discovered that the Native American tribes all practiced some style of wrestling, with rules and techniques differing by tribe. Some tribes specialized in leg or arm wrestling, and others practiced a style similar to catch wrestling, where the goal was to throw your opponent. Early European settlers wrote about witnessing indigenous wrestling matches. There aren't a lot of records of Native Americans and European settlers wrestling each other, but some exist.

Wrestling became a popular pastime in North America over the ensuing generations. The early matches resembled Greco-Roman wrestling, allowing only holds above the waist, with the object being to throw your opponent for a *fall* (when both of a wrestler's shoulders touch the mat). Newer settlers coming from Europe preferred a more open style, and over the centuries aspects of various European styles, including Cornish, Scottish Backhold, and Cumberland, melded their way in.

By the late-1700s, wrestling was a full-on spectator sport. Historians can't identify for sure when the sport first became worked; but most likely, as soon as money became involved, the pure sanctity of the sport went out the window. Newspaper articles dating back to the early 1800s discuss numerous matches that the reporters believed were fixed. And by the late 1800s, you had full-on professional wrestling, including larger-than-life characters and primitive storylines designed to draw money.

Comparing then to now

Well into the 20th century, whether you mostly did theatrical wrestling or not, you absolutely needed to know how to legitimately wrestle. That's not necessarily the case anymore:

- **Pioneer Era wrestlers:** A wrestler had to be able to legitimately wrestle because the bouts weren't always fixed. If someone decided that they wanted to try to steal a championship, or if someone out of the crowd wanted to try to test the mettle of one of the wrestlers, that wrestler had to have the ability to legitimately hold their own on the mat.
- **Modern pro wrestlers:** Nowadays, a high-level athlete, such as a volleyball player, can be trained to be a world champion professional wrestler despite having never gotten into a legitimate fight in their lives.

Gambling and side bets

Gambling and *side bets* (each wrestler allegedly puts up money toward the total purse) helped define modern professional wrestling. Because of gambling and side bets, some wrestling matches were fixed from Day One; and by the late 1800s, likely the vast majority of them were predetermined. Money drove the evolution of wrestling from a:

- Fun pastime on the frontier
- Rough and rowdy — and frowned-upon — endeavor in the mid-1800s
- Full-on touring entertainment spectacular after the American Civil War

ABRAHAM LINCOLN — NO STRANGER TO WRESTLING

Wrestling exploded in popularity following the American Civil War. You may have heard that the man who led the United States through the American Civil War, 16th President Abraham Lincoln, was a wrestler in his younger years. The stories of Lincoln's prowess, like anything, have grown in the retelling, to the point that some sources now list him as being an undefeated champion who won 200 straight matches. According to verifiable records, Lincoln appeared to be a good wrestler who both won and lost the few matches that we have records of. His most famous bout took place around 1831, when Lincoln was in his 20s, against a fellow by the name of Jack Armstrong, the leader of a local gang in Salem, Illinois.

Although what happened during the match varies among different accounts, eyewitnesses relate that the match went to a draw when neither man could throw the other. Regardless of the outcome, Lincoln and Armstrong — as often happens in both real-life and theatrical pro wrestling — became good friends.

Also, during this match, spectators gambled. Townspeople who showed up bet money, drinks, knives, and anything of value. This is one of the most important things you'll read in this book.

In the 2020s, a pro wrestling promotion in British Columbia, Canada held matches that featured a wrestler named Abe Lincoln — who was, in fact, supposed to be the actual Abe Lincoln, complete with a stovepipe hat, which he wrestled in.

Pro wrestling very quickly became a way to fleece *marks* (the spectators being conned) out of their money. Fans placed bets on matches, and the wrestlers or their promoter determined how the match finished based on how much money the wrestlers and their representation could make. After the match, they then split the profits and moved on to the next town. Wrestlers could easily move from town to town, staying ahead of the newspapers that might reveal their shady practices.

By the late 1800s, traveling carnivals had come into vogue, and pro wrestling became a sideshow act. Sometimes, two top wrestlers squared off, and spectators made bets. Other times, the wrestler faced a local tough guy (sometimes actually a local tough guy if the wrestler himself was skilled, but often just another pro wrestler masquerading as the local tough guy). The wrestling matches took place alongside the other worked carnival games, and the *carny* (carnival worker) lingo and pro wrestling lingo merged to create the insider's vocabulary still used today. (We talk about the carny connection and this lingo in Chapter 2.)

ONE OF THE FIRST GIMMICK WRESTLERS

The first wrestler in world history who was largely a *gimmick* (larger-than-life pretend persona) was King of the Wrestlers Charles. History doesn't know much about Charles, other than he went from town to town in 1840s United States, declaring himself King of the Wrestlers Charles and offering to take on all comers. He was flamboyant, wacky, and a national newspaper favorite, the first big pro wrestling star. He either charged admission to his matches or took side bets to make his money, depending on the city. He had a friend, Eugene Carriere, who traveled with him and appeared to play opponent for most of his worked matches. By the 1850s, he essentially vanished from the historical record.

Meeting three notable wrestlers of the Pioneer Era

To the average person, Abraham Lincoln was the most famous wrestler of the Pioneer Era (see the sidebar "Abraham Lincoln — No stranger to wrestling" in this chapter). But to wrestling historians, he was far from the most notable. The three biggest stars of the Pioneer Era who didn't outwardly work a *gimmick* (fake persona) were Colonel James H. McLaughlin, William Muldoon, and John McMahon, whom we talk about in the following sections.

Colonel James H. McLaughlin

Arguably the most important middle Pioneer Era figure when it comes to catch-as-catch-can wrestling and *collar-and-elbow wrestling* (an Irish style of wrestling that began with the wrestlers gripping each other by the collar and elbow and trying to force a fall — the grip itself is still used today in judo, jiu-jitsu, and professional wrestling) was Colonel James H. McLaughlin. Although many titles in wrestling are gimmicks, McLaughlin was a legitimate Union Army colonel during the American Civil War.

In 1870, McLaughlin won the Detroit International Tournament, the biggest national wrestling tournament of the Pioneer Era, and was awarded a leather belt that had a gold buckle. And then several weeks later, he beat American Collar and Elbow Champion Homer Lane (who was supposed to be in the Detroit tournament but no-showed). The Detroit tournament itself was a major national news story, the biggest in American professional wrestling up to that point in time, and McLaughlin became a favorite of the national press for decades afterward. After he defeated Lane in Titusville, Pennsylvania, on April 30, McLaughlin was recognized as the singular American Collar and Elbow Champion.

He remained one of the three biggest stars in the industry for decades afterward. He wrestled through the early 1900s, where he toured the Yukon with Frank Gotch (see the section "Entering the Heavyweight Wrestling Champion Era — Frank Gotch" later in this chapter) and Joe Carroll, almost certainly performing worked three-way programs in different towns.

William Muldoon

William Muldoon was the most influential figure of the middle Pioneer Era when it comes to the popularity of Greco-Roman wrestling. Muldoon was a legitimate wrestler, but also a *worker* (he fixed matches), like most wrestlers during that period. Until very recently, historians believed that he served in the Civil War, but while he researched his biography of Muldoon, *The Last Gladiator* (University of Texas Press), historian Scott Beekman discovered that Muldoon's brother served; Muldoon himself forever lied that he had served in the Union Army.

Muldoon won the World Greco-Roman Championship from Thiebaud Bauer in 1880. His most famous match took place in 1881, when he allegedly went to a seven-hour draw with Clarence Whistler at Madison Square Garden in New York City.

Prior to his title win, Greco-Roman wrestling had a poor reputation in America, with the public seeing it largely as a farce (which it was). Muldoon went around the country in the 1880s performing technical demonstrations, which helped convince the public that Greco-Roman wrestling was, in fact, a legitimate sport.

TECHNICAL STUFF

Because he was a New York City policeman, in addition to being a pro wrestler, the New York press loved to cover his exploits, making him one of the most famous mainstream wrestlers of the era.

John McMahon

John McMahon (no relation to the Vince McMahon family) looked like a 19th-century stereotypical male — big handlebar mustache, trousers pulled up a little too high, and suspenders. He was a great wrestler — and also a carny (see our discussion of carnival workers and wrestlers in Chapter 2). And when we say carny, he even wrestled in P.T. Barnum–promoted circuses near the end of his career (all worked matches).

He served in the Civil War as a Union soldier. He debuted as a professional wrestler in June of 1861 and allegedly went undefeated for 17 years (almost certainly untrue, like all Pioneer Era records).

TIP

During his heyday, the press often compared him to McLaughlin (see the section "Colonel James H. McLaughlin" earlier in this chapter). But they never actually wrestled each other until 1878, when they had a classic three-match program. The series was almost certainly worked; the contemporary newspaper accounts of the matches were very skeptical of their legitimacy. The results also fit into the standard pro wrestling format of splitting wins:

- McMahon won the first bout (after which he claimed McLaughlin's Detroit International Tournament belt).
- McLaughlin won the second (after which McMahon returned the belt).
- The third match went to a draw (so McLaughlin kept the belt).

Entering the Heavyweight Wrestling Champion Era — Frank Gotch

Wrestling exploded in popularity during the heyday of wrestler Frank Gotch, from around 1908 to 1913, and it went into a steep decline for many years following his retirement in 1915. Historians consider him the first American World's Heavyweight Wrestling Champion, and he was a legitimate gigantic mainstream sports superstar. Because of Gotch, amateur (legitimate) wrestling is a mainstay of middle and high schools and collegiate wrestling programs today.

The following sections look at professional wrestling during this era. Chapter 11 provides specifics about Gotch.

Battling George Hackenschmidt

In 1905, George Hackenschmidt defeated wrestler Tom Jenkins to become the first-ever recognized Undisputed World's Heavyweight Wrestling Champion. Gotch was ready to take the title. Gotch and Hackenschmidt had two of the most famous matches in pro wrestling history (the first match helped popularize wrestling in the United States, and the second did the opposite):

- **The first battle:** Took place on April 3, 1908, in Dexter Park Pavilion in Chicago, Illinois. Although scheduled to go *three falls* (meaning who could win two-out-of-three), Hackenschmidt gave up after a two-hour first fall and relinquished the title to Gotch, the first American to ever hold that title. He became a national sports icon with the win and went undefeated through the rest of his career.

WARNING

Gotch had a dark side. Eyewitness reports from the first match suggest that he thumbed Hackenschmidt in the eyeball, headbutted him, and may have even greased his body, all of which were illegal tactics.

» **The rematch:** Their rematch took place on September 4, 1911, at the new Comiskey Park in Chicago, in front of nearly 30,000 fans. Hackenschmidt injured his knee before the match (whether the Gotch camp paid to have him suffer an injury or whether it was bad luck is a fact lost to history).

  On the day of the match, the wrestlers made an agreement: Gotch claimed he would *carry* Hackenschmidt in the match (do a fixed performance where he would help the injured Hackenschmidt look impressive), they'd each "win" one fall, and then Gotch would beat him in the end. But when the bell rang, Gotch did the opposite. He quickly and decisively legitimately beat Hackenschmidt in two straight falls by using his dreaded *toe hold* (a submission hold), which attacked the knee. Hackenschmidt hated Gotch for the rest of his life. (You can read more about Hackenschmidt in Chapter 11.)

Facing the truth about reality

Pro wrestling in the United States fell on tough times following 1915. At the time, your average person's grasp of wrestling history was specific to their own lifetime memories, so a generation grew up thinking that pro wrestling during the Gotch era was 100 percent legitimate. For many reasons, following his death, questions again arose in the press regarding pro wrestling's legitimacy. The second Gotch-versus-Hackenschmidt match, discussed in the preceding section, certainly didn't help matters — newspapers called it "a farce," "the stinker of the century," and "a fix."

Many in academia claim that pro wrestling was legitimate competition through the era of Gotch and Hackenschmidt, and it didn't become show-business wrestling until the early 1920s. Only recently, with the explosion of interest in the history of wrestling and newly available digitized newspaper archives online did historians understand that pro wrestling had mostly been a work dating back a century before Gotch.

The 1920s — The Gold Dust Trio era

Professional wrestling changed forever in the 1920s with the rise of the Gold Dust Trio, which consisted of the wrestlers Toots Mondt and Ed "Strangler" Lewis, and the manager Billy Sandow.

At this time, many wrestlers trained and wrestled in carnivals. They were both *workers* (performance wrestlers) and masters of legitimate submission wrestling. The wrestler terminology in those days identified:

- **Shooter:** A great legitimate wrestler.
- **Hooker:** A shooter who was adept at applying debilitating submission holds that could break bones and tear ligaments (the submission holds were referred to as *hooks*).

  REMEMBER

  Mondt was trained in the art of hooking and was said to have become very dangerous.
- **Policeman:** Physically handled problems when they cropped up amongst unruly wrestlers, giving those who got out of line a *stretching* (beating).

Creating modern pro wrestling

Toots Mondt, who was a great wrestler, found his greatest strength was his mind. He came up with the idea of starting a promotion (with Lewis and Sandow) in the early 1920's that completely changed the way professional wrestling was presented:

- Instituting time limits
- Presenting a more exciting, theatrical style of wrestling
- Using more modern moves, including high-risk *bumps* (falls) such as bodyslams, punches, and kicks
- Signing wrestlers to the very first exclusive contracts
- Establishing longer-term storylines and programs

The changes were revolutionary, and within a year, the Gold Dust Trio had taken over American professional wrestling. Their success allowed them to promote shows in larger buildings, make more money (hence the name), and thus sign more talent. What Mondt dubbed *Slam-Bang Western-Style Wrestling* dominated the business for most of the next decade.

Witnessing the first big pro wrestling screwjob

The Gold Dust Trio didn't have a monopoly on professional wrestling. Other promoters ran events, and the main competition for the Trio was a promotion headed by a man named Joe Stecher. On April 15, 1925, this rivalry led to the first high-profile *screwjob* (essentially, going against the script) in the history of wrestling.

The Trio wanted to capitalize on the fame of Wayne Munn, a well-known college football player from the University of Nebraska, by making him their World Heavyweight Champion (a very controversial decision because every previous World Heavyweight Champion had some legitimate wrestling background to speak of).

Munn won the title from the Trio's "Strangler" Lewis on January 8, 1925, in Wichita, Kansas. On April 15, Munn was scheduled to defend the title against Stanislaus Zbyszko (a wrestler signed to the Gold Dust Trio) at a show in Philadelphia, Pennsylvania.

Unbeknownst to the Trio, Joe Stecher's team offered Zbyszko a payoff to steal the title from Munn. Zbyszko quickly double-crossed and pinned Munn, who had no legitimate wrestling ability whatsoever. Zbyszko then jumped ship from the Trio to Stecher's group and lost the title to Stetcher on May 30 in St. Louis, Missouri.

The Stecher group had effectively stolen the World Heavyweight Championship from the Gold Dust Trio. Although some promoters did award versions of the world championship to non-wrestlers after this screwjob, for the next several decades, if you wanted to be in line for a major-league World Heavyweight Championship, you needed to know how to legitimately wrestle.

Making up and breaking up

As a result of Zbyszko taking the title from Munn (see the preceding section), from 1925 through 1928, two different groups promoted two different World Heavyweight Titles. The dispute ended on February 21, 1928, with Stecher "losing" his version of the title (which was originally Lewis's version anyway) back to Lewis, ending the dispute and unifying the titles.

In 1928, the Gold Dust Trio split up because of differences between the members. All three remained in the business in different capacities: Sandow as a manager, Lewis as a perennial World Champion through the late 1940s, and Mondt as the mastermind behind several of the biggest names and promotions in the history of wrestling over the next 50 years (flip to Chapter 7 for more about Mondt's illustrious career).

Entering the Great Depression/WWII

Because the *Great Depression* (a severe global economic downturn from 1929 to 1939 that left nearly everyone in financial straits) and World War II dominated headlines from the 1930s to mid-1940s, most fans know next to nothing about that era in professional wrestling. But it was a very successful time for pro wrestling, highlighted by one of the biggest and most forgotten stars in the history of the sport, Jim Londos.

Wrestling during the Great Depression — The Jim Londos era

Historians have largely overlooked Jim Londos because, during the era in which he was at his peak:

- His biggest-drawing shows occurred outside the United States.
- He fought for United States sports coverage with press favorites such as "Strangler" Lewis (discussed in the section "The 1920s — The Gold Dust Trio era" earlier in this chapter).
- The early histories of the era covered wrestlers such as Lou Thesz (flip to the section "Thesz leads the way" later in this chapter), whose mentorship by and friendship with Lewis led to an emphasis on Thesz's career and dealings.

Rising in popularity

Adjusted for inflation, Londos (see Figure 4-1) was very likely the biggest draw in the history of professional wrestling, made even more impressive because Londos set his records during the Great Depression.

FIGURE 4-1: Jim Londos.

Jim Melby photos from Dr Mike Lano's Collection

Londos, called "The Golden Greek", was born January 2, 1894, in Argos, Greece. His birth name was Christos Theofilou, making him one of the rare wrestlers who arguably had a better real name than his stage name (he quickly changed his name to Jim Londos because a sports editor in Oregon, believe it or not, advised him to get a name that was easy for English-speaking Americans to pronounce). He broke into professional wrestling in 1914 and, within a few years, had already become a somewhat big star.

Londos was on the smaller side (he stood about five-foot-eight feet and weighed about 200 pounds), and although he almost certainly was a good legitimate wrestler (you pretty much had to be in those days), his calling card was his movie-star good looks and physique. The newspapers focused their coverage mostly on wrestlers such as Ed Lewis and Joe Stecher, who wrestled throughout the large media centers in the United States, but he quietly amassed a following both in the States and his homeland of Greece.

Living life as a champ

In July of 1930, Londos faced top star Dick Shikat for promoter Ray Fabiani's version of the World Heavyweight Championship, and Londos emerged victorious. He then began an incredible run as champion, turning around business at Madison Square Garden to the point that newspapers claimed the turnstiles spun so many times and generated so much heat that custodians had to cover them in ice. Although the turnstile stories are obviously exaggerated, in reality, attendance at the Garden increased seven-fold after Londos began headlining.

In 1933, he returned to Greece a hero, having achieved his goal of becoming World Heavyweight Champion (although, interestingly, he had been stripped of the title a year earlier for refusing to face "Strangler" Lewis.

TIP

On October 22, 1933, he faced Kola Kwariani at Panathenaic Stadium in Athens, Greece. Londos claimed the show drew 100,000 fans. The newspapers reported a crowd of 65,000. Because professional wrestlers are prone to hyperbole, we'd usually recommend that you take the word of the newspapers. However, in the 21st century, historians discovered film from the match in the Greek national newsreel archives and uploaded it to YouTube — and although 100,000 people may not have been there, if the number was less, it was not much less.

TECHNICAL STUFF

Although no one can verify the true number, if you exclude the two New Japan/WCW Collision in Korea shows on April 28 and 29, 1995 (in which the North Korean government basically ordered the fans to attend — see Chapter 14), Londos versus Kwariani may have been the legitimately most-attended event in the history of pro wrestling.

Experiencing highs and lows

Londos regained a version of the World Title in 1934 and continued drawing gigantic crowds and record-breaking gates. On September 20, 1934, the dream match of that era — Londos versus "Strangler" Lewis — finally took place at Wrigley Field in Chicago. Londos beat Lewis in a match that drew what was at the time the all-time United States attendance and gate records for pro wrestling: 35,625 attendees and $96,000 brought in ($2.6 million at the time of writing, adjusted for inflation).

Londos lost his version of the World Title to Danno O'Mahoney in 1935 and traveled the world for several years afterward, drawing large crowds everywhere he went. He regained the title from Bronko Nagurski on November 11, 1938. And although he continued to wrestle on and off through the late 1950s, a new era of stars was beginning to rise.

Wrestling during World War II

World War II (WWII; 1939–1945) changed the real world and the world of pro wrestling forever in many ways. Many current or future American pro wrestlers ended up enlisting or being drafted, and others helped entertain the troops or even train them in hand-to-hand combat. In Japan, the war was responsible for the explosion in popularity of professional wrestling that continues to this day.

Thesz leads the way

Although pro wrestling was basically 100 percent worked by the time WWII broke out, and although the style had evolved to become far more theatrical and entertaining (some would say preposterous), the biggest stars of the late 1930s and early 1940s still came from an era where they were trained in legitimate hooking and shooting techniques.

Arguably the biggest star of the 1940s, Lou Thesz (whom we talk about in Chapter 5) was one of the last great old-school hookers (in part simply because he outlived everyone else). Thesz had been involved in legitimate Greco-Roman and folkstyle amateur wrestling since he was 8 years old. And when he broke into professional wrestling in the early 1930s, he trained with George Tragos, Ad Santel, and "Strangler" Lewis, all of whom added dangerous legitimate submissions to his repertoire.

During WWII, the U.S. military recruited Thesz and others, including future legend Verne Gagne and Joe Stecher, to help teach hand-to-hand combat to troops. The U.S. Navy's Training Division of the Bureau of Aeronautics also distributed a *Wrestling* manual, which featured illustrations and photographs of various wrestling techniques.

Among the legendary professional wrestling characters who served in World War II were "Classy" Freddie Blassie, Paul Boesch (who received a Silver Star, Bronze Star, and Purple Heart), Sam Muchnick, "The Sheik" Ed Farhat, Lord James Blears, and even Vince McMahon, Sr.

Making special attractions (including women) the focus

Women's professional wrestling exploded during WWII, in part because so many men were being drafted, so the promotions needed to find new talent. Wrestling shows, which had always featured *special attractions* (usually meaning matches that didn't involve men), increased the number of matches between women, little people (known then by the derogatory name *midget wrestling*, now called *micro or minis wrestling*), and even animals.

The women, who often wrestled in risqué (at the time) one-piece swimsuits, became big draws. Back in the 1930s, many matches that involved women had a woman wrestling a man, but by the 1940s, more and more woman-versus-woman matches took place.

REMEMBER

Although the biggest stars of midget wrestling got their start in the 1940s, their heyday kicked off with the advent of U.S. national television, because people loved watching their comedic matches on TV.

Rikidōzan and Japanese pro wrestling

Japan's defeat in World War II was the catalyst for the sport of professional wrestling exploding into the mainstream in that country. Having suffered a devastating defeat in the war, surrendering to the Allies after the United States dropped atomic bombs on Hiroshima and Nagasaki in 1945, the Japanese people wanted a hero. Although you might think that Japan choosing a pro wrestler as a national hero sounds absurd on the surface, it was reality. (Check out Chapter 10 for a deep dive into Japanese professional wrestling.)

GETTING FOREIGN HEELS

World War II spawned decades of foreign menace *heels* (bad guy personas), from evil Japanese salt-throwing heels (often portrayed by Hawaiians) to goose-stepping German Nazi heels. Wrestling didn't move away from foreign stereotypes for decades (and, of course, they got a renewed push with the rise of the evil Russian heels during the Cold War in the 1980s, most of whom weren't actually Russian).

Japanese wrestling before the war

Before World War II, the Japanese had come to the United States to engage in combat sports since at least the late 1800s. Koujiro Matsuda, a Japanese sumo wrestler, emigrated to the States in 1883 and became the first famous Japanese professional wrestler.

Several years later, Matsuda and another wrestler who had traveled to America, Shokichi Hamada, staged the first professional wrestling show in Japan, advertised as a demonstration of Western-style wrestling. The concept failed to catch on with the public. Various Japanese grapplers continued to come to America, however, until World War II made the countries enemies.

Giving Japan a victory

After the war, in 1951, Japanese wrestler Mitsuhiro Momota (ring name: Rikidōzan) trained and wrestled with U.S. promotions Mid-Pacific Promotions in Honolulu and National Wrestling Alliance (NWA) San Francisco. Rikidōzan then started the first official professional wrestling promotion in Japan in 1953, the Japanese Wrestling Association (JWA). The home-grown talent consisted largely of former sumo wrestlers and *judokas* (people who trained in judo). At first, Rikidōzan, the top star, feuded largely with other Japanese wrestlers.

REMEMBER

In 1954, JWA ran shows at Tokyo Sumo Hall that were broadcast on national television. On the first night, Rikidōzan teamed with another legendary *judoka*, Masahiko Kimura, to face the Sharpe Brothers (a pair of Canadian professional wrestlers) in a tag team match. The Japanese watching on television were enthralled by two big, powerful Japanese wrestlers pummeling two even larger white wrestlers (no one cared that the Sharpes weren't actually from the States).

Rikidōzan's televised destruction of foreigners — often large Americans — became a sensation in the country:

- His televised matches drew tens of millions of viewers and set worldwide records.
- The sport itself exploded to match the popularity of sumo and baseball in Japan.
- Rikidōzan became a cultural icon. He was legitimately responsible for selling millions of television sets, like the professional wrestler Gorgeous George in the United States (see the section "Making an immediate impact" later in this chapter).

WRESTLING MONEY MAKERS BEFORE TV

In the beginning of pro wrestling, wrestlers made money through side bets. For example, on March 16, 1872, Col. James H. McLaughlin bet $1,000 versus Homer Lane's $600 that he could throw Lane twice in 30 minutes (he failed). Other times, spectators set up a side for each man, and each side bet that a particular wrestler would win.

Later, promoters staged events built around one big super fight — say Frank Gotch versus George Hackenschmidt. They rented a venue and sold tickets, and then the wrestlers split a portion of the ticket sales. While wrestling evolved, promoters formed troupes of wrestlers, and they *ran cards* (wrestling shows) regularly in their specific territories around the country. Usually, the *undercard wrestlers* (preliminary match wrestlers underneath the main event) received a predetermined flat fee, and the main eventers (or just the champion himself) got a percentage of the money earned at the gate.

Watching the Television Era

The birth of television changed pro wrestling forever by bringing the action to a wider audience than it had ever been exposed to before. From literally the dawn of television all the way through today, professional wrestling has always been one of the most popular programs on TV. In the following sections, we explore how pro wrestling became popular in the TV era.

Making an immediate impact

In the United States, by far the most famous name of the early television period was George Wagner, otherwise known as "Gorgeous George."

Wagner developed the "Gorgeous George" character (also called the "Human Orchid") in the early 1940s when working shows on the West Coast. Although he was a strong amateur wrestler and had been in the business a decade, his career didn't take off until he went full gimmick with the effeminate character.

REMEMBER

So much of modern pro wrestling dates to Wagner's popularization of it, including the following:

- **Ring music:** He used the "Pomp and Circumstance" classical march (that you hear all the time at graduations), which Randy Savage also used during his peak in the 1980s.

» **Bleached blonde hair:** Pretty much every top star from the 1960s through the 1980s bleached their hair.

» **His valet:** Less a manager and more a personal manservant who removed George's robes and sprayed perfume around ringside, "Jeffries" was a model for many future valets both male and female.

» **Elaborate sequined robes:** The outlandish sequined glittering wrestling robe became a staple of flamboyant bad guy wrestlers.

» **Gimmicks:** He threw "Georgie Pin" orchid souvenirs to the crowd (a practice he stole from wrestler "Dizzy" Davis in Mexico, who threw flowers to the crowd at his matches).

TIP

The character, which generated tremendous *heat* (fans hated him), turned Wagner's career around in the 1940s. And he really shot to superstardom because George built his character for the new medium of television. "Gorgeous George" was larger than life. He made his TV debut on November 11, 1947, from the station KTLA in Los Angeles, California, against Sam Menacker (Sam got lucky that history remembers him — often newspapers that reported on George's act wouldn't even bother to mention his opponent).

"Gorgeous George" almost immediately became:

» One of the biggest celebrities in the nation

» One of the first bona-fide television stars

» The subject of articles in the national press, *TIME* and *Newsweek* magazines

» The top draw in the entire pro wrestling business

» Allegedly able to command half the gate of any show that he headlined (likely an exaggeration, but he made a lot of money)

Businesses that sold TVs placed them in the windows facing out, and huge crowds gathered outside to watch his matches. People who had televisions would host parties where people would come over just to watch George wrestle. (Co-author Bryan Alvarez can attest to these parties because his grandmother Gladys, still alive at the time of writing at 96, witnessed and even took part in such parties). Some of the biggest stars in the history of entertainment, including James Brown, Bob Dylan, and Muhammad Ali all claimed that they either stole portions of George's act, or that meeting the superstar that was Gorgeous George helped change their life.

How pro wrestling's presence on TV evolved

Although the national television boom that centered around "Gorgeous George" was relatively short-lived, it changed the business:

- **Cheap programming:** One of the reasons wrestling was such a huge hit in the late 1940s and early 1950s was because television needed programming, and wrestling was a cheap way to get it. At its peak in the early 1950s, wrestling aired on television in some form every day of the week. And unlike today, viewers had only a small number of available channels, so everybody saw it at one point or another.
- **Going local:** Television was also expanding to feature local programming specific to a given market, and those stations needed programming: Once again, pro wrestling fit that bill. In the ensuing decades, pro wrestling airing on local TV stations helped further the growth of the *territorial system* (wrestling promotions running only in specific geographic markets) around the United States, which we talk about in Chapter 5.

IN THIS CHAPTER

» Exploring the territorial system

» Discovering the top territories

» Seeing how the National Wrestling Alliance (NWA) formed and fell apart

» Meeting the territories that broke away from the NWA

Chapter 5
Examining the Midcentury Territory Era

The only thing certain in life is change. For good or bad, change is unavoidable. The professional wrestling industry has changed dramatically since the early days of the Pioneer Era (which we talk about in Chapter 4). The two biggest changes of all involved the creation and eventual death of a geographic network of wrestling promotions called the *territorial system*, part of the Territory Era.

This chapter focuses mostly on the territorial system in the United States (with a little Canada mixed in). Pro wrestling existed all over the world during this timeframe, but the United States was the center of the pro wrestling universe. We discuss important historical events in Japan, Mexico, and elsewhere in Part 4.

Getting the Lowdown on Territories

In professional wrestling, a *territory* was basically a geographical region run by a particular promoter and promotion. By the mid-20th century, you could find territories not only all over the United States and Canada, but all over the world.

The territorial system can realistically trace its roots back to Harry Hill's Variety Theatre, which we discuss in Chapter 12. Hill was basically the first-ever professional wrestling promoter. After opening his theater, he rose to prominence as a promoter of pro wrestling, boxing, and more, all centered in the New York market.

While time passed and more promotions began popping up in the early decades of the 1900s, the territorial system began to evolve. The system worked for a while, and promoters and wrestlers benefited, but the system did eventually die:

- **Staying local:** The territorial system worked from the 1940s until the 1980s because news traveled slowly prior to the explosion of cable television and the development of the internet. Every territory basically had its own local television and ran live events exclusively in that territory.

  TIP

  Even though organizations in close proximity had occasional promotional wars, in general, everyone stayed exclusive to their particular territory. And because no real national pro wrestling television aired from the late 1950s through the late 1970s, and because VCRs, which allowed tape-trading among rabid fans to explode, weren't commonplace until the mid-1980s, promoters could easily run the pro wrestling show in their own little neck of the woods and nobody outside that area would know what was happening.
- **Finding success:** Even though wrestling newsstand magazines carried the news around the country (very slowly), fans in a particular territory really got exposed to only their local brand of wrestling, which was great for everyone:
  - *Wrestlers:* If you were a top star, you could make big money in a particular territory until the fans grew tired of you. At that point, you lost some big matches and then left the territory for another. Because most fans wouldn't know you (other than maybe reading your name in wrestling magazines), you stepped into the new territory with a new name, ready for another run before a brand-new set of eyes.
  - *Promoters:* Could use these rotating stars to constantly keep things fresh.
  - *Fans:* Regularly got to see new stars come and go. Things never got stale.
- **The end of the territories:** The territories died when Vince McMahon, Jr., decided to break all the rules and go national in the early 1980s. By the end of the decade, the territorial system was dead, and pro wrestling was basically left with two big-time national promotions: World Wrestling Federation (WWF) and World Championship Wrestling (WCW), which you can read about in Chapter 6. Chapter 6 explains how cable TV, and then the internet, changed the pro wrestling promotion landscape.

Identifying the Territories during the Territory Era

Vince McMahon, Jr.'s national expansion of the WWF and the explosion of national cable television ultimately killed off the territorial system. The following sections give you a brief overview of some of the top territories in the United States and Canada during the 1950s to early 1980s.

REMEMBER

Although some promotions shared the same names, they weren't affiliated with each other.

West Coast

The West Coast of the United States featured promotions with very good wrestling action, but the top stars didn't achieve the same success as those in the larger media markets of the Northeast:

- **Los Angeles, California (World Wrestling Association [WWA]):** Also called NWA Hollywood or NWA Los Angeles, the territory ran from 1958 through 1982. Cal and Aileen Eaton were the original owners, and Mike LeBell took over in 1966 until it closed in 1982. It used the Grand Olympic Auditorium as its main venue.
- **Portland, Oregon (Portland Wrestling):** Also known as Big Time Wrestling and Pacific Northwest Wrestling. Founded by Herb Owen in 1925. It was one of the original 1948 NWA territories, and Herb's son Don continued to run the territory through 1992, making it basically the last old-school wrestling territory.

  REMEMBER

  Wrestlers loved working the Portland Wrestling territory because Don was an honest promoter and paid well — and, honestly, the wrestlers loved all the women who frequented the matches.
- **San Francisco, California (Big Time Wrestling):** Otherwise known as NWA San Francisco. Ran from 1960 through 1981, the entire time under the auspices of former wrestler Roy Shire. Running big shows from the legendary Cow Palace arena, the promotion was among the strongest in the country because of a combination of strong booking and a highly-rated television program. Some of the best in-ring matches in the nation took place through Big Time Wrestling in the 1970s.

- **Vancouver, British Columbia (All Star Wrestling [ASW]):** Started in 1960 and active through 1989 under various owners, including founder Rod Fenton, famed wrestler and former World Champion Gene Kiniski, and finally Al Tomko. ASW hung on until the bitter end, likely in part because of its geography.

TECHNICAL STUFF

When co-author Bryan Alvarez broke into wrestling in 1998, he worked for International Championship Wrestling, a promotion out of British Columbia run by Tim Flowers, and many of the older ASW wrestlers were still working. He was always told that if you want to make it, you have to get out of the Northwest because it was like "an island" where nobody outside of the region ever really heard of you.

Midwest

The Midwest had a strong wrestling history, the birthplace of Frank Gotch and thus modern amateur wrestling:

- **Calgary, Alberta (Stampede Wrestling):** Founded in 1948 by wrestler Stu Hart, patriarch of the legendary Hart family, and controlled by the Harts through its initial death in 1984 (it reopened multiple times). Stampede was among the top promotions in Western Canada for almost 50 years. Besides promoting, Stu was a legendary trainer who broke in multiple greats, including his sons Bret and Owen, as well as famed tag team Edge and Christian, Japanese star Hiroshi Hase, and Chris Jericho and Lance Storm, all of whom became big stars and decorated champions.
- **Detroit, Michigan (Big Time Wrestling):** Ran from 1945 through 1980, promoted first by Harry Light, and most famously by notorious bloodbath wrestler "The Sheik" Ed Farhat.
- **Indianapolis, Indiana (World Wrestling Association [WWA]):** Founded by top star Dick "The Bruiser" and former great Wilbur Snyder, WWA ran from 1964 through 1989. It was the birthplace of such legends as Bobby "The Brain" Heenan, one of the greatest managers in history (see Chapter 12), and was largely built around feuds involving "The Bruiser," who was the first champion and went on to win the WWA Title 13 different times over the following two decades.
- **Kansas City, Kansas and Missouri (Central States):** One of the original NWA territories that was also one of the last to shut down, it ran from 1948 through 1989. It was originally promoted by Orville Brown, the first NWA World Heavyweight Champion, and later by wrestler Bob Geigel and finally Jim Crockett, Jr. (Flip to the section "Jim Crockett Promotions" later in this chapter for more about Crockett).

REMEMBER

- **St. Louis, Missouri (St. Louis Wrestling Club):** One of the strongest territories for decades, it ran from 1959 through 1985, largely under the direction of founder Sam Muchnick. It ran a weekly television show called *Wrestling at the Chase* on local TV station KPLR for more than 20 years, renowned for taping in the Khorassan Ballroom inside the Chase Park Plaza Hotel before a crowd often dressed in suits and evening gowns.
- **Toronto, Ontario (Maple Leaf Wrestling):** Technically, named the Queensbury Athletic Club, this territory ran from 1930 through 1984 and had the Maple Leaf Gardens arena as its home base. And so fans referred to it as Maple Leaf Wrestling. The Tunney family essentially controlled the territory for most of its existence.

South

Southern "Rasslin," as it was often termed, often featured very entertaining characters and a strong in-ring wrestling style:

- **Atlanta, Georgia (Georgia Championship Wrestling [GCW]):** A powerhouse of wrestling, GCW's flagship television show of the same name was the first NWA television program broadcast nationally on cable television in 1976. Airing on what became Ted Turner's SuperStation TBS (see Chapter 6 for more discussion of Turner's role in pro wrestling), GCW was a huge success (the first TV show of any type to draw more than 1 million viewers on cable).
- **Tampa, Florida (Championship Wrestling from Florida [CWF]):** Ran from 1949 to 1987, its heyday being under the control of Eddie Graham. Some of the biggest stars in wrestling passed through the territory, from all-time great NWA Champion Ric Flair to one of his biggest rivals, Dusty Rhodes, to legendary attraction Andre the Giant and the face of the NWA for a decade, Lou Thesz.
- **Tulsa, Oklahoma and New Orleans, Louisiana (Mid-South Wrestling Association):** Founded as NWA Tri-State in the 1950s, it underwent several name changes. Its biggest success, while short-lived, came in the mid-1980s when former wrestler Bill Watts, promoting it as Mid-South Wrestling, heavily invested in an attempt to go national. But the collapse of the oil industry in Oklahoma spelled the end of the brief golden age and quickly led Watts to sell the territory to Jim Crockett Promotions (JCP). (We talk more about this ill-fated territory in Chapter 6.)

Texas

Texas was a large enough state to host multiple territories:

- **Amarillo (Western States Sports):** This promotion ran from 1946 through 1981 under a variety of owners, including legendary grappler Dory Funk and his two sons, Terry and Dory, Jr. The promotion enjoyed a heyday in the 1960s and 1970s under the Funks and expanded to multiple cities outside of Texas, including Albuquerque, New Mexico, and Colorado Springs, Colorado.
- **Dallas (World Class Championship Wrestling [WCCW]):** Founded in 1966 by Fritz Von Erich, the promotion was built around the Von Erich family. It was part of the NWA until 1986, when Fritz decided he was going to try to break free and go national. WCCW closed its doors in 1990.

  The territory is most famous for its 1982 through 1986 heyday built around the rivalry of the Von Erich Sons versus the Fabulous Freebirds (Michael Hayes, Terry Gordy, Buddy Roberts and Jimmy Garvin), which was an enormous box-office success. The 2023 theatrical film *The Iron Claw* recaps the tragic deaths of all the Von Erich brothers, save Kevin.
- **Houston (Houston Wrestling):** The Houston territory ran from 1925 through 1987. Houston had television on local KHTV for more than 30 years. During its heyday (under former wrestler Paul Boesch), it promoted such legendary acts as the Junkyard Dog, Jake "The Snake" Roberts, King Kong Bundy, Hacksaw Jim Duggan, Rock & Roll Express, and the Midnight Express.

  TIP

  Among its fans was a man who would become President of the United States, George H.W. Bush.

Islands

Territories were not exclusive to the Continental United States:

- **Halifax, Nova Scotia (Atlantic Grand Prix Wrestling):** Former wrestler Emile Dupree ran this territory during the 1960s and 1970s, and it was famous for its very popular tours of the Maritimes (New Brunswick, Nova Scotia, and Prince Edward Island), where stars could gain experience working sometimes 30 days straight. In the final days of the territory, future worldwide stars such as Edge, Christian, Masahiro Chono, and Don Callis worked Maritime tours.
- **Honolulu, Hawaii (50th State Big Time Wrestling):** Operated from 1936 through 1988, its final owner was Lia Maivia, Dwayne "The Rock" Johnson's grandmother (if you somehow weren't aware, the Rock was a gigantic pro wrestling star in WWE before he became a Hollywood A-lister). It peaked

in popularity in the 1960s and 1970s, when its television show, *50th State Big Time Wrestling,* was one of the most popular TV programs.

TIP

Unsurprisingly, wrestlers loved working the Hawaii territory, essentially getting paid to wrestle at night and hang out at the beach all day.

- **San Juan, Puerto Rico (World Wrestling Council [WWC]):** Founded in 1973 in the U.S. territory of Puerto Rico, WWC remained a part of the NWA through 1988. The promotion was often built around the Colon family (its patriarch Carlos being one of the original founders, alongside Victor Jovica and former wrestler Gorilla Monsoon), and continues promoting to this day, more than 50 years later — and yes, it still often builds its matches around members of the Colon family.

Creating the National Wrestling Alliance (NWA) to Unify Territories

On July 14, 1948, a promoter named Paul "Pinkie" George got together with six other promoters — Orville Brown, Al Haft, Harry Light, Sam Muchnick, Don Owen, and Tony Stecher (brother of Joe Stecher) — to create the National Wrestling Alliance (NWA). They wanted to create a national governing body for professional wrestling that would oversee a singular World Heavyweight Champion.

REMEMBER

Essentially, any promotion or territory affiliated with the new NWA could create their own secondary singles or tag team championships. But the NWA Board of Directors would elect only one globally recognized NWA World's Heavyweight Champion, and that champion would travel from territory to territory around the world to defend that title.

Before the death of the territories (which we talk about in Chapter 6), the two strongest organizations in professional wrestling were:

- **The National Wrestling Alliance (NWA):** An alliance of territories around the world. The dominant force in the business for more than 30 years, from the 1950s to the 1970s.
- **The Capital Wrestling Corporation (CWC):** Later renamed World Wide Wrestling Federation (WWWF), then World Wrestling Federation (WWF), and finally World Wrestling Entertainment (WWE). Ultimately became the last promotion standing (read about that battle in Chapter 6).

REMEMBER

In fact, for much of that period, CWC itself was an NWA territory (although because CWC ran the gigantic New York market, it had more power than any other territory). And for many fans, the most prestigious title during this period was the NWA World Heavyweight Championship.

Making an NWA World Heavyweight Champion

The first NWA Board of Directors chose Orville Brown as the inaugural NWA World Heavyweight Champion. Brown fit the champion mold for several reasons. He was:

- A talented wrestler who understood the showbiz aspect of the business
- A very good (but not world-class) legitimate *shooter* (he was also a real wrestler and could defend himself if another wrestler tried to steal the title)
- A good *draw* (he sold tickets) throughout the Midwest

He also just happened to be the champion of his own small promotion in Iowa that he had started several years earlier named the National Wrestling Alliance. He was recognized at the time as the Midwest Wrestling Association World Champion and held the Iowa version of the World Title, both of which were unified to create this new NWA World Heavyweight Title.

WARNING

But his reign was short. On November 1, 1949, he was involved in a very serious car accident that ended his career. The NWA then chose as his successor a wrestler named Lou Thesz, who shaped the NWA for much of its first decade.

Passing the NWA Championship torch

Lou Thesz (shown in Figure 5-1), the second wrestler to hold the NWA World Heavyweight Championship Title, started professional wrestling in the 1930s (which we talk about in Chapter 4). Although pro wrestling matches were mostly predetermined in that era, nearly everyone working in the business at that time was a legitimate, trained *grappler* (a real wrestler). He had a high-level amateur wrestling background, as well as intense training in *submissions* (hold designed to make an opponent quit, also called *hooks*).

Before every promotion had 15 or 20 different championships (which started around the 2020s), promoters heavily protected the World Title. Not everyone who deserved it got their turn. Only a very small, select number of the absolute biggest superstars ever became the World Champion, and the World Championship was the most valuable prize in wrestling, both in storyline and in real life.

FIGURE 5-1: Lou Thesz.

Photo by Wrealano@aol.com

TIP

World Title matches and the World Champion always drew the biggest crowds and generated the most revenue. Fans held the NWA World Championship in high regard because legend said that the NWA Title (and the NWA itself) traced its roots directly back to legendary wrestler George Hackenschmidt in 1905. (See Chapter 4 for more about him.) This great pro wrestling story isn't true at all, but fans of the time didn't know that and wanted to know the real World Heavyweight Champion of professional wrestling, who could trace their victory back to the beginning.

Thesz — A model World Heavyweight Champion

Thesz was the perfect choice for NWA World Heavyweight Champion because he possessed it all:

- Tall and good-looking
- Kept himself in great shape
- Carried himself like a world-class athlete
- Had a legitimate wrestling background (so nobody could steal the title from him)

From the beginning of his career in 1932 through his retirement in 1990 (not a typo!), Thesz officially held some version of the World Heavyweight Championship on seven different occasions. The NWA Board of Directors voted on the World Heavyweight Champion in the Territory Era, choosing a champion to:

- Represent the organization inside the ring. Not necessarily as a shooter or as a *hooker* (real wrestler who could also snap your bones), but at the very least as someone who could have entertaining matches.
- Serve as a big draw wherever they traveled.

The middle of the 20th century was unique. Despite what anyone says, in reality, most everyone knew that pro wrestling was largely a predetermined athletic performance art (rather than an actual athletic competition). But from the days of the Gold Dust Trio in the 1920s (flip to Chapter 4) up through probably the late 1970s, many fans did believe that the top wrestlers were, if nothing else, legitimately tough human beings. And some fans did believe that, although the *undercards* (opening matches below the main event) were fake matches, the main event championship matches were often legitimate.

LOU THESZ'S IMPACT ON JAPANESE PRO WRESTLING

Thesz was one of pro wrestling's biggest stars for decades, not only in the United States, but particularly in Japan, where he was known as the "God of Wrestling."

Japanese wrestler Rikidōzan (whom you can read about in Chapters 4 and 10) and Thesz had a legendary feud in Japan. An October 6, 1957, match that lasted an hour and ended in a *draw* (no winner) drew a ridiculous 87.0 rating (meaning 87 percent of the entire TV-owning population of Japan watched the match live). Also, in the NWA International Championship match on August 27, 1958, Thesz *put over* (lost to) Rikidōzan, which drew an 85.0 rating.

Later in his career, Thesz (along with catch wrestler Karl Gotch — helped train a new generation of Japanese pro wrestlers, teaching them not only how to perform showbiz matches, but also legitimate hooking and shooting techniques, helping shape the more-realistic submission wrestling, and focusing on strong style of Japanese wrestling that sets it apart.

A TALE OF TWO NWAS

We need to clarify something about the NWA. Wrestling history actually has two NWAs, organizations that used the same abbreviation but were completely different entities:

- **National Wrestling Association:** A regulatory body created in the early 20th century. With pro wrestling having exploded in the Northeast under the Gold Dust Trio and Joe Stecher's promotion (see Chapter 4), the National Boxing Association created the National Wrestling Association to try to make sense of professional wrestling.
- **National Wrestling Alliance:** A promotion formed in the mid-20th century. (See the section "Creating the National Wrestling Alliance [NWA] to Unify Territories" in this chapter for the details about this organization.)

Replacing Thesz with a dud

When Thesz traveled to Japan and saw how culturally important the sport was there, in comparison to in the United States, he gave his notice as NWA Champion and agreed to drop the title to an old friend, Dick Hutton.

WARNING

Hutton was a great legitimate wrestler, but unfortunately he wasn't charismatic, so he was the wrong choice to replace Thesz. Pro wrestling was already on a downswing in the States during the late 1950s, and Hutton's title win furthered the spiral. Not until the rise of Buddy Rogers and the World Wide Wrestling Federation (see the section "World Wide Wrestling Federation (WWWF)" later in this chapter) did things begin to turn around.

Finding some Flair

The wrestler Ric Flair (see Figure 5-2) was such an incredible *worker* (showbiz wrestler) and talker that he ended up dominating as multi-time NWA Champion from his debut in the early 1970s into the late 1980s (and his run hardly ended at that time).

FIGURE 5-2: Ric Flair.

Photo by Wrealano@aol.com

Flair became not only one of the best in-ring workers in history, but also one of the greatest *promos* (interviews), and he had such charisma that the NWA Board of Directors voted him World Champion over and over again.

Even when, in his 40s, promoters said he was too old for the role, after those promoters tried out one star after another to replace him, time and time again, they realized that, in fact, nobody could play World Champion as well as Flair. He won his first NWA World Title from Harley Race (see the section "Jim Crockett Promotions" later in this chapter for more about Race) on September 17, 1981, in Kansas City, with Thesz (whom we talk about in the section "Thesz — A model World Heavyweight Champion" earlier in this chapter) as special guest referee. And Flair held that belt on and off until 2000.

If you add up all of Flair's NWA Title wins, including those unacknowledged (and there were many), he actually won some version of the World Championship on anything from 21 to 25 different times. Flair himself has always claimed 21. But for those hardcore historians out there, we can say for sure that the number was more than 16, and therefore when John Cena supposedly broke the record by winning 17, he broke a fake record (in a fake sport, to boot), and the real record is a long way away from being broken.

WARNING

FIGHTING THROUGH TRAGEDY

Harley Race and Ric Flair were two of the most iconic NWA Champions in history. In both cases, their careers nearly ended as quickly as they started.

Race, a huge figure in NWA wrestling, almost didn't live to leave his mark. On Christmas night 1961, Race and his wife Vivian were driving during a heavy snowfall. A tractor trailer full of eggs slid out of control and smashed into their car, completely destroying it. Vivian, who was pregnant at the time, didn't survive. Race's right leg was so shattered that doctors determined they had to amputate it. His promoter at the time, Gust Karras, rushed to the hospital and told the doctors not to do the amputation. Because Karras was a powerful figure in the city, the doctors ultimately agreed, but they did say that Race would very likely never walk again — and certainly never wrestle. But Race did recover and ultimately became one of the most famous NWA World Heavyweight Champions.

Flair also almost became a footnote in history, rather than the huge pro wrestling star he did become. On October 4, 1975, just three years after his professional debut, Flair was involved in a small plane crash, along with executive David Crockett (promoter Jim Crockett, Jr.'s brother), and wrestlers "Mr. Wrestling" (George Woodin), Bob Bruggers, and Johnny Valentine. The pilot was killed, Valentine was paralyzed, and Flair broke his back in three places. Doctors told him that his career was over, he would never wrestle again. But Flair went through intense rehabilitation and not only returned to the ring but became the most decorated World Champion in the history of professional wrestling.

Breaking Away from NWA

By the end of the 1950s, pro wrestling in the United States was in serious decline, in part because televisions were so popular. In 1950, basically 20 percent of the homes in the United States had a television set. By the end of the decade, that number had skyrocketed to 90 percent. TV saw an explosion of programming — everything from sitcoms to game shows to children's programming. With such intense competition, professional wrestling programming went from appearing as a nightly feature on multiple networks to essentially not appearing at all by the end of the decade.

PUTTING THE BELT ON BOND

The NWA Board of Directors voted the Champion into that position. Thesz, the perennial champion, was a legitimate bad dude. And if the bad dude doesn't want to lose the title, how do you get it off him in the ring?

The answer in the Territory Era involved making the chosen champion put up a real-life $25,000 bond. (A $25,000 bond in the mid-1950s was equivalent to about $300,000 at the time of writing.) When you became NWA Champion, you had to post this $25,000 bond, and when you dropped the title when NWA requested it, you got your money back. If they asked you to drop the title and you refused, you lost your bond. Although the top wrestlers in that era made a great living, $25,000 was still a lot of money to forfeit.

When the NWA wanted current Champion Buddy Rogers to turn over his belt to Thesz, they threatened to donate Rogers' $25,000 to charity if he didn't appear and drop the title as requested, so Rogers showed, and Thesz became Champion again.

WARNING

In addition to its disappearance from mainstream television, the National Wrestling Alliance (NWA) itself had to deal with a great deal of internal discontent. Thesz was the dominant NWA Champion, but by the mid-1950s, he already had one foot out the door. Promoters struggled to get Thesz scheduled to wrestle at their events because he had so many different places he had to appear in, and they were upset about the monopolistic control the Alliance had over the business as a whole.

During the late 1950s, many promoters began to split from the NWA to form their own separate territories with their own recognized World Champions, which the following sections discuss.

World Wide Wrestling Federation (WWWF)

The World Wide Wrestling Federation (WWWF; now World Wrestling Entertainment [WWE]) is the largest professional wrestling organization in the world and got its start in the early 1960s after splitting from the NWA over a promotion dispute.

Breaking off from NWA

Buddy Rogers — a tanned, bleached-blonde, jacked-up, and charismatic professional wrestler — was one of the big stars of Vince McMahon, Sr.'s Capitol Wrestling Corporation (CWC) in the latter half of the 1950s. Because of his popularity in various territories, Rogers won the NWA World Championship in 1960.

CWC, the most powerful NWA territory (New York), controlled the charismatic Rogers, with his great look and outlandish *heel* (bad guy) persona. And you'll never guess — they wanted priority over his *bookings* (where he wrestled and when), so the other promoters struggled to get him scheduled to perform in their territories.

Sam Muchnick, the many-time NWA President and head of the powerful St. Louis territory, wanted former World Champion Lou Thesz (check out the section "Thesz — A model World Heavyweight Champion" earlier in this chapter) to return, and beat Rogers for the NWA Title.

CWC's McMahon and Mondt didn't want the title change, but the Alliance voted for it. The NWA demanded Rogers lose the title to Thesz. On January 24, 1963, at the Maple Leaf Gardens arena in Toronto, when Thesz and Rogers stepped into the ring, Thesz whispered the famous line: "We can do this the hard way, or the easy way." In other words, "Either give me the title, or I'm just going to take it from you." Rogers chose the easy way.

REMEMBER

That was it for McMahon and Mondt, the heads of CWC (see Chapter 6 for more on these figures). Rogers as Champion was a great draw in their territory; Thesz wasn't. They didn't want to battle for dates for a worse-drawing NWA Champion. They quickly withdrew from the NWA and renamed CWC the World Wide Wrestling Federation (WWWF).

McMahon and Mondt created a storyline where Willie Gilzenberg, playing the role of a CWC authority figure, came on TV and announced that although Rogers had lost to Thesz in Toronto, it wasn't a sanctioned title match — therefore, Rogers was still the Champion. And because CWC had withdrawn from the NWA, Gilzenberg presented Rogers with a brand-new belt — the newly-christened World Wide Wrestling Federation Championship.

A record-breaking title run

Because Buddy Rogers, the first WWWF Champion (see the preceding section), had heart problems, in 1963, the WWWF set up Sammartino (a rising pro wrestling star) to defeat Rogers in a title match. That win for Sammartino began an almost eight-year reign as WWWF Champion. Sammartino became one of the biggest *drawing cards* (ticket sellers) and most beloved babyface wrestlers in history.

Sammartino (see Figure 5-3) worked a crazy schedule and became such a cultural icon in the Northeast that he even once held court with the Pope. By the late 1960s, he demanded a break from WWWF's McMahon, Sr., which started a series of Championship changes:

FIGURE 5-3: Bruno Sammartino.

Photo by Wrealano@aol.com

- **Sammartino loses to Ivan Koloff:** On January 18, 1971, in Madison Square Garden, the beloved babyface WWF Champion Sammartino was pinned in the middle of the ring by the heel Koloff. Fans were stunned into complete silence — it remains one of the most shocking losses in professional wrestling history.
- **Koloff loses to Pedro Morales:** In those days, WWWF was built around babyface champions. When the heel Koloff beat babyface Sammartino, Koloff held the belt for only 21 days before losing it to babyface Pedro Morales.

REMEMBER

Two years later, WWWF begged for Sammartino to win the title back, but Sammartino wanted none of the crazy schedule. The McMahons offered multiple concessions, including a limited schedule and a percentage of the gate of every show he worked on. Sammartino finally agreed to return.

WHEN THE UNBEATABLE SAMMARTINO WAS BEATEN

Nobody, and we mean *nobody,* could even conceive of the idea that the great Bruno Sammartino (whom we talk about in the section "A record-breaking title run" in this chapter) might ever lose a match. During his match with Ivan Koloff in 1971, Koloff hit the flying kneedrop off the top rope, then covered Sammartino. The ref counted three.

Years later, Sammartino explained in a *Wrestling Observer Live* podcast interview with co-author Bryan Alvarez that the arena suddenly went completely silent, and he thought maybe a hit had ruptured his eardrums. But that silence is what happened, backed up by witness accounts of that night.

When the ref counted three, the crowd was literally stunned into absolute complete silence. Several moments passed, and then the first sound that broke the silence was weeping. Both men and women alike quietly began crying when the enormity of what they had just witnessed set in. The organizers didn't publicly announce a winner for fear of a riot. But Sammartino's first reign was over.

- **Morales loses to Stan Stasiak:** Although the McMahons wanted to replace Morales with Sammartino, they didn't want to have a babyface-versus-babyface match. So, on December 1, 1973, Morales and heel Stan Stasiak did a *double-pin finish* (both men's shoulders were pinned at the same time) in their match, and Stasiak became the new champion (something they held off announcing because they didn't want a riot at the match).
- **Stasiak loses to Sammartino:** Ten days after the Morales-versus-Stasiak match, Sammartino beat Stasiak to win the title. Fans said that the reaction when he regained the title was one of the loudest in WWWF history.

Sammartino held the title for almost four more years before losing it for the last time to "Superstar" Billy Graham on April 30, 1977, in Baltimore. This loss, along with the Koloff loss, were the only two decisive pinfall or submission losses that Bruno Sammartino ever suffered in his entire WWWF career.

McMahon tries to steal the NWA Title

When Vince McMahon, Jr., first bought the WWWF from his father in 1982 and planned to go national, he had a secret meeting with wrestler Harley Race (see the section "Jim Crockett Promotions" later in this chapter), who was at that point the NWA World Champion scheduled to lose the belt to Ric Flair (whom we talk about in the section "Finding some Flair" earlier in this chapter). McMahon offered Race a huge sum of guaranteed money to no-show the Flair match and jump to the WWWF — bringing the NWA World Title with him. Insiders say that McMahon's plan was to take the most widely recognized title in the world, the NWA World Championship, and:

- Have WWWF wrestler Hulk Hogan (discussed in Chapter 6) beat Race for the Championship.
- Hogan, as NWA Champion, would then beat "The Iron Sheik" for the WWWF Title.
- This win would unify the belts, creating the new undisputed World Heavyweight Championship controlled by the WWWF.

We know for a fact that Race turned McMahon down, saying he couldn't betray everyone who had invested in him as NWA Champion for so many years.

TIP

We *don't* know for a fact Race's claim that McMahon was so upset to be turned down that he made a foolish error — he tried to attack Race, which Race put an end to quickly in the public bathroom where they had this discussion (it's what Race said happened). Just a few years later, with his NWA career winding down, Race did take an offer to jump to the then-World Wrestling Federation (WWF). Back in McMahon's good graces, Race stopped telling the story of the bathroom attack. But when asked years later if it was true, he refused to deny it.

American Wrestling Association (AWA)

Verne Gagne, a legendary wrestler from Minnesota, was the man behind one of the strongest regional promotions of the Territory Era, the American Wrestling Association (AWA). He was a big star during the first big TV boom in the mid-1950s, the clean-cut amateur babyface standout who was a college football star and a two-time NCAA champion (one of his most famous rivals being the same Dick Hutton who beat Lou Thesz for the NWA Title a decade later, which we talk about in the section "Replacing Thesz with a dud" earlier in this chapter).

In 1960, Gagne and promoter Wally Karbo split off from the NWA to form the AWA. The new AWA did a storyline claiming that Pat O'Connor, the NWA Champion at the time, would be the first AWA Champion; however, if he didn't defend his title against Gagne (who had defeated a previous NWA Champion, Eduard Carpentier) within the next 90 days, he would be stripped of the title. No one ever planned for O'Connor to defend the title, and so 90 days later, O'Connor lost it. Gagne was awarded the AWA Title.

Building the AWA into a power

For most of the next two decades, Gagne was the face of the territory, the perennial AWA Champion feuding with some of the biggest stars in the business, including "The Crusher," "Dr. X" (Dick Beyer), Nick Bockwinkel, "Mad Dog" Vachon, and later, a big, tall, tanned muscleman by the name of Hulk Hogan (whom you can read about in Chapter 6).

The AWA also helped kick off the careers of many of the greatest stars of the next generation, including Ric Flair (see the section "Finding some Flair" earlier in this chapter), Shawn Michaels, the Road Warriors, Ricky Steamboat, "The Iron Sheik," and even future Minnesota Governor Jesse "The Body" Ventura.

Focusing on the power of TV

One of Gagne's strengths was the ability to produce high-quality television programs, which usually featured his preferred style of technical, scientific wrestling.

REMEMBER

Gagne was also one of the first promoters to break the rules of expansion. First in 1968 and later in 1981, he made moves to gain television in Los Angeles and San Francisco, respectively, which upset the promoters in those territories. Roy Shire, the promoter in San Francisco, complained to the NWA, but because the AWA wasn't part of the NWA, they couldn't do much (plus, Shire's promotion was pretty much dead at that point anyway).

Jim Crockett Promotions

Jim Crockett Promotions (JCP), controlled by Jim Crockett, Jr., became the most powerful NWA territory, the only one to really give Vince McMahon, Jr., and WWF a real fight in the 1980s. JCP was ultimately purchased by Ted Turner and became World Championship Wrestling (WCW; flip to Chapter 6 for the details on WCW and WWF).

Crockett, Jr., was the son of Big Jim Crockett, Sr., who began promoting pro wrestling in 1935 at the behest of a wrestling promoter in the New York territory named Jack Curley who wanted someone to run his territory in the Carolinas.

Crockett's son, Junior, took over when Senior passed away. He teamed up with a man named George Scott as booker, and the two of them created a very successful territory in a very short period of time.

They booked some of the biggest stars of the era including Harley Race, Ric Flair, Terry and Dory Funk, and Jack and Gerry Brisco. Their business model involved running shows at the Greensboro Coliseum arena weekly (drawing 8,000 to 10,000 fans per week during JCP's heyday in the late 1970s and early 1980s).

TIP

Race was the big star of Jim Crockett Promotions from the time that Crockett, Jr., took over through 1981. Race, who grew up watching 1950s televised wrestling on the DuMont Network, broke into the business in 1959 and became one of the biggest stars in the world within just a few years. (Flip to the section "McMahon tries to steal the NWA Title" earlier in this chapter for more about Race.)

IN THIS CHAPTER

» Seeing how Hulkamania helped change the business forever

» Watching a promotion's death and rebirth

» Reviving a flagging industry with the Monday Night War

» Figuring out what really killed WCW

Chapter 6 Going National

Sometimes, in life, change happens slowly. Other times, it happens at breakneck speed. The same philosophy applies to the professional wrestling industry.

In the mid-1980s, the pro wrestling business drastically shifted from territories (which we talk about in Chapter 5) to national promotions. Although certain economics of the wrestling business have changed, pro wrestling at the time of writing really isn't much different than it was in the late 1990s. But the late 1990s pro wrestling scene was drastically different from the 1980s, and the wrestling of the 1980s was drastically different than it was even in the 1970s. This chapter focuses on those pivotal changes.

Delving into the 1980s WWF Boom

Pro wrestling experienced a fundamental change when Vince McMahon, Jr., bought the World Wrestling Federation (WWF) from his father in the early 1980s (which we talk about in Chapter 12), moving wrestling from the territory system (that we discuss in Chapter 5) to a national structure.

The WWF went mainstream, and its top stars became household names. The company itself became synonymous with the term *pro wrestling.* And the man that WWF built its empire around was a fellow by the name of Terry Bollea, otherwise known by his ring name, "The Incredible" Hulk Hogan.

WWF was best known in the 1980s for two things:

- The explosion of Hulk Hogan as the biggest star in United States wrestling history
- The creation of *WrestleMania,* what is today the biggest annual wrestling show in the world

The following sections explore Hulk Hogan and his impact on the WWF and professional wrestling and discuss the creation of *WrestleMania.*

Introducing Hulk Hogan

Hulk Hogan didn't have an immediate impact on pro wrestling. Rather, Terry Bollea spent several years in the biz before he became the Hulk Hogan persona.

He wrestled his first match under a mask in 1977, using the ring name Super Destroyer. Because the promoters saw his potential but also realized that, at this point in his career, he was very green (meaning, he sucked), they put him back under a mask for the rest of the year so that he could develop in anonymity.

McMahon, Sr., brought him in to the World Wide Wrestling Federation (WWWF, yet to drop the "Wide" in its name) near the end of 1979 and had him work television tapings as a heel named "The Incredible" Hulk Hogan. He had a strong two-year run as a heel, but in those days, WWWF would bring in a heel, *put them over strong* (have them achieve many victories) for a while, then have them do a bunch of losses and cycle them out of the territory. Following this pattern, Hogan lost a series of matches over his last six weeks and left in April of 1981. The idea was likely to have him go elsewhere for a while, then return in a few years for another run.

Creating Hulkamania with Hollywood's help

REMEMBER

In the early '80s, Hogan got an offer to appear in Sylvester Stallone's 1982 movie *Rocky III,* in which he played a jacked-up wrestler named Thunderlips. After filming wrapped, he ended up going to work for Verne Gagne's American Wrestling Association (AWA; see Chapter 5 for more about the AWA).

Gagne initially planned to continue with Hogan being a heel, but the fans were having none of it. They went wild for him from day one, so Gagne quickly shifted plans. Over the next year, Hogan wrestled as a *babyface* (a good guy persona) and lit the AWA territory on fire; the AWA did bigger business than they'd ever done previously.

On May 28, 1982, *Rocky III* came out, and Hogan's character in some ways stole the film. He was quickly booked as a guest on the *Tonight Show*, which in those days virtually never had anyone from pro wrestling on. The only legitimate wrestling guest up to that point in history was Lou Thesz, who did the *gimmick* (persona) of a professional sportsman (check out Chapter 5 for more on Thesz). Hogan's popularity exploded further, and *Hulkamania* (AWA's term for Hogan's popularity) was born.

At his peak in the AWA (in 1983), Hogan was the biggest drawing *card* (ticket-seller and moneymaker) the company had ever had, and he parlayed that into a second career in New Japan Pro Wrestling (NJPW), where he made $10,000 per week — ridiculous money for a pro wrestler. (You can read all about NJPW in Chapter 10.)

Returning to the WWF

One day, a photographer named Steve Taylor gave Hogan a message from Vince McMahon, Jr., that said McMahon wanted Hogan back in the WWF. He was willing to pay; he planned to make Hogan the WWF Champion and the first wrestler in history to make more than $1 million a year. Hogan immediately gave his notice to Gagne at the AWA.

The entire business changed in a three-day period in 1983:

» **December 25:** Despite Hogan giving his notice, Gagne continued to advertise Hogan for AWA events. At the St. Paul Civic Center, Gagne ran a sold-out Christmas Night show. Hogan didn't appear, despite being advertised. Fans were deeply disappointed.

» **December 26:** The following night at Madison Square Garden, Bob Backlund defended the WWF Title against "The Iron Sheik."

» **December 27:** At the Chase Hotel in St. Louis, not just Hogan, but also the AWA's Roddy Piper, David Schultz, and announcer "Mean" Gene Okerlund, three of Gagne's big stars, all arrived for a television taping, signaling their jump to the WWF.

WARNING

HOGAN'S TARNISHED LEGACY

Although Hogan was a complicated person in real life, his wrestling character was the most famous professional wrestler of all time. When he died on July 24, 2025, he was persona non grata with World Wrestling Entertainment (WWE), largely because of a leaked tape in which Hogan himself admitted that he was a racist "to a point." He dropped the n-word multiple times.

The matter only worsened when he returned to WWE in the aftermath of the tape's release and instead of apologizing while addressing the locker room, he talked about how you need to be careful that you don't get caught when saying something questionable. His final appearance for WWE was on the Netflix Monday Night *RAW* debut on January 6, 2025, where the fans watching live in Inglewood, California, booed him out of the building. WWE never used him again.

The WWF version of Hulkamania was born on January 23, 1984, at Madison Square Garden. Coming to the ring to Survivor's "Eye of the Tiger," the theme song for *Rocky III*, Hogan beat The Iron Sheik in just five minutes to win the WWF Title.

Helping create big booms

Hogan was the centerpiece of two of the biggest boom periods in professional wrestling history:

- **1980s:** When he catapulted WWF into the stratosphere (see the preceding section)
- **1990s:** When he turned WCW's fortunes around to the point that for a brief period they actually beat WWF at their own game (which we talk about in the section "Moving to the New World Order" later in this chapter)

REMEMBER

Incidentally, WWE built the 21st-century boom period that's ongoing at the time of writing around an ensemble cast, not a single standout professional wrestler. So, as far as a singular *draw* (money generator and ticket seller) who turned around the business of a national promotion, Hogan is far and away the number one performer in history, followed by "Stone Cold" Steve Austin (see the section "Ending the Nitro winning streak — "Stone Cold" Steve Austin" later in this chapter), who took a promotion that was already gaining momentum and sped it up.

Taking WWF national

Hogan's WWF Championship win (discussed in the section "Returning to the WWF" earlier in this chapter) exploded the fortunes of McMahon and the WWF. And McMahon wanted to rule the world. In the beginning, ruling the wrestling world meant taking the WWF national, breaking all the rules of the old territorial system, and becoming the brand name in pro wrestling to your average Joe on the street:

- **Going to cable:** In the early 1980s, WWF programming began airing on the USA Network, first in 1983 with the weekly *All American Wrestling* TV show, and then in 1985 with the weekly *Prime Time Wrestling.* Anyone in the country who had the USA Network could watch, but cable TV was still pretty limited.
- **Going local:** McMahon wanted to extend his reach quickly, so he offered to pay local TV stations to air WWF's weekly television programs. One by one, territories lost their television shows, and without that promotional vehicle, they began going out of business. The only way to survive was to try to compete with McMahon by going national.
- **Going for other promotions:** But McMahon also wanted control of the entire national scene. He convinced major shareholders in Georgia Championship Wrestling (GCW), which aired on TBS, to sell him the majority of their GCW stock.

  TIP

  McMahon, in purchasing a majority interest in GCW, got what he actually wanted — the TBS time slots, Saturday and Sunday nights at 6:05 p.m. Eastern time. (Flip to Chapter 7 for more on McMahon's WWF business maneuvers.)

Coming up with *WrestleMania*

In order to try to make back some of the money he had sunk into trying to gain control of the wrestling business, McMahon decided to promote a giant event, a supershow: the very first *WrestleMania* from Madison Square Garden. He wanted to make it the biggest event in the history of wrestling and air it live around the country on closed circuit television, in the hopes of turning the fortunes of his company around.

Of course, professional wrestling had held gigantic events dating back to 1911, when Frank Gotch and George Hackenschmidt battled it out (which we talk about in Chapter 4). And rarely did a single event turn an entire business around. McMahon knew that he had to create more than your average supershow. It had to draw in not just the hardcore wrestling fans, but also the mainstream viewer.

THE PRO WRESTLING CABLE WARS

On July 14, 1984 — a day fans and insiders dubbed *Black Saturday* — fans tuned in to cable channel TBS to see their Georgia Championship Wrestling (GCW). Instead, they found a World Wrestling Federation (WWF) syndicated show. They were furious. Thousands of fans called and sent letters saying they wanted their "Gordon Solie wrestling" back. Ted Turner, who owned TBS, had no loyalty to McMahon, so he allowed multiple promotions to air on his channel:

- **Championship Wrestling from Georgia:** The promoter behind GCW, Ole Anderson, created this promotion when McMahon bought a majority share in GCW (see the section "Taking WWF national" in this chapter for this story).
- **Mid-South Wrestling:** A year after giving Championship Wrestling from Georgia a time slot, Turner did the same for this promotion, run by Bill Watts.

McMahon was furious, and even more furious when Mid-South started crushing his WWF syndicated shows in the ratings.

Jim Barnett, a long-time wrestling promoter, brokered a deal where McMahon sold the WWF time slots to rival organization Jim Crockett Promotions (JCP) for $1 million. Because it was an exclusive deal, Mid-South Wrestling lost its time slot (and Championship Wrestling from Georgia had already gone under). So, in terms of national professional wrestling, the last two standing were:

- WWF on the USA Network (which we talk about in the section "Taking WWF national" in this chapter)
- JCP on TBS (see the section "Exploring the Death of JCP and the Birth of WCW" later in this chapter)

REMEMBER

WWF had already gone mainstream with the help of pop singer Cyndi Lauper and actor tough-guy Mr. T. (Chapter 16 talks about these culture cross-overs.) The main event for *WrestleMania* featured Hulk Hogan and Mr. T versus Roddy Piper and "Mr. Wonderful" Paul Orndorff.

McMahon rented out 200 different buildings where he planned to air the show via closed circuit television (the first *WrestleMania* actually predated pay-per-view television). But the ticket sales a week before the event were so poor that 30 percent of the buildings canceled their showings of *WrestleMania*.

Whether true or not (and pro wrestling is a business built on lies), McMahon and others have claimed over the years that the first *WrestleMania* was a make-or-break proposition. If it was a success, the WWF survived; if it was a flop, WWF went out of business.

Hitting the mainstream despite a lawsuit

One week before the show, Hogan and Mr. T managed to get booked on both the talk show *Late Night with David Letterman* and the sketch comedy show *Saturday Night Live*, which drew huge mainstream attention. But what really exploded into the mainstream on that final week was Hogan's appearance on the TV talk show *Hot Properties* hosted by comedian Richard Belzer.

WARNING

Belzer asked Hogan to show him a wrestling hold. Hogan didn't want to, but Belzer kept pushing. Finally, Hogan relented. He put Belzer in what was at the time called a *front face lock*, where you bend the person in front of you over and wrap your arms around their neck in a choke hold (nowadays, it's called the *guillotine* in mixed martial arts). While Hogan calmly explained how the move that he was doing on Belzer worked, Belzer legitimately passed out. Hogan felt Belzer go limp and let go of the hold, so Belzer crashed to the floor, smashing his head on the ground.

Belzer filed suit against Hogan, Mr. T, McMahon, and Titan Sports (WWF) for $5 million and later settled out of court for about a half million dollars. What could have been a disaster for the WWF was instead the opposite. Everyone was talking about what happened with Hogan and Belzer; and they were talking about *WrestleMania*.

On March 31, 1985, *WrestleMania* was a gigantic success, drawing almost 20,000 fans to Madison Square Garden and more than a million viewers on closed circuit television. All told, it generated $5 million in revenue. Hogan came out of the first *WrestleMania* far and away the biggest star in American professional wrestling, and McMahon's dream of becoming the brand name in national professional wrestling had come true.

Reaching its peak with *WrestleMania III*

The peak of the 1980s WWF boom was *WrestleMania III*, which occurred on March 29, 1987, in the Pontiac Silverdome arena in Pontiac, Michigan, headlined by Hogan, who had to defend the title against his longtime friend-turned-foe André the Giant (see Figure 6-1).

FIGURE 6-1: André the Giant and Hulk Hogan.

Photo by `Wrealano@aol.com`

REMEMBER

WWF, unlike almost every other wrestling promotion in that era, pretended no other American wrestling promotions existed. And they invented or changed history as it suited them. They came up with some real whoppers for *WrestleMania III* as we identify in Table 6-1.

TABLE 6-1 **Debunking *WrestleMania III***

WrestleMania III Fiction	Truth
Hogan and André had never wrestled.	Hogan had many matches around the country with André the Giant in the late 1970s and early 1980s, including a very famous match on August 9, 1980.
André the Giant was 7 feet 4 inches tall.	He was actually about 6 feet 10 inches.
André had never lost a match in 15 years.	The records show many losses, including a loss to Antonio Inoki in New Japan the previous year and dozens of losses in tag team matches in WWF.
André had never been bodyslammed.	A *bodyslam* is a wrestling move in which a wrestler picks up their opponent and slams them to the mat. Numerous wrestlers had slammed André over the years, including Hogan himself in WWF at Shea Stadium in 1980.

Despite all the false claims, fans bought tickets in droves. Unlike today, where World Wrestling Entertainment (WWE; which changed its name from WWF) announces *WrestleMania* a year in advance and puts tickets on sale shortly after the announcement, WWF announced the date and location for *WrestleMania III* about six weeks prior to the event. They almost immediately sold tens of thousands of tickets.

In the end, more than 78,000 fans packed the building for the match. WWF inflated the attendance to 93,173 — and for years it promoted *WrestleMania III* as the biggest show in WWF/WWE history (you can find more on those claims in Chapter 14). Hogan, of course, bodyslammed André, hit the *big legdrop* (he jumped in the air and dropped his leg on him), and pinned the Giant to retain the WWF Championship.

Exploring the Death of JCP and the Birth of WCW

By the late 1980s, the country was down to two major national organizations: World Wrestling Federation (WWF) and Jim Crockett Promotions (JCP). Most long-time hardcore fans preferred JCP because they felt the wrestling matches were more authentic and more exciting, but for the average person, WWF was far out in the lead as the brand name they knew.

Although the Crocketts had national television on TBS, they came in a distant number two behind WWF — and worse, they spent money like it was going out of style, including flying the top stars around the country in not one, but two, very expensive private jets. Also, as good as the in-ring wrestling product was, the *booking* (storytelling) of the programs was leading to a great deal of dissatisfaction, even amongst the most hardcore of fans.

As we discuss in the section "Coming up with *WrestleMania*" earlier in this chapter, according to the McMahons, the concept of *WrestleMania* was make or break for the company. Although we don't know what would have happened to WWF had it failed, we do know what happened to JCP when they tried something similar and it failed — it sped up their decline.

JCP and WWF engaged head to head in an old fashioned wrestling war:

- **JCP makes a play.** Crockett booked his fifth annual *Starrcade* mega-event (JCP's equivalent to *WrestleMania*) for Thanksgiving night 1987. (Back in those days, Thanksgiving was a huge night for pro wrestling.) This was the first show that Crockett ever tried to run on pay-per-view (PPV) television. Crockett was deep in the hole and banking on the idea that the *Starrcade* PPV revenue would keep him afloat.
- **WWF counters.** McMahon quickly announced that WWF was going to run their *Survivor Series* PPV event on the same day at the same time.
- **JCP backs off.** Crockett, who knew that JCP would lose going head-to-head with WWF, opted to move the start time to earlier in the day.

REMEMBER

- **WWF goes in for the kill.** McMahon, who at this point was the king of pro wrestling on PPV by a wide margin, gave the cable operators an ultimatum: If they aired Crockett's PPV, he would deny them access to *Survivor Series* and the following year's *WrestleMania.* Of course, every cable operator in the country, with the exception of five markets (San Jose, Charleston, South Carolina, Charlotte, Greensboro, and Raleigh, North Carolina — the Carolinas were JCP's strongest market) iced out Crockett.
- **JCP goes on offense.** With JCP on death's door, Crockett booked JCP's *Bunkhouse Stampede* PPV event at the Nassau Coliseum, in Uniondale, New York — smack dab in the middle of McMahon's home market.

  WARNING

  It was a stupid idea for many reasons, including that most everyone in the market was a WWF fan, so the show didn't sell a lot of tickets.
- **WWF crushes JCP.** McMahon put his WWF *Royal Rumble* mega-card event on head-to-head with *Bunkhouse Stampede,* and not on PPV — on free television. The Rumble drew a gigantic number of viewers, badly hurting the business (ticket sales and PPV buys) of Crockett's *Bunkhouse Stampede.*
- **JCP makes a desperate play.** Crockett tried getting revenge by airing a free *Clash of the Champions* show on TBS head-to-head with the 1988 *WrestleMania IV* PPV event. The Clash did well, but the next day, all the national press that covered wrestling wrote only about one thing — the brand-name *WrestleMania.*

  WARNING

  The cable companies were furious that JCP had, in theory, cost them millions of dollars in revenue from *WrestleMania* PPV buys (in those days, the cable operators took about half the PPV revenue, and the wrestling promotion got the other half). They flat-out said that head-to-head PPV battles could never happen again.

The Crocketts were cooked.

Watching Pro Wrestling Decline in the Early 1990s

Because pro wrestling had always done great ratings for Ted Turner (and because he was a fan, all of which we talk about in Chapter 7), in the summer of 1988, Turner purchased JCP for $9 million and created World Championship Wrestling (WCW). But the early 1990s saw the pro wrestling industry overall fall into a steep decline for a number of reasons. Here's where the promotions stood:

- **World Wrestling Federation (WWF):** Still on fire, but Hulk Hogan as the top attraction (see the section "Introducing Hulk Hogan" earlier in this chapter) was getting long in the tooth, and McMahon was looking for his successor. Then a steroid scandal struck the WWF. The following sections dive into some of the WWF struggles.
- **World Championship Wrestling (WCW):** The distant number two national promotion — and number two is never a great place to be. They had stars, such as multi-time NWA Champion Ric Flair, Sting, Big Van Vader, the Road Warriors, and Lex Luger, but none of them approached the mainstream name recognition and drawing power of the top WWF stars such as Hogan, "Macho Man" Randy Savage, "Rowdy" Roddy Piper, André the Giant, and the Ultimate Warrior. Everything about WCW at this time, frankly, sucked, including business.
- **Every other territory:** Either dead or dying. The American Wrestling Association (AWA; see Chapter 5) was gone by 1991. Portland Wrestling finally closed its doors in 1992, ending the era of the territories forever. (Flip to Chapter 5 for talk of the Territory Era.)

The following sections examine why pro wrestling faltered in the early 1990s and how it tried to bounce back.

Looking for a replacement for Hogan

By the early 1990s, McMahon was looking for a fresh star for the WWF — someone new to carry the company. Although Hogan had been on top for years (with the exception of a short period in the late 1980s when he left to make movies, so Randy Savage had a run as WWF Champion), McMahon believed that Hogan was getting too old to remain his star.

TIP

Because McMahon's emphasis was on his new star having a muscular physique, rather than demonstrating genuine wrestling ability, he chose a bodybuilder by the name of Jim Hellwig, who wrestled as "The Ultimate Warrior." Warrior wasn't a great wrestler in the ring at all, but he had an incredible physique and an extremely memorable persona — he painted his face, pounded his chest, wore extremely colorful ring gear, and screamed gibberish. He was a living cartoon character.

So, on April 1, 1990, at *WrestleMania VI* at the Skydome in Toronto, Ontario, Warrior pinned Hogan clean for the first time in Hogan's WWF career since 1983; Warrior won the WWF Title. The torch was passed.

Unfortunately, Warrior was no Hulk Hogan. He wasn't as good a wrestler as Hogan (who wasn't particularly good by this point either), he wasn't a good talker (Hogan was an incredible talker), and he didn't connect with the crowd in the same way — and business began to fall. Within a year, McMahon panicked and put the title back on Hogan. This didn't turn business around.

Dealing with a WWF steroid scandal

McMahon's love of gigantic physiques resulted in a roster chock-full of men on steroids. Anyone could easily obtain steroids in the United States before the federal government's 1988 Anti-Drug Abuse Act made sweeping restrictions to drug access. Then, in 1990, the Anabolic Steroids Control Act classified them as Schedule III controlled substances, so using them without a valid medical reason became a federal crime. (Of course, these laws didn't stop steroid use in pro wrestling at all; it just meant wrestlers had to find a friendly doctor or black market dealer to supply them.)

WARNING

In 1991, an estimated 70 to 95 percent of the WWF roster was on steroids. That year, a federal court convicted Dr. George Zahorian III, a ringside physician for WWF based out of Pennsylvania, of illegally supplying steroids. He testified during the trial that he had supplied steroids to numerous WWF wrestlers. McMahon was ultimately indicted on charges of conspiring to distribute steroids, possession of illegal steroids, intent to distribute, and embezzlement (the indictment alleged that he used company funds to purchase the illegal drugs). Ultimately, because of a simple jurisdictional issue, McMahon was found not guilty.

The steroid scandal rocked the WWF in many ways:

- **The corporation ordered everyone to get off steroids.** Very quickly, physiques across the WWF changed, and many top stars went from looking like living superheroes to actually resembling normal people.

» **Some wrestlers refused to go off steroids.** They tried to fool the testing so that the results came back that they weren't on steroids, but many who tried failed. The WWF ended up firing them as a result.

» **Their star fell from grace.** After putting the WWF Title back on Hogan (discussed in the preceding section), Hogan's name came up repeatedly in the press as a steroid user. Because his *gimmick* (persona) was that he was a God-fearing, honest man who built his body through training, prayers, and vitamins (which WWF marketed to children), his reputation took a massive hit.

At this point, McMahon had no choice but to rebuild his company around smaller, more athletic wrestlers and attempt to create a future without Hulk Hogan. Following the 1993 *King of the Ring* PPV event, Hogan left the company.

REMEMBER

Although the matches in the mid-1990s, which featured a new generation of stars such as Bret Hart, Shawn Michaels, and "Mr. Perfect" Curt Hennig, provided significantly better wrestling matches than the in-ring product of the steroid era, the shows had their problems. The *undercard* (matches underneath the main event) featured a parade of wacky gimmicks that fans didn't like at all:

» **"The Red Rooster":** Terry Taylor pretending that he was, well, a chicken

» **"Repo Man":** Barry Darsow coming to the ring with a hooked rope and a Zorro mask to conceal his identity

» **Voodoo master "Papa Shango":** Charles Wright, who supposedly made opponents vomit green goo

WARNING

Business collapsed. And it fell even further in the wake of an underage ring boy sex scandal that rocked the company in 1992 (and is still in litigation at press time). By 1995, the mighty WWF was actually losing money and in legitimate danger of folding.

Starting the Monday Night War

By 1995, the long-struggling WCW was doing better than WWF was, and both organizations could thank one person (or blame, depending on which side you were on): Hulk Hogan.

When Hogan left WWF in 1993 (see the preceding section), he toured Japan for a while. In 1994, WCW offered Hogan an almost ridiculous agreement, including a multi-million dollar signing bonus, creative control, a gigantic PPV percentage, and more. But with Hogan headlining, WCW saw a sharp increase in business.

WCW then began hiring other stars from the WWF 1980s boom period, including former WWF Champion and long-time Hogan friend and rival (both on TV and in real life) Randy Savage.

TIP

Ironically, McMahon considered the wrestlers that WCW hired too old. But a funny thing happened: Fans not only didn't see them as too old, but the generation that grew up with the 1980s WWF were now teenagers, and the stars of their childhood became deeply nostalgic characters. Nostalgia draws money. And WCW saw an immediate boost to arena gates and attendance, as well as PPV buy rates.

Creating *Nitro* to challenge *RAW*

On September 4, 1995, WCW *Monday Nitro*, a fast-paced hour of WCW wrestling, debuted on TBS — on a night when WWF's *Monday Night RAW* was pre-empted for the Westminster Dog Show.

Prior to *Nitro*, WWF and WCW television shows featured largely boring one-sided *squash matches* (a star would give a nobody an often-boring one-sided beating) and an *angle* (story arc) here or there to help build live events and PPV. Promotions didn't want to give everything away on TV because they wanted to tease the big matches and then make people pay for them — either by buying tickets to live events or spending money on PPV. Furthermore, WWF never acknowledged that its competition even existed.

Nitro changed all that. The first *Nitro* featured three big matches:

- Brian Pillman versus Jushin Liger in a high-flying spectacular
- Sting versus Ric Flair in a battle of all-time WCW legends
- Hogan versus Big Bubba in a rematch of a famous main event WWF feud of the 1980s

TIP

On the show, WCW also not only acknowledged the existence of WWF, but took one shot after another at the competition.

The show did well. The big question was what would happen the following week, when WWF and WCW went head-to-head for the first time. Most people involved in pro wrestling at the time thought it was going to be a disaster — they thought half of *RAW's* audience would choose WCW, leading to both companies getting a portion of the viewers they would have without competition.

But the predictions were wrong. That week, *RAW* drew its normal audience in its normal time slot, and *Nitro* on the other channel actually beat *RAW* head-to-head in the ratings, 2.5 to 2.2. An entire new audience had sprung up to watch *Nitro.*

Moving to the New World Order

For the first six months of the Monday Night Wars, *RAW* and *Nitro* battled with no clear winner. Some weeks, *Nitro* won the ratings battle; and some weeks, *RAW* won. Fan interest in professional wrestling, in general, was really heating up.

With WWF struggling financially, WCW made a huge offer to two top wrestlers at WWF — former WWF Champion Kevin Nash (ring name Diesel) and former WWF Intercontinental Champion Scott Hall (ring name Razor Ramon) — when their deals came due in the spring of 1996, and they accepted. WCW had found success with former WWF stars, most notably Hogan, but also Randy Savage and Lex Luger.

One week after wrestling his final match for WWF, Hall showed up on WCW *Monday Nitro*. Although he didn't outright say that he was Razor Ramon or from the WWF, he essentially did his Razor Ramon gimmick and voice, and stated, "You people, you know who I am." To fans, Razor Ramon had come to WCW and challenged them to a WWF-versus-WCW war.

Two weeks later, Nash debuted. Like Hall, he didn't say he was Diesel or coming from WWF, but obviously fans were supposed to assume. The two men called themselves "The Outsiders," and every week, they would run roughshod on the WCW wrestlers for two months.

Then, Hulk Hogan joined Nash and Hall in a spectacular moment (which we talk about in Chapter 7), turning heel for the first time since McMahon took WWF national in 1984. They called themselves the New World Order of wrestling.

REMEMBER

The turn was a sensation. WCW, which had been trading ratings wins with WWF for the previous nine months, skyrocketed. The NWO angle had already gotten them three straight weeks of wins, but after Hogan joined the NWO, they didn't lose another Monday night head-to-head battle until April 13, 1998 — a whopping 83 consecutive weeks.

Ending the Nitro winning streak — "Stone Cold" Steve Austin

"Stunning" Steve Austin was fired by Eric Bischoff in 1995 — the same Eric Bischoff that created the NWO and lit the wrestling world on fire with the creation of WCW *Monday Nitro* — because Bischoff felt that Austin wasn't very marketable.

You can't win them all.

> **WARNING**
>
> ### BREAKING KAYFABE AND ANGERING THE HIGHER-UPS
>
> Originally, WWF had planned for Triple H to win the 1996 WWF *King of the Ring* tournament. But a few months prior, Paul Michael Levesque (ring name, Triple H — which was short for his original ring name, Hunter Hearst Helmsley) really pissed off McMahon. Because Scott Hall and Kevin Nash were leaving for WCW (see the section "Moving to the New World Order" in this chapter), they celebrated with their best friends Levesque and Shawn Michaels in the middle of the ring following Hall's and Nash's last match at Madison Square Garden.
>
> You might ask, "Who cares? Four friends celebrated together at an untelevised event! What difference does that make?" If such a celebration happened today, nobody would care because the pro wrestling world is long past the point where promoters try to convince fans that wrestling is real. But because this happened in 1996, when promoters still fought very hard to protect the secrets of the business, management was furious that two heels, Levesque and Nash, celebrated with two babyfaces, Michaels and Hall. These four men broke *kayfabe* (the inner workings of pro wrestling) and exposed the secrets of the business. And worse, some fan filmed the celebration — and the footage ended up getting out on the dreaded World Wide Web (which had launched to the public only in 1993).

This same Steve Austin, the one deemed not very marketable, ended up being the wrestler who not only turned around the fortunes of WWF, but was also the reason that *Nitro's* win streak finally ended. His rise set the table for WCW's collapse and eventual death, and as far as marketability is concerned, his most famous T-shirt, plain black with "Austin 3:16" printed in white letters, sold more units than any other piece of merchandise in the history of professional wrestling, generating tens of millions of dollars.

Happenstance begins WWF's turnaround

After wrestler Triple H (real name, Paul Michael Levesque) angered the head of the WWF, Vince McMahon (check out the sidebar "Breaking kayfabe and angering the higher-ups" in this chapter), McMahon (see Figure 6-2) decided to award the *King of the Ring* victory originally intended for Triple H to wrestler Steve Austin.

FIGURE 6-2: Vince McMahon, Jr.

Photo by Wrealano@aol.com

TIP

In the finals of the tournament, Austin faced Jake Roberts, whose gimmick was that he was a God-fearing humble Christian. After beating Roberts, Austin cut a promo in which he stated, in part: "You sit there and you thump your Bible, and you say your prayers, and it didn't get you anywhere. Talk about your Psalms, talk about John 3:16. Austin 3:16 says I just whipped your ass!"

But it was only after a feud with wrestler Bret Hart that "Austin 3:16" took off in wrestling fandom. Both men were great *workers* (believable in-ring wrestlers) who portrayed themselves as real people: Bret the babyface master technician and Austin the heel beer-drinking brawler. At a match at *WrestleMania 13*, the two wrestlers performed one of the most famous *double-turns* in wrestling history — meaning, when it was over, the babyface Hart became a new top heel, and the heel Austin became the new top babyface. "Stone Cold" Steve Austin had himself a huge fan base.

Meanwhile, McMahon made himself (at first, unintentionally) a heel by tricking Hart into losing his WWF Championship belt before Hart went to work for WCW. (It was called the Montreal Screwjob, which we talk about in the next section.)

Getting screwed over: The Montreal Screwjob

Pro wrestling history is rife with instances where someone did a bad thing, but it paid off for them with great success. The Montreal Screwjob, which we talk about here, along with Rikidōzan's destruction of famed judo legend Masahiko Kimura in 1954 (a famous double-cross where Rikidōzan went against the pro wrestling script and legitimately knocked out an unsuspecting Kimura, a despicable act that launched Rikidōzan to superstardom in Japan), are arguably the two most famous examples in history.

The entire story of the Montreal Screwjob could be its own book someday, but the following sections give you the short version.

Managing money woes

WWF was financially strapped in 1996, but the last thing McMahon wanted was for another top star and former WWF Champion to jump ship to WCW. So, when Bret Hart's deal came due, McMahon offered Hart an unprecedented deal — a 20-year contract worth approximately $10 million over that period and "reasonable creative control" over his storylines.

McMahon instantly regretted it. By mid-1997, he was so concerned about finances that he told Hart that WWF would allow Hart to negotiate with WCW, and if they made him an offer he liked, he could take it. Eric Bischoff, who ran WCW, quickly offered Hart $7.5 million over three years. Hart agreed to take the deal.

But the Hart transition from WWF to WCW had issues centered around Hart being the current WWF Champion and his refusal to lose the belt to McMahon's chosen wrestler, Shawn Michaels, because of legitimate bad blood between the two.

Protecting the WWF Title

In those days, each professional wrestling organization's World Championship Title was considered that organization's centerpiece. The Championship was the prize that the main wrestlers sought to attain; and, in theory, championships and championship matches drew the big money by getting people to buy live event tickets and PPV events.

Under no circumstances, McMahon believed, could the WWF Title go to WCW.

Now granted, the WWF Title couldn't go to WCW. A few years earlier, the WWF Women's Champion, Madusa, jumped to WCW as champion, and in a very famous moment threw the WWF Women's Title belt in the trash can on *Nitro*. But this led to a bitter lawsuit, and long story short, Bischoff wasn't about to put another WWF Title belt on television. But, in McMahon's mind, even if Hart didn't show up on WCW *Nitro* carrying the physical belt, under no circumstances could he enter WCW as the WWF Champion. He had to lose the title before leaving WWF.

McMahon wanted Hart to lose to Michaels. Hart and Michaels had a very bitter real-life hatred for each other, which McMahon himself stoked because he thought the real hatred led to good on-screen chemistry. But on June 9, 1997, the two wrestlers got into a legitimate fight in the locker room; Hart pulled out clumps of Michaels's hair, and Michaels threatened to quit. Bitter feelings ran high.

Negotiating for a title change

In the weeks leading up to *Survivor Series 1997*, the event at which WWF wanted Hart to lose his title, Hart said he had no problem losing the title to anyone, anywhere, with two exceptions:

- **Not to Michaels:** Hart absolutely refused to lose it to Michaels because of their mutual dislike.
- **Not in Canada:** He didn't want to lose it at *Survivor Series,* an event happening in Montreal, Quebec; Hart was legitimately considered a Canadian national hero.

If McMahon wanted Hart to lose to perennial *jobber* (a wrestler who never wins) Brooklyn Brawler in New York, great! But he wasn't losing to Michaels in Canada.

After weeks of negotiations, McMahon offered a suggestion: Hart could beat Michaels in Montreal; and then, in a four-way PPV main event in Springfield, Massachusetts in December, Michaels would beat Hart to win the belt on Hart's way out. Hart agreed to this scenario because he'd have gotten a win over Michaels in Canada, and he'd be losing the title in the United States.

But this plan had problems:

- **Contract timing:** Hart's WCW contract started on December 1, a week before the Springfield event. After discussions with WCW head Bischoff, they agreed to delay Hart's debut for a week so that Bret could drop the title. And although McMahon was wary of trusting Bischoff that did solve one problem.
- **Reputation concerns:** When McMahon approached Michaels with the idea, Michaels talked to his buddy, wrestler Triple H (real name, Paul Michael Levesque). Triple H said that under no circumstances should Michaels lose to a guy who's about to go to WCW, because Shawn was about to become the WWF Champion and the top face of the company. So, Michaels called McMahon and said no dice to losing in Montreal.

Going in without a finish

When the big day arrived, November 9, 1997, with more than 20,000 fans in the building, McMahon, Michaels, and Hart didn't have an agreed-upon finish to the match.

McMahon met Hart before the show. Unbeknownst to McMahon, Hart was wearing a wire, supplied to him by High Road Productions, a production company working on a documentary of Hart's life and career called *Wrestling with Shadows*. McMahon asked Hart what he wanted to do. Hart said he wanted to leave with his head held high and suggested they do a *schmozz* finish, where the match would end in a countout or disqualification so that the title wouldn't change hands. And then Hart could show up on WWF *Monday Night RAW* the following night and vacate the title. McMahon said, "I'm all for that."

Before the match, Hart also met with referee Earl Hebner, who told Hart that he swore on the life of his children that he wouldn't screw Hart in the match. Well, Hebner apparently was willing to risk his kids because he did, in fact, screw Hart.

Former wrestler, backstage agent and longtime McMahon ally Pat Patterson suggested a sequence near the finish of the match, where:

- Michaels would put Hart in Hart's own *sharpshooter submission* (an entangled leg hold).
- Hart would reverse the hold into a sharpshooter of his own.
- When it looked like Michaels was done for sure, his friends, Degeneration X (which consisted of wrestlers Triple H, Rick Rude, and Chyna), would *hit the ring* (jump inside), causing a disqualification — the big schmozz.

Instead of following the plan, when Michaels put Hart in the sharpshooter, Hebner immediately turned and told the timekeeper to ring the bell. The ring announcer ruled Michaels the winner via submission, awarding him the WWF Championship. Hart had legitimately been screwed out of the title live on worldwide PPV. Hart went backstage and punched McMahon so hard that McMahon was knocked unconscious.

Creating a monster

McMahon, of course, felt that he did the right thing in the Montreal Screwjob, and he didn't want fans (and even many of the WWF wrestlers) to think that he was a horrible person who had done a terrible thing. He went on *Monday Night RAW* and cut what he thought was a babyface promo, defending his decision. It completely backfired because he came off as a total heel, and the fans who hated him for his decision just hated him even more.

REMEMBER

When McMahon realized he could never convince the fans that he was a babyface, he decided to embrace being a heel and become an on-screen character, the evil WWF boss Mr. McMahon. His top babyface, Steve Austin, was a blue-collar character, a beer-drinking redneck who hated authority. The feud of Steve Austin versus McMahon, common man versus evil boss, exploded WWF business in every aspect, from attendance, to merchandise, to television ratings, to PPV revenue.

The heel Mr. McMahon, created unintentionally through the Montreal Screwjob, turned the tide in the Monday Night Wars and gave WWF a definitive victory.

Adding Some Attitude with The Rock

The two biggest stars of the Attitude Era (which also made them two of the biggest stars in wrestling history) were "Stone Cold" Steve Austin (see the section "Ending the Nitro winning streak — "Stone Cold" Steve Austin" earlier in this chapter for more on how Stone Cold helped shoot the WWF into the stratosphere) and "The Rock" Dwayne Johnson.

Johnson was the son of Rocky "Soulman" Johnson, one of the biggest wrestling stars of the 1970s. Dwayne's first dream was to be a pro football star, but when he was cut from the Canadian Football League in 1995, he asked his dad to train him to be a professional wrestler. The wrestling business during Soulman's heyday wasn't an easy or necessarily lucrative life, and he didn't want his son to become a wrestler. But his son wanted it bad, and eventually Soulman relented and began to train Dwayne with the help of another wrestler, Ron Slinker.

Unlike most wrestlers, Dwayne had a foot in the door; his father contacted his close friend Pat Patterson, a WWE agent and one of McMahon's closest confidantes. Patterson attended a training session and called McMahon and said this Dwayne kid had more potential to be a pro wrestling star than anyone he had ever seen. Johnson was immediately signed to a WWF contract.

The early road for Johnson was rocky. WWE debuted him in 1996 as "Rocky Maivia" (his dad's name was Rocky and his mom's maiden name was Maivia) and presented him as a babyface, the "The Blue Chipper." Fans quickly grew to hate him, feeling the company was giving him too much too soon, and soon he was met with "Rocky Sucks!" and "Die Rocky Die" — Attitude Era chants.

What turned his career around was going heel, taking on the cocky persona of "The Rock," and developing a legendary trash-talking style of bad guy promos. Within a few years, he had proved Patterson right and was dominating WWF as the top star in the business, neck-and-neck with Austin. Along with Austin versus McMahon, the Austin versus Rock rivalry (see Figure 6-3) was the biggest money-drawing feud of the late-'90s Attitude Era.

FIGURE 6-3: "The Rock" faces off with "Stone Cold" Steve Austin.

Photo by Wrealano@aol.com

Even after retiring to Hollywood, Rock made several short-term returns to wrestling, including in 2012 and 2013 when matches with John Cena drew the biggest pay-per-view numbers of all time for professional wrestling, more than 2.4 million combined buys generating hundreds of millions of dollars. Rock was arguably a bigger star in Hollywood than he was in wrestling. From around 2016 through 2021, Johnson was the biggest and highest-paid A-list star in all of Hollywood. His three biggest films to date, *Furious 7* in 2015, *The Fate of the Furious* in 2017 and *Jumanji* in 2017, together grossed nearly $4 billion, and to date his films have grossed more than $12 billion worldwide.

Addressing the Death of WCW

We can't point to one single reason that WCW went out of business, but we can tell an overarching story that tracks its decline, which we do in the following sections.

Keeping the NWO around too long

The NWO (discussed in the section "Moving to the New World Order" earlier in this chapter) was a massive box office success for WCW. But it was an angle that had an incredible beginning with no satisfying end. These dudes, who allegedly came from WWF, showed up and ran amok on WCW. Because the good guys were (in theory) the WCW wrestlers, in the end, WCW needed to prevail over NWO and rid the company of them.

But the NWO was big business, so WCW wouldn't wrap up the storyline. The peak of the storyline happened at *Starrcade 1997*, where WCW wrestler Sting (real name, Steve Borden) challenged Hogan for the WCW Title.

Sting, who hadn't wrestled in a year because of the WCW's storyline, got tired during the match. And Hogan was Hogan. He didn't want to lose his top spot, and he didn't want to *sell* (make Sting look good) in the match, so he dominated Sting the entire match.

The planned and WCW-approved finish went something like this:

1. **Hogan would hit Sting with his Legdrop of Doom finisher.**

   A *finisher* is something every wrestler has. It's their big move that they end most matches with.

   REMEMBER

   Having Sting get pinned at all in the big climactic finale to this storyline, even with a crooked referee involved, was an impossibly bad idea given this was the alleged end of the story and Sting was portrayed as the only remaining possible savior of WCW.

2. **Referee Nick Patrick would count a lightning-fast pin.**

   This speed-up would suggest that the NWO paid him off to help Hogan win.

3. **Bret Hart, fresh off Montreal, would arrive and proclaim that he wasn't going to stand for another screwjob.**

   Read all about the Montreal Screwjob in the section "Getting screwed over: The Montreal Screwjob" earlier in this chapter.

4. **Hart would restart the match.**
5. **Sting would run wild and *submit* Hogan (make him give up) by using his famed *Scorpion deathlock* (an intertwined leg hold).**

But what actually happened made Sting, who was supposed to be the hero, look like a bad wrestler who got beaten fair-and-square and then needed help to win:

1. **Hogan hit Sting with the Legdrop of Doom, as planned.**
2. **Nick Patrick, however, counted a perfectly normal three-count.**

   Patrick met with Hogan before the match and Hogan told him in no uncertain terms to not speed up his count.

   It wasn't fast at all, so everyone in the building saw Sting get beat up the entire match and then pinned clean in the middle of the ring.
3. **Hart made his return and claimed he wouldn't stand for another screw-job (even though Patrick's count was fair).**
4. **Hart restarted the match, and Sting won.**

   So Sting didn't come out of the match looking like the top star (nor was he portrayed that way), the NWO dragged on, and Hogan remained top star.

WARNING

Clinging to Hogan

To WCW's head, Eric Bischoff, Hogan was the golden ticket to professional wrestling success, a man who would never stop generating revenue. To be fair, Hogan did generate more revenue for WCW than the company had ever generated before, to the point that for 83 weeks, they crushed WWF and held the number-one position in pro wrestling (see the section "Moving to the New World Order" earlier in this chapter).

WARNING

But in 1998, Hogan was 45 years old, and his body was falling apart, racked with injuries. And worse, fans who had been watching him for decades grew tired of him. Although McMahon was objectively wrong in 1990 when he thought Hogan was too old to draw money in pro wrestling (as we talk about in the section "Dealing with a WWF steroid scandal" earlier in this chapter), he wasn't wrong about the fact that, at some point, the wrestling world would need to replace Hogan.

But Bischoff was riding so high on the back of Hogan's success that he didn't even consider pulling Hogan out of main events.

And so, Hogan headlined show after show. And even when someone else scored a big win over him (such as Lex Luger, Sting, and Bill Goldberg), WCW never truly elevated the winner into the position of the new top star. WCW always set a loss up as a bump in the road, with the goal of getting the top spot and the WCW Title back onto Hogan sooner rather than later.

Hogan, along with Scott Hall, Kevin Nash, and a few of the other aging top stars, refused to relinquish their main event spots, so the great young wrestlers on the *undercard* (matches below the main event) never got elevated. The older wrestlers continuously looked for every opportunity to stall the ascent of the new kids.

Making terrible booking decisions

The storytelling in WCW fell off a cliff around 1999. Bischoff, who ran WCW, had overseen the storytelling since around the time that Hogan signed with WCW in 1994, but other people played the role of *head booker* (the top person who crafts the storylines), including Kevin Sullivan, for much of the NWO's rise (discussed in the section "Moving to the New World Order" earlier in this chapter).

REMEMBER

WCW's storytelling first showed signs of weakness when Bischoff (see Figure 6-4) inserted himself into the NWO as a heel television character, which moved his focus toward his own on-screen antics, as opposed to storytelling. The booking suffered further in the wake of Sting's inability to decisively beat Hogan at *Starrcade 1997*, because fans had been waiting almost two years for a happy ending that did not end up satisfying, and NWO Hogan continued to be pushed as the top star (see the preceding section).

FIGURE 6-4: Eric Bischoff during an NWO match.

Photo by Wrealano@aol.com

The two big promotions saw huge changes simultaneously in 1998:

- **WWE exploded in popularity.** With the ascent of Austin to the Championship, WWF was elevating new talent and creating new megastars. As a result, *Nitro's* multi-year unbeaten ratings streak came to an end.
- **WCW was stagnating.** It ran with the same old *pat hand* on top (meaning they continued pushing the same people and made little effort to create new stars), and none of the younger stars could move up the *card* (be put into main event positions). WCW was still running strong financially in early 1998, but wrestling history made it clear that they were heading toward a fall.

In late 1998, Bischoff gave Kevin Nash head booking power. Unfortunately, Nash's main concern was Nash:

- **He booked himself to be the man who ended Bill Goldberg's 173-0 unbeaten streak.** The streak was so legitimately valuable that most fans and insiders widely assumed that some young promising talent would finally beat him and become an instant superstar. Instead, Nash chose himself.
- **Nash immediately gave the title back to Hogan.** On *Nitro* the week after Nash booked himself a win, he defended the belt against Hogan in a massive main event. When the bell rang, Hogan touched Nash with one finger — called the *Fingerpoke of Doom* — and Nash took a giant fake bump and got pinned by Hogan. The match was a ruse to set up yet another NWO reunion with Hogan back on top as champion. Fans absolutely hated it, and not in a money-drawing way.

WCW began to collapse in 1999, to the point that they were soon losing millions of dollars per month. It hired new booking blood, including the WWF's Vince Russo and Ed Ferrara (which you can read about in Chapter 7).

Turns out Russo didn't have the booking chops that he said he did. Add to that the fact that WCW awarded Russo bonuses based only on TV ratings. Therefore, all the other very important revenue generators (such as attendances and pay-per-view buys) fell to the wayside.

From late 1999 through 2000, WCW hired, fired, and hired back Russo; and then it even paired him with Bischoff (of all people). By the time the year was over, WCW had lost more than $60 million in a single year.

TIP

WHY WCW REALLY DIED

They say the winners write history, but the losers try to write history, too. If you listen to the history of the death of WCW as told by WCW figures such as Vince Russo, Eric Bischoff, and Kevin Nash, they tell you that WCW died because AOL merged with Time Warner in 2001, media mogul and pro wrestling fan Ted Turner lost power, and the new guy put in charge, Jamie Kellner, canceled all their TV, rendering WCW worthless.

On the surface, that's true: That all happened.

WCW folks might tell you that Kellner canceled their TV spots because he hated pro wrestling. But the real reason Kellner canceled WCW was because WCW was bad business. The people who blamed the AOL/Time Warner merger were the same people who ran WCW into the ground, destroyed its value, and took it from being a massive money generator to a massive money loser in a scant two years. Had WCW generated $125 million in 2001, like it did just a few years earlier, Kellner would have had virtually no reason to cancel the programming. But when Kellner was hired, WCW was losing tens of millions of dollars, with no indication that it was about to turn things around. It had to go.

3 Identifying the Major Promotions

IN THIS PART . . .

Delve into the most popular companies of the 20th century and how they impacted modern professional wrestling.

Look at the professional wrestling promotions that carried the torch into the 21st century.

Examine the rise of independent wrestling.

IN THIS CHAPTER

» Following the path of World Wrestling Entertainment (WWE)

» Competing as World Championship Wrestling (WCW)

» Watching the Extreme Championship Wrestling (ECW) become extreme

Chapter 7
Highlighting the Big Three

Many American fans consider American professional wrestling the be-all and end-all, particularly because World Wrestling Entertainment (WWE) regularly produces documentaries that get a little creative with facts to push this narrative. But pro wrestling has had legions of fans all over the world for as long as this sort of entertainment has existed in the form recognized today. As big as the name Hulk Hogan was in the United States, he was far less of a main-stream name here than El Santo was in Mexico or Rikidōzan was in Japan.

This chapter focuses mostly on American professional wrestling, specifically an overview of the three big national U.S. wrestling promotional groups in the 1990s.

Eyeing World Wrestling Entertainment (WWE)

For much of modern history, WWE (previously WWWF and WWF) has been the largest wrestling company in the world. But there were periods when they really struggled, faced stiff competition from other companies, and even at one point found themselves in second place. The following sections walk you through the ups and downs and the name changes that take it where it is today.

Every company, from the smallest start up to the largest mega corporation has an origin story. For the World Wide Wrestling Federation (WWWF) (later the World Wrestling Federation [WWF] and then World Wrestling Entertainment [WWE]), their beginnings mirror so many other notable promotions in the past in that they decided to forge their own path by breaking away from the National Wrestling Alliance (NWA).

Forming the CWC: The beginning days

Vincent J. McMahon (father of the more famous Vince McMahon, Jr.), and Toots Mondt ran the Capitol Wrestling Corporation (CWC) when it was founded in 1953, originally as a northeastern territory of the NWA. Because the territory encompassed the northeastern part of the United States — including the most powerful media market in the country, New York City — many fans and wrestlers considered the CWC the most dominant NWA territory.

The CWC promoted shows throughout the Northeast and built stars such as the following:

» **Antonino Rocca:** One of the biggest names of the first national television era (the late 1940s through the mid-1950s).

» **Buddy Rogers:** Among the biggest worldwide drawing cards of the era, he won the NWA World Heavyweight Title from Pat O'Connor on June 30, 1961, before more than 35,000 fans at Comiskey Park in Chicago.

REMEMBER

As a wrestler, personality, and ticket-seller, Rogers was a great choice for a champion, but the title reign was very controversial. The NWA Champion, who was voted on by the NWA Board of Directors, was expected to travel around the country defending the title in various territories. But Mondt had a stranglehold on Rogers's bookings, making it very difficult for other promoters to schedule him for events. Ultimately, the Board decided to switch the title from Rogers back to perennial champion Lou Thesz to allow other promoters to book the champion for appearances.

Going out on their own

Mondt and the CWC promoters weren't happy about the decision to make Thesz the champion, instead of their wrestler Rogers (see the preceding section). As a result, in 1963, they pulled out of the NWA, formed a new promotion dubbed the WWWF, and named Rogers their new champion.

Unfortunately, Rogers had health issues, including suffering a heart attack, and so couldn't play the role of champion. So the WWWF very quickly moved the title to Bruno Sammartino in a very famous 48-second title change.

Sammartino dominated WWWF for more than a decade, including two long reigns as WWWF Champion — the first lasted 2,803 days, and the second lasted 1,237 days. Fans loved Sammartino, and he probably could have had an unending championship run from his first title win through his retirement, but the incredible number of dates and appearances took its toll, and he basically had to demand his way out of his title reign.

TIP

In the 1960s and early 1970s, WWWF was built around babyface champs, so a heel won only to provide a transitional reign to get the title from one babyface to another without having two babyfaces face off.

In 1971, the belt went from babyface Sammartino to heel Ivan Koloff to babyface Pedro Morales during a short period of time. Morales was the biggest Hispanic star in the history of the company, selling out Madison Square Garden 21 times in 30 title matches during his two-year run. Morales was a gigantic draw specifically in the New York market, but not elsewhere. Therefore, the WWWF talked Sammartino into returning for his second and final WWWF Title run. (At this point, Vince McMahon, Sr. and Jr. ran the WWWF because McMahon forced Mondt out of the company in the 1960s.)

The latter part of the 1970s was dominated by two champions:

- **Superstar Billy Graham:** An incredible heel *draw* (meaning he sold a lot of tickets) who was champion from April 1977 to February 1978.
- **Bob Backlund:** Played the humble babyface All-American wrestler and held the title from February 1978 until December 1983.

McMahon, Sr. had the WWWF rejoin the NWA in 1971, which allowed them to once again book big-name NWA talent that they wouldn't otherwise have access to. By the end of the 1970s, McMahon, Sr. was winding down, and McMahon, Jr. was taking steps to prepare for his eventual takeover.

Getting a new name: The WWF

In 1979, the McMahons renamed the company the World Wrestling Federation (WWF). A year later, McMahon, Jr. incorporated the name *Titan Sports* and trademarked *WWF* for wrestling operations. A few years later, he bought the company from his father and business partners, Phil Zacko, Arnold Skaaland, and Gorilla Monsoon for $1 million, which he then proceeded to pay off by using proceeds from his wrestling operations.

McMahon then began to break all the old rules of the territorial system of professional wrestling. He:

- Pulled out of the NWA again (after his father rejoined in 1971; see the preceding section)
- Began a national expansion that included raiding multiple territories of their top stars, buying airtime for his programming in rival territories, and numerous other cutthroat tactics designed to not only compete, but to also put all of the other territories out of business
- Put the title on a jacked-up blonde All-American muscleman named Hulk Hogan (perfect for the larger-than-life patriotic decade of the 1980s) — see Chapter 6 for more about Hogan
- Within six years of taking control, had basically put 95 percent of the wrestling territories in the United States out of business

Taking some hits

In the early 1990s, WWF business was hurt by a steroid and ring boy sex scandal (flip to Chapter 6 for more information), combined with an overall declining interest in professional wrestling. For several years, McMahon tried to rebuild his company around a new generation of smaller, more athletic wrestlers, but business continued to suffer.

WCW — which we talk about in the section "Focusing on World Championship Wrestling (WCW)" later in this chapter — signed Hogan in 1994 and created the New World Order (NWO). For the first time in its history, WWF briefly became the number two promotion in the United States.

Coming out on top

Through a series of both planned and unplanned circumstances, WWF began to turn business around while WCW began to cool off (check out the section "Focusing on World Championship Wrestling (WCW)" later in this chapter).

REMEMBER

McMahon capitalized on one of the most infamous moments in pro wrestling history, the Montreal Screwjob (which we talk about in Chapter 6) by making himself the top heel evil-boss character. His feud with common-man wrestler Steve Austin exploded the company into the stratosphere. Business turned around to the point that McMahon, in the summer of 1999, took the company public and almost immediately joined the ranks of American billionaires.

The company remained on fire through 2001 to the point that both WCW and the number three U.S. promotion, Extreme Championship Wrestling (ECW), went out of business (flip to the section "Looking into Extreme Championship Wrestling (ECW)" later in this chapter, for more about the ECW). WWF ultimately purchased them both.

Although it took him 17 years, McMahon finally achieved his dream of heading the sole big-time professional wrestling organization in the United States.

Losing a court battle and going with another name change: WWE

In 2002, the company changed its name to World Wrestling Entertainment (WWE) after they lost a lawsuit to the other WWF: the World Wildlife Fund. The two sides had battled in court for years:

- **Trademark:** The World Wildlife Fund had trademarked *WWF* in 1961, and McMahon had been using the letters *WWF* since he renamed the company World Wrestling Federation in 1979.
- **Usage agreements:** Twice, the two sides had come to an agreement on the wrestling company's usage of the initials, with McMahon agreeing that outside of the company's WWF *block logo* (a very famous block-style logo used in the 80s and early-'90s), the promotion would never refer to itself as WWF, only as World Wrestling Federation. McMahon agreed to the terms and then flagrantly disregarded them (which has happened multiple times during his career).
- **Violation:** The World Wildlife Fund began proceedings at the High Court of Justice in England, arguing that the World Wrestling Federation had agreed to terms in 1994 and then violated the agreement. The court sided with the Fund.

TIP

Ultimately, the promotion opted to change the name to WWE. And to save face, they claimed that the rebrand allowed them the ability to emphasize the entertainment aspect of the company. The WWE then started an ad campaign entitled (seriously) "Get the F out!"

Getting fresh leadership

Winning the U.S. wrestling war (see Chapter 6) didn't guarantee success for the WWF; business fell in the wake of the death of WCW and ECW, and the WWF sank into a two-decade period of stagnation that only turned around after McMahon was replaced as head of creative by his son-in-law Paul Levesque.

REMEMBER

Most in wrestling, from fans to wrestlers to promoters, had always believed that without McMahon, WWE might not survive. In fact, without him, WWE rose to its greatest financial height in history. (Chapter 6 goes into the details of the modern WWE.)

Focusing on World Championship Wrestling (WCW)

World Championship Wrestling (WCW) is the only promotion in history which, for a time, beat WWF at its own game (see the section "Taking some hits" earlier in this chapter) and became the biggest wrestling organization on Earth. The following sections walk you through how the WCW started, prospered, and eventually ended.

Eyeing the WCW's beginnings and struggles

When businessman Ted Turner purchased Jim Crockett Promotions (JCP) in 1988, he changed the name to WCW. Even before this purchase, Turner was an influential name in professional wrestling, ever since the launch of his cable television station Turner Broadcasting System (TBS) in 1976. Here's a general overview of what happened:

- **1976:** TBS aired Georgia Championship Wrestling (GCW), which was the first television show (of any type!) on cable TV to draw more than 1 million viewers. GCW was run by Ole Anderson and several shareholders, including legendary wrestlers Jack and Jerry Briscoe and promoter Jim Barnett.
- **1982:** The show changed its name to WCW because Anderson deemed the name *Georgia Championship Wrestling* too region-specific.
- **1984:** McMahon bought GCW out from underneath Anderson by making a deal with the Briscos and Barnett. The purchase gave him the time shots in which World Championship Wrestling aired, in his attempt to take full control of pro wrestling in America; but as it turned out, Georgia Championship

Wrestling fans didn't want to see McMahon's WWF version of wrestling. The ratings collapsed, and Turner wasn't happy.

- **1985:** A year later, McMahon ended up selling the time slots to JCP for $1 million. McMahon told Crockett, "You'll choke on that million." He then proceeded to do everything in his power to put Crockett out of business.
- **1988:** Because of both McMahon's predatory tactics and Crockett's poor business maneuverings, JCP was on death's door. Because professional wrestling programming had been instrumental in his own cable and satellite television success, Turner stepped in and purchased the company for $9 million.

REMEMBER

For the first seven years of WCW under Turner, business basically sucked. WCW had some good wrestlers who had good matches, but it also had bad matches, bad stories, and one problem after another. But Turner was loyal to wrestling and everyone who worked for WCW believed that no matter what happened, no matter how bad it got, no matter how much money it lost, WCW would always be around. The top brass at TBS broached the idea of shutting down WCW — Turner said it wasn't happening and to never bring up the subject again.

Trying to be more competitive

Everything turned around for the WCW in the middle of the 1990s. It had gone through one management figure after another before a former announcer named Eric Bischoff somehow got the role of executive producer of WCW. Within a year, he got promoted to executive vice president, and he used his power to make big moves. For example, he:

- **Hired Hogan for a ridiculous amount of money:** Hogan had left WWF a year earlier, basically in disgrace following a steroid scandal, and was working in Japan. Bischoff hired him and pushed him straight to the top, making him WCW Champion and the centerpiece of the company. As wild as the Hogan deal seemed when it was first signed, he more than paid for himself because business turned around immediately.
- **Requested a weekly prime-time cable TV show:** A year after Bischoff hired Hogan, Turner wanted to make WCW more competitive with the WWF, so he gave Bischoff a Monday night prime-time slot, head-to-head with WWF's flagship *Monday Night RAW.* Even though many in the business thought this move would hurt both companies and split their audience, in fact, the Monday night audience for wrestling immediately doubled.
- **Brought more former WWF stars to the WCW:** Both the WWF and WCW shows ran neck-and-neck for several months until Bischoff hired two of the bigger stars in WWF at the time, former WWF Champion Kevin Nash (who used the name Diesel) and former multi-time Intercontinental Champion Scott Hall

(called Razor Ramon). Without outright saying so, they were presented as WWF invaders looking to take over WCW. This marketing led to trademark infringement lawsuits between WWF and WCW — but also big business success.

- **Made Hogan go heel:** In the summer of 1996, Hogan turned heel for the first time in 15 years, joining Nash and Hall as the NWO. WCW business exploded, because a group of bad guys headed by a newly-turned-evil Hogan made for compelling television shows.

Recognizing the beginning of the end

From 1996 to 1998, WCW business hit all-time peaks. But as much good as Bischoff did, he did even greater damage, which ultimately put the company completely out of business. A primary issue was that he refused to elevate new talent, younger talent — *any* talent:

- **He didn't move WCW past the NWO.** A new babyface wrestler never definitively got one over on the NWO. The NWO storyline dragged on and on and on. The closest the good guys came to finally destroying the NWO was WCW wrestler Sting's victory over NWO Hogan at *Starrcade 1997*. Bischoff and Hogan completely bungled that victory, and Hogan continued as top star (see Chapter 6 for details).
- **He missed the chance to create a new megastar.** Bill Goldberg, a muscular former football player who wrestled explosive short matches that fans loved, was the obvious choice to become the new WCW Champion, but that storyline didn't go anywhere because Hogan and other top stars worked to sabotage him behind the scenes (see Chapter 6 for more).

WARNING

- **His hiring decisions didn't turn around business.** WCW hired writers Vince Russo and Ed Ferrara away from WWF, supposedly the geniuses behind WWF's recent turnaround in business. But Russo in particular misrepresented himself. He came up with some good ideas when in WWF, but McMahon was the true genius behind the company's success. Without McMahon, Russo's WCW shows often made little sense, presented bad matches, and frustrated fans, causing many to switch to WWF.

Sticking a fork in it

While business declined for WCW, panic set in:

- **Too many changes:** A rotating cast of different writers came and went: Kevin Nash, Kevin Sullivan, and Russo again. Each time, damage was piled on top of damage, and by 2000, WCW as an organization was losing more than $60 million in a calendar year.

- **New management:** At the same time, Time Warner (of which Turner was vice-chairman) and AOL merged. So Turner — who had vowed that as long as he was around, nobody would ever get rid of WCW — no longer had a say in WCW's fate. The new management did what new management does — they looked at the books and saw WCW hemorrhaging money, so they made the decision to sell.
- **Bought out:** McMahon and the WWF purchased the company for $2.5 million and the agreement to buy a few million dollars in ads on Turner stations.

The story of the most rapid and astounding rise and fall of a big-time wrestling promotion in world history came to an end in the spring of 2001 when WWF bought WCW, which as a company ceased to exist, but continued on for a short time as a brand on WWE television.

Looking into Extreme Championship Wrestling (ECW)

The story of Extreme Championship Wrestling (ECW) could take up a full book (and has). ECW was a national wrestling promotion that started in the Philadelphia area in 1992. During the Monday Night Wars, it was a distant number three behind WWF (which we talk about in the section "Eyeing World Wrestling Entertainment [WWE]" earlier in this chapter) and WCW (see the section "Focusing on World Championship Wrestling [WCW]" earlier in this chapter).

REMEMBER

No matter what, it could never move into even the number two position. It was, as promoter Paul Heyman famously said, "too big to be small, and too small to be big." It never had the means to compete with its much larger and much better-funded rivals. The following sections focus on ECW's history — a story that might seem undervalued or overvalued, depending on whose perspective you choose.

A pivotal part in the Monday Night Wars

The history of wrestling would almost certainly be completely different today if ECW had never existed. In 1996, when WCW had overtaken WWF in the Monday Night Wars on the back of the success of *Monday Nitro* and the NWO, WWF was in dire straits financially.

TIP

Even though many characters and moments get the credit for WWF's turnaround — deservedly — the turnaround first began and then accelerated when McMahon began testing out more hardcore concepts that he flat-out stole from ECW, such as edgier:

- **Storylines:** Brian Pillman pulling a gun on Steve Austin, a very controversial TV moment that almost got *RAW* kicked off the USA Network.
- **Promos:** "Austin 3:16 says I just whipped your ass." WWF had always been a very PG product, and Austin's bad language helped usher in a more PG-13 era.
- **Gimmicks:** Shawn Michaels, Triple H, and Chyna as the original Degeneration X (DX) featured three grown adults acting like teenagers and making teenage jokes about genitalia and such. Their catch phrase was, "Suck it!"
- **Presentations:** Sunny and Sable appearing on television half naked every week — another very PG-13 transition.

The Monday Night Wars boom period (from 1995 to 2001) happened because professional wrestling suddenly became the hot thing to the young male audience of that period, teenagers and those in their very early 20s. And both WWF and WCW attracted them in different ways:

- **WCW:** Pushed the big stars of the 1980s, wrestlers those fans had first watched when they were kids. WCW's '80s wrestlers — such as Hogan and Randy Savage — offered teenage viewers a sense of nostalgia.
- **WWF:** Moved to a more hardcore, raunchy product, which of course attracted young males in the teenage demographic (and, not surprisingly, children under 13 found PG-13 programming really attractive because it was forbidden, so the under-13 crowd became a gigantic audience for WWF during that era).

WARNING

Ultimately, if you put all the other issues that WCW faced aside, their strategy was doomed to failure because nostalgia has a shelf life, whereas generations of young men (and not-so-young men, in many cases) will continue to enjoy raunchy content.

Seeing where ECW started

ECW began as a little company called Eastern Championship Wrestling:

- **Beginning in Pennsylvania:** A Philadelphia man named Tod Gordon partnered with Joel Goodhart, a local radio host, in 1989 to run a promotion called the Tri-State Wrestling Alliance.

- **Going solo:** Goodhart wanted to get out of the business, so in 1992, Gordon bought Goodhart's shares, renamed the promotion Eastern Championship Wrestling, and joined what was left of the National Wrestling Alliance (NWA); see Chapter 5 for the history of NWA.
- **Getting a booker:** In 1993, Gordon hired wrestler Eddie Gilbert as his *booker* (someone who primarily writes the storylines for a wrestling company). Gilbert's booking was mostly about getting himself over (meaning because he was also a wrestler, as the booker he made himself one of the top stars). Within a year, he and Gordon had a big falling out.
- **Going extreme:** Gordon replaced Gilbert with a man recently fired from his job as a manager in WCW, Paul Heyman. After Heyman came onboard with ECW, he turned it up a notch on the Memphis-style brawls and hardcore action. On his very first show, he teamed up two local guys, Ted Petty and Mike Durham, as The Public Enemy, and booked them in a blood feud with legends Terry and Dory Funk. At the time, WWF and WCW rarely featured bloody, wild, brawling matches involving weapons, so ECW stood out.

Getting extreme

By 1994, both WCW and New Japan had abandoned the NWA Championship, so because the NWA was a governing body and not a promotion, the title sat vacant. The NWA still had a Board of Directors, and the man in charge, Dennis Coralluzzo, decided to promote a tournament to resurrect the NWA Title.

ECW's Heyman and Gordon offered to host the tournament, arguing that ECW's television show had the widest reach of any current NWA affiliate; and they suggested their champion, Shane Douglas, win the tournament. ECW had a plan to garner headlines by legitimately double-crossing the NWA and creating a new championship:

- **Out with the old:** After Douglas won the tournament, he took the mic and accepted the NWA Title "in the tradition" of all the greats who came before him. But then he announced that all those legends could kiss his ass. He threw down the NWA Title and said the era of the ECW World Heavyweight Champion, Shane Douglas, had begun.
- **Getting a new name:** On the very next ECW television show (*ECW Hardcore TV*), Gordon announced that the company had withdrawn from the NWA and would henceforth be renamed Extreme Championship Wrestling.

TIP

If you ask any fan to tell you what the first thing they think of is when they hear the moniker *ECW*, they probably rattle off a list of extreme events:

- **Violence:** Bloodbaths, broken tables, and hard unprotected chairshots to the head
- **Weapons:** Kendo sticks and barbed wire
- **Adult content:** Foul language and strippers; plus all the stuff that you never saw on TV but everyone knew existed, including copious usage of alcohol and street drugs backstage (and sometimes you saw that on TV)

ECW ran shows out of the ECW Arena, a bingo hall located at 2300 South Swanson Street in Philadelphia (which was renamed the 2300 Arena in 2013 and still hosts combat sports and concerts at the time of writing). It sat around 1,100 fans, and ECW packed the building for television tapings. The ECW Arena crowds were legendary, for both good reasons and bad, and the promotion had an underground outlaw vibe that WWF and WCW couldn't touch.

Peeking behind the rivalry

REMEMBER

Even though ECW was, in theory, competing for supremacy with WWF and WCW (publicly, Heyman pushed WWF and WCW as ECW's mortal enemies), ECW had working relationships with both companies — sometimes, secretly, at the same time:

- **WWF:** McMahon, the head of the WWF, helped fund ECW for years, sending a check every week to HHG Corporation, ECW's parent company (which, of course, Heyman owned).
- **WCW:** Worked together with ECW behind the scenes (while Heyman promoted WCW as ECW's arch enemy), most notably during a very famous angle involving Brian Pillman (see the sidebar "What a pill," in this chapter).

WHAT A PILL

The story of Brian Pillman could only happen in professional wrestling. Pillman was working as a wrestler for WCW in 1995 but wasn't happy with his lot in life. He wanted to make more money and get a better *push* (move up higher on the cards, be portrayed as a bigger star), but WCW clearly didn't plan to help him. He saw his best chance as going to WWF, where he could feud as a top heel with the babyface champion at the time, Shawn Michaels. Pillman came up with an idea. He wanted to make his character,

"The Loose Cannon," appear to simply be Pillman himself, a real-life maniac whom management couldn't control. Because fans knew wrestling stories and characters weren't real, his idea was to try to blur the lines and make them believe "The Loose Cannon" was actually real.

Pillman convinced WCW's head, Eric Bischoff, that if they could fool everyone — fans and wrestlers alike — into thinking that he was an unhinged maniac, somehow, that would draw money. So, they came up with a story where Pillman supposedly went off script on television and got himself fired. But Pillman suggested they take it a step further. Nobody would believe this firing, he explained, because wrestlers got fired in storyline all the time. For this angle to work, everyone had to believe that he was really out of his mind and really went off script; and the only way to convince everyone of that was for Bischoff to really fire him.

So, Pillman talked Bischoff into giving him a legitimate release, meaning that he was no longer under contract with WCW. Bischoff and Heyman then worked together to get Pillman to ECW, continuing the story that after he was fired, Pillman went to work for Heyman's rogue outsider group. WCW paid Heyman to use Pillman because WCW was trying to convince their fans that Pillman's firing was legitimate.

And then, in the end — and this is the best part — because Pillman had gotten himself a legitimate release, he signed with the WWF in 1996.

Finding success in the Monday Night Wars

ECW built themselves up to likely the biggest level of success they could achieve while playing third wheel in the Monday Night Wars by doing the following:

- **Starting careers:** They created stars such as Sandman, New Jack, Raven, Sabu, Taz, Tommy Dreamer, Rob Van Dam, and the Dudleys, who parlayed that success into decades-long careers.
- **Giving folks a shot:** They introduced smaller, high-flying wrestlers to many American fans for the first time, guys such as Rey Mysterio, Jr., Eddy Guerrero, and Dean Malenko. After appearing in ECW, these wrestlers were quickly hired away by WCW.
- **Letting legends come back:** They gave a platform to older stars, such as Terry Funk, who became legends to a brand-new younger audience.
- **Taking stars higher:** They helped make wrestlers who had already achieved some level of stardom, such as Cactus Jack, even bigger stars.

- **Making money:** They generated revenue from touring business and even saw moderate success running pay-per-view (PPV) events.
- **Getting on cable TV:** In 1999, they got the holy grail for professional wrestling— a national cable television slot on The Nashville Network (TNN).

WARNING

But when compared to WCW (which had massive resources with the backing of the Turner Networks) and WWF (a billion-dollar company after going public in 1999), ECW had no resources to fall back on. Heyman and his family funded the company. If ECW consistently lost money, Heyman would go bankrupt (which eventually happened). Their resources included only the revenues that they generated minus expenses — and unfortunately, you can't fight with limited resources against seemingly unlimited resources and expect to come out on top.

ECW was a small company forced to operate as if it was a much larger company:

- **Paying for talent:** When ECW got the TNN television deal and subsequently a video game deal, the broadcasting and video game companies wanted ECW to lock up their top talent, and the only way to do so was to offer the top talent guaranteed six-figure contracts.
- **Paying for PPV:** In 1997, ECW began running PPV events more frequently to try to remain competitive with WWF and WCW. The PPVs were expensive to run, and in those days, the event organizer didn't receive revenue from the PPV until three months after it aired.

Having money troubles

ECW had to face the big money of the WWF and WCW in more ways than one. If ECW created a big star, both WWF and WCW would make a play for that person, and they could offer more money than ECW could.

REMEMBER

ECW benefited from its relationship with WWF in some ways, but because of the power disparity, WWF always came out on top:

- When ECW wrestlers appeared on WWF TV, the ECW wrestlers never walked in and got big wins over WWF superstars.
- The bottom-tier WWF wrestlers would invariably beat the top ECW wrestlers, including ECW's champions.

- In the 1990s, ECW stars being booked as prelim wrestlers on WWF and WCW television hurt ECW business because it convinced some ECW fans that ECW's top wrestlers were just third-tier stars nationally.

The TNN deal (see the preceding section), while initially incredibly valuable for ECW, was the beginning of the end in many ways:

- **Losing TNN:** Very shortly after signing the deal, ECW realized that TNN planned to make a very large bid for WWF's *RAW,* which had provided the cable channel USA Network enormous success over the past several years. After TNN got *RAW*, they canceled the ECW show in October 2000.
- **Finding no other cable TV takers:** At that point, the only hope was for a high-paying television deal on another network. But USA Network had no interest in non-WWF wrestling, and TBS and TNT still owned WCW (and after selling, had agreed to a clause where no other wrestling promotion could get televised on a Turner station for years afterward).
- **Getting no financial bailout:** ECW had lost $2.5 million in 2001 — which was a drop in the bucket compared to the $60 million-plus that WCW had lost. But that $2.5 million was the Heyman family's money, and Heyman didn't want to lose another $5 million struggling along with no major national television.

Fizzling out

ECW had no grand finale, no final celebratory show similar to WCW's last *Monday Nitro*. Instead, wrestlers just stopped being paid. Heyman stopped going to shows. Most of the wrestlers had no idea what was going on because nobody told them anything.

The hardest of the hardcore ECW loyalists held out hope that Heyman had a great grand plan that was about to be unveiled (almost exactly how it went when WCW was on death's door, which you can read about in the section "Sticking a fork in it" earlier in this chapter — WCW diehards thought the end of WCW was all some grand storyline by Bischoff, the executive producer of WCW).

ECW went out with a whimper, their last show taking place on January 13, 2001, in Pine Bluff, Arkansas, headlined by Justin Credible versus Sandman. At the end of the event, the wrestlers who remained in the locker room had an impromptu farewell celebration.

On March 5, 2001, Heyman showed up on *Monday Night RAW* to replace Jerry Lawler on commentary.

REMEMBER

Of course, various promoters revived the "ECW" concept many times (although under different names for trademark reasons). The most notable was WWE, which even incorporated ECW as a third brand, alongside *RAW* and *SmackDown*, for several years in the 2000s. But no matter who from the original company appeared in the events, those events were always the WWE version of ECW, not the real spirit of ECW. Extreme Championship Wrestling was, maybe more than any other single promotion in wrestling history, a product of its time and place that couldn't have survived before or after its heyday of the mid-1990s, because society itself moved on from the hardcore grunge ethos of the mid-'90s.

IN THIS CHAPTER

» Succeeding where WCW failed: Total Nonstop Action (TNA)

» Creating Ring of Honor (ROH)

» Going all in with All Elite Wrestling (AEW)

» Following the path of WWE's newest boom period

Chapter 8
Moving into the 21st Century

The day: March 26, 2001 — World Championship Wrestling (WCW) aired its final episode of WCW *Monday Nitro.* About a week prior, parent company Time Warner/AOL not only cancelled any future episodes, but they also sold all of WCW's assets to longtime rival World Wrestling Federation (WWF).

In other words, WCW died on this day. The end of WCW only a few months after the number three U.S.-based promotion Extreme Championship Wrestling (ECW) folded changed the landscape of professional wrestling.

The millions of fans who watched wrestling each week dwindled while the months went on. Even though the *Attitude Era* (from 1997 to 2001) — the modern peak of pro wrestling popularity — had ended, the professional wrestling industry didn't die in North America. Many new promotions sprouted throughout the first two-plus decades of the 21st century, each one sporting its own unique identity and cultivating its own niche audience. This chapter looks at the new age of professional wrestling in the United States and shows more of a bucking of the traditional presentation of pro wrestling.

Exploring Total Nonstop Action (TNA)

Although Vince McMahon purchased WCW and became an on-screen storyline *heel* (bad guy persona) for his WWF, the legitimate successor to WCW was essentially Total Nonstop Action (TNA). Although they may not have ever reached the popularity of peak WCW, TNA was a steady presence in the 21st century, and at its peak had 1.5 million regular viewers each week. Here we dive into TNA and what pro wrestling looked like during this time.

Creating NWA-TNA

In 2000, with WCW on death's door, several groups put together offers to purchase the company. One of them was headed by longtime wrestler and promoter Jerry Jarrett. Although WCW was losing $5 million per month, Jarrett felt that if he cut costs and ran a far more streamlined business operation, the company could be saved. Historians claim that Jarrett's group bid $20 million for WCW, but that WCW's owner, Ted Turner, never even considered his offer and sold WCW to McMahon, head of WWF, for approximately $2.5 million. If Turner didn't consider Jarrett's bid, no one has really ever adequately explained why.

WARNING

Jerry Jarrett's son, Jeff Jarrett, worked for WCW as a wrestler, but WWF didn't want to bring Jeff back when they bought WCW because of bad blood. Jeff had demanded WWF pay him approximately $200,000 for his last night working as a wrestler with the company in 1999. WWF wanted him to lose the Intercontinental Title to Chyna (one of the most prolific women's wrestlers in WWF history), but his contract had already expired, so he didn't have to do anything he didn't want to do — and he demanded the healthy bonus, which McMahon resented.

So, with nowhere to go, Jeff and his friend, pro wrestling journalist Bob Ryder, came up with the idea for a new promotion, and they talked Jeff's father Jerry into funding it. They planned to name it National Wrestling Alliance-Total Nonstop Action (NWA-TNA) because of the intended affiliation with NWA. But NWA-TNA couldn't get a TV deal, where a television network would pay for the company to air their product on said network. So, they came up with a solution: They'd air their weekly show exclusively on pay-per-view (PPV) for $10 a pop.

If you think this idea sounds crazy, well, that's because it was. The Jarretts came up with every reason, stat, and theory under the sun to explain why this income structure would work. But they were asking fans to pay $10 every week to watch a two-hour PPV wrestling show, which wasn't a popular or sustainable business model.

Becoming TNA Entertainment

By the end of the first month, NWA-TNA had around 8,000 to 10,000 PPV buys per week — which, if we're honest, is a rather impressive number. But the Jarretts thought that they could do perhaps as many as 500,000 buys per week, and so they budgeted accordingly. Because the viewership didn't soar as they anticipated it would, within three months, NWA-TNA was on the verge of declaring bankruptcy.

TIP

However, one of the people working for them in their marketing department, Dixie Carter, happened to be the daughter of Bob Carter, who (along with his wife, Janice) owned Panda Energy International, a company that maintained and operated power plants. They quickly purchased a 71-percent interest in what would become TNA Entertainment, and the company was saved for the first (but certainly not the last) time. (See the section "Becoming a business" later in this chapter for other rescues.)

Carter became President of TNA Entertainment. And the wrestler going by the moniker of "Abyss" named a gimmick, a 2-by-4 board that had nails sticking out of it, after Janice Carter. (Really. We're not making that up.)

For the first several years, TNA Wrestling ran shows from the Tennessee State Fairground Sports Arena. The arena was affectionately referred to as the TNA Asylum.

Joining the team early on was former WWF and WCW writer Vince Russo — the same Russo who helped bring down WCW, which we talk about in Chapter 6. TNA initially kept Russo's involvement a secret because of the concern that if wrestlers or backstage employees found out he was involved, they would quit. Ultimately, many of the people who had assisted in steering WCW into the iceberg — from wrestlers to people working behind the curtain — joined TNA.

Making an impact

Although TNA still exists to this day, the mid-2000s are considered the company's glory period. In 2004, TNA launched its weekly television program, *TNA iMPACT!*:

- **Buying time:** Initially airing as a *time buy* on Fox Sports (meaning TNA paid for the airtime, rather than Fox Sports paying to air it), the production was handled at Universal Studios in Orlando, Florida, where the soundstage they used became known as the Impact Zone.
- **Setting up PPV:** TNA transitioned to monthly PPVs beginning with the *Victory Road* event on November 7, 2004.

- **Landing a cable deal:** Momentum picked up in 2006 because of a number of factors. The company landed a major (paying!) cable television deal with Spike TV, and *iMPACT!* debuted on the network on October 1, 2005.

  REMEMBER

  This deal allowed TNA to sign more mainstream talent, such as Olympic gold medalist Kurt Angle (whose feud with submission specialist Samoa Joe drew the two biggest PPV buy rates in company history, more than 60,000 for each), former WWE, WCW, and ECW talent such as Christian Cage, Mick Foley, Kevin Nash, Booker T, Sting, Team 3D (formerly known as the Dudley Boyz), and various other talents who had broken through to the mainstream via the now-named World Wrestling Entertainment (WWE), WCW, and Extreme Championship Wrestling (ECW), all of which we talk about in Chapter 6.
- **Going international:** The next year saw the company's first round of international touring, leaving a noticeable industry footprint in Europe (France, Germany, and the United Kingdom) and Asia (India and the United Arab Emirates).
- **Merchandising:** TNA saw further growth in 2008, with business deals coming to fruition for toys (with toy manufacturer Jakks Pacific,), trading cards (with sports collectible event promoters Tristar Productions), and even a video game (through Midway Games).

When it comes to innovation, TNA was willing to be more experimental than most promotions, aside from the weekly PPVs. They were one of the first major promotions to partner with YouTube (2007):

- **TNA YouTube channel:** Provided content to fans, including replays of prominent angles from *TNA iMPACT!*
- **TNA U TV:** A series of YouTube-exclusive podcasts that featured TNA content

Innovating and reinventing

TNA Wrestling's innovations when it came to the *presentation* (the overall vibe of the television show) made it stand out. One of the more cutting-edge aspects of TNA involved the type of matches that they created:

WARNING

- **Some misfires:** A few match innovations just didn't work, such as the Reverse Battle Royal, one of the silliest matches in history, where wrestlers fought to get inside the ring from outside and had to pretend the fight was difficult.
- **The X Division:** Featured some of the most amazing high-fliers in the industry. Advertised as "not about weight limits, but about no limits."

Heavyweights who could pull off impressive aerial maneuvers, such as the "Samoan Submission Machine" Samoa Joe, could compete for the title.

- **Ultimate X:** The X Division Title match. Either the title belt or (in the case of a non-title match) a giant X would be suspended above the ring, and wrestlers would have to climb the turnbuckle posts and make it up to the cables suspended above the ring. Like a ladder match (which we talk about in Chapter 3), the first person to climb across the cables and procure the belt or the giant X was ruled the winner.

REMEMBER

- **Knockouts Division:** The women of TNA came to prominence in the late-2000s. At the time, WWE was primarily hiring fitness and lingerie models for their women's division. TNA focused on hiring talented female wrestlers, women such as former WWE stars Mickie James and Gail Kim, as well as two-time TNA Knockouts Champion Awesome Kong, who put on matches of the same caliber as the men — and sometimes surpassing them.

Competing at the next level — A double-edged sword

For TNA to get to the next level, they had to go mainstream. Majority owner Panda Energy International opened up the pocketbook. Star wrestler Hulk Hogan and former WCW executive producer Eric Bischoff debuted with TNA on January 4, 2010, and business briefly picked up. TNA then signed more big names —everyone from Kevin Nash and the "Nature Boy" Ric Flair to Jeff Hardy and Rob Van Dam.

Hogan and Bischoff made multiple changes to TNA:

- Moved to a four-sided ring (old guys hate change).
- Rebranded TNA's TV show to *Impact Wrestling* (the entire promotion was renamed *Impact Wrestling* when they were purchased by Anthem in 2017, a name change which lasted for seven years).
- Attempted to launch a new Monday Night War (check out Chapter 6 for this pro wrestling moneymaker). Unlike in 1995, WWE wasn't struggling to survive, and it handily crushed TNA. The entire war lasted less than two months.

These changes put a huge financial strain on the company:

- Trying to challenge WWE on Mondays caused massive debt.
- Moving the weekly television tapings out of Universal Studios and taking them on the road live every week was very expensive because running live weekly

shows, with all the setup and teardown, costs much more than taping multiple shows in one night in one location.

- Signing Hogan, as well as all the other big names, came with a big price tag.

WARNING

By 2012, Panda Energy wanted out, and Dixie Carter ended up acquiring their stake to become the majority shareholder. The company was careening headlong toward doom. Over the next couple of years, financial issues cost them one big-name talent after another.

Finally, in July of 2015, Spike TV canceled the show. The company, which had lost millions of dollars over the prior decade, appeared dead in the water.

Becoming a business

In 2016, Leonard Asper's company Anthem Sports and Entertainment purchased TNA, in a deal brokered by booker, manager, and promoter Scott D'Amore and commentator Don Callis. The company survived, but Anthem ran TNA like a business — meaning it had to not lose money hand-over-fist like it had done for its entire prior existence. Because of this restructuring, TNA operated a rather low level from a budgetary and from a visibility standpoint, nowhere near the glory days of the mid-2000s. They had television on various networks, including the Denver-based and Canadian-owned AXS TV (which was also purchased by Anthem), but none of them had a vast reach.

REMEMBER

By the time All Elite Wrestling (AEW; which we talk about in Chapter 2) launched in 2019, TNA was, at best, a distant number three promotion in the United States. TNA and AEW had a working agreement in the early days which helped keep the TNA name in the news, particularly when Canadian-born and New Japan Pro-Wrestling–forged Kenny Omega won the Impact Title and took the belt on AEW television, and when former WWE and TNA star Christian Cage won the Impact Title on AEW television and then lost the belt back on Impact TV.

In recent years, the company experienced a minor renaissance:

- **Nostalgia:** The company announced at its event *Bound for Glory 2023* that *Impact Wrestling* was being rebranded back to TNA. The name *TNA* had become a laughingstock in wrestling for various reasons (not the least of which was hilariously bad programming, terrible booking, and all-time horrible matches throughout their entire existence), but the rebrand back to its old name made TNA come across as a cool retro promotion.

- **Deals:** TNA's PPV buys began slowly creeping up, and in December of 2025, they announced a television deal with AMC Networks, their strongest TV deal since Spike TV dropped them in 2015.
- **Alliances:** TNA formed a working alliance with WWE — technically, they worked with *NXT*, but WWE owns and operates that developmental brand. This alliance, which often featured WWE stars winning TNA Titles, which was rarely reciprocated, favored WWE, but it still benefitted TNA in terms of national exposure.

TIP

Entering the Ring of Honor (ROH)

Like TNA (discussed in the section "Exploring Total Nonstop Action [TNA]," earlier in this chapter), the wrestling promotion Ring of Honor (ROH) sprouted up from the ashes of ECW and WCW, which you can read about in Chapter 6. ROH stood out because of their no-frills, sports-forward presentation of professional wrestling.

If you look at the wrestling landscape of the last 20 years, it's not hard to see that many who are considered to be top stars in major promotions, stars such as Bryan Danielson, CM Punk, Samoa Joe, Seth Rollins, AJ Styles, the Young Bucks, and several others, all blazed their path through Ring of Honor.

These sections take a closer look at ROH during this timeframe.

Inspecting the beginnings

ROH was founded by Rob Feinstein, Gabe Sapolsky, and Doug Gentry in 2002. All three had ties to ECW, which had gone out of business a year earlier:

- **Feinstein:** Owned a company called RF Video, which sold wrestling tapes mostly for the now-defunct ECW
- **Sapolsky:** Had worked for ECW for years as a savant of marketing and event promotion
- **Gentry:** Worked behind the scenes as a jack-of-all-trades production staffer for both ECW and RF Video

REMEMBER

They got the idea for ROH in 2001, after watching the second King of Indies tournament in Galt, California, which featured one incredible match after another. The three concluded that you could find more than enough great talent to start a high *work-rate* (more physical, technical, and faster-paced style of wrestling) independent promotion to perhaps fill the gap left by the death of ECW and provide shows to market for RF Video.

Like ECW, ROH's touring stuck primarily to the Northeast: Massachusetts, Maryland, New Jersey, New York, and Pennsylvania. Over time, the company expanded west (Ohio) and south (all the way down to Florida).

Forgoing the heavier *sports entertainment-style* storylines (less soap operatic and talking, but more action), just like ECW did in the 1990s, ROH went with a more smash-mouth product. What separated ROH from other smaller promotions that popped up after ECW failed (such as Combat Zone Wrestling and Game Changer Wrestling, promotions inspired by the more extreme violence that ECW inspired) was its Code of Honor, a set of rules that the athletes of ROH had to abide by, including wrestlers having to shake hands before the ring bell sounded.

TIP

ROH provided a mix of different wrestling types. It didn't try to force everyone to wrestle the same style of match, which led to entertaining results:

- **Brawlers:** Less scientific, more just rugged fighters (CM Punk, Homicide, and Jay and Mark Briscoe)
- **MMA-inspired strikers:** Wrestlers with mixed martial arts (MMA) background (Samoa Joe, Kyle O'Reilly, Bobby Fish, and Sumie Sakai)
- **Mat technicians:** Shoot or catch wrestling background (Bryan Danielson, Nigel McGuinness, and Katsuyori Shibata) — Chapter 11 explains catch wrestling in greater detail
- **Lucha libre-inspired high-fliers:** People relying heavily on aerial high risk offense (Tyler Black [Seth Rollins] and AJ Styles)
- **Powerhouses:** Wrestlers that show unique feats of strength in the ring (Claudio Castagnoli, PCO, and Brian Cage)

Going international

Rob Feinstein (see the preceding section) resigned and sold his stake in ROH after a TV news sting alleged he tried to solicit sexual relations with a minor. Because of this scandal, TNA ended their working relationship with ROH, which meant they lost the larger exposure that TNA granted them.

Without TV, ROH was a big money loser. In 2004, Cary Silkin, a New York–based ticket broker, took over operations of the company. Many fondly remember this change of hands as the start of ROH's golden age.

REMEMBER

Under Silken, the company initiated more international relationships, working with the Japanese promotions Dragon Gate and Pro Wrestling NOAH (see Chapter 10 for more information). Although ROH's success in its early years was heavily contingent upon its DVD sales, after it started participating in international shows, the promotion's visibility saw a marked increase. ROH signed:

- A PPV and on-demand deal with the marketing and consulting firm, Funk Sports & Entertainment, in the spring of 2007
- A television deal with TV outlet for sports and MMA, HDNet, in 2009

Although visibility increased, it was still quite limited, and ROH continued to lose money.

Giving Sinclair Broadcasting the reins

By 2011, the company was essentially on death's door. Losses were piling up, and HDNet canceled their television slot. A sale to Sinclair Broadcasting, the largest owner of station affiliations, saved ROH. All the local Sinclair affiliates around the United States started airing ROH events, with the idea that ROH would tour those markets, draw between 500 and 1,000 fans per event, and become profitable.

WARNING

But local TV didn't have the reach that it did even a decade prior; they couldn't draw those numbers, and the company continued to struggle financially.

It was, however, a growing artistic success. By the mid-2010s, fans had begun to greatly sour on WWE programming, and TNA had collapsed to its lowest level in a decade. ROH essentially became the second-biggest promotion in North America for a few years and signed several big names, including the Young Bucks, Cody Rhodes, and Adam Page.

During this same late-2010s period, New Japan (which you can read about in Chapter 10) also began to heat up when they signed a deal with AXS TV and started a New Japan World streaming service. ROH and New Japan worked together to raise each other's profiles. This period also marked a strong boom in North American independent promotions because fans wanted a WWE alternative.

Surviving the pandemic and its aftereffects

The end of the glory period for ROH was a combination of two things:

- **The birth of All Elite Wrestling (AEW) in 2019:** AEW signed a television deal with broadcaster TNT, which immediately made it the second-most-watched promotion in North America; the top ROH stars all jumped ship to the more successful AEW.

- **The COVID-19 pandemic that began in 2020:** When wrestling re-opened, ROH had the strictest COVID-19 safety requirements of any wrestling promotion in the world, which further hurt attendance and business.

REMEMBER

Finally, in October of 2021, with no turnaround in sight, the company went on hiatus. Shortly thereafter, Tony Khan (whom you can read about in the next section) purchased the company and its most important asset, the tape library that dated back to 2002 and featured matches with some of the biggest stars of the 21st century.

A multitude of wrestlers got their big break in ROH, many of whom are household names today, such as Bryan Danielson, Samoa Joe, CM Punk, and Seth Rollins.

Recognizable names became top stars and main-event acts in ROH from other promotions:

- **U.S.-based TNA:** Jay Lethal, AJ Styles
- **Japanese promotion Pro Wrestling NOAH:** Kenta Kobashi, Takeshi Morishima
- **Mexican lucha libre AAA:** Bandido, Rush

Today, ROH largely serves as a sort of developmental arm of AEW.

Going All In at a Pay-Per-View Event: All Elite Wrestling (AEW)

Prior to 2019, there was a vacuum in the North American nationally televised cable wrestling landscape. Once you could watch WWE, WCW, and ECW, now just one — WWE — existed. The creation of All Elite Wrestling (AEW) changed the industry. We can't really tell the story of AEW without talking about the PPV event known as *All In*.

Finding the origins of AEW

In 2017, a fan on Twitter asked *Wrestling Observer Newsletter* editor Dave Meltzer whether he thought wrestling promotion Ring of Honor (ROH; see the section

"Entering the Ring of Honor [ROH]" earlier in this chapter) could sell out a 10,000-seat arena. Meltzer responded in the negative. Former WWE star Cody Rhodes saw the tweet and said he'd take that bet.

A year and a half later, Rhodes and the ROH tag team the Young Bucks did it with ROH's *All In* event at the Sears Centre Arena in Hoffman Estates, Illinois.

They got to that point by heading a media blitz:

- Bringing in mainstream stars such as actor Stephen Amell, a friend of Rhodes who was starring in the TV series *Arrow*
- Building hype on their very popular YouTube series, *Being the Elite*
- Procuring funding and getting ROH's blessing

TIP

In the weeks leading up to the show, only one match had been announced. However, the rumored other talent being involved and the hype surrounding the event were enough to ensure that tickets sold out less than 30 minutes after going on sale, and it was the largest-attended North American wrestling show outside of WWE or WCW in 25 years.

Wrestlers from every promotion imaginable appeared on the show:

- **ROH:** Frankie Kazarian, Jay Lethal, and Hangman Page
- **National Wrestling Alliance (NWA):** Tim Storm
- **TNA:** Chelsea Green and Deonna Purrazzo
- **New Japan Pro-Wrestling (NJPW):** Kota Ibushi, Kazuchika Okada, and Kenny Omega
- **Major League Wrestling (MLW):** Maxwell Jacob Friedman
- **Lucha Underground:** Matt Cross, Penta El Zero, and Rey Fenix
- **Original WCW:** Former world champion Diamond Dallas Page, wrestler and martial artist Glacier

REMEMBER

A businessman (and long-time pro wrestling fanatic since childhood) named Tony Khan, seeing the success of *All In*, hired the Bucks, Rhodes, and Omega and created a brand new promotion, All Elite Wrestling (AEW) in 2019. Khan also set himself up as the president and head booker. Khan's experience in sports (because his father Shahid owned both an NFL team and a Premier League soccer team and Tony served as an executive for both), as well as his family's vast resources, made him the perfect business partner for the former ROH stars who wanted to change the world of professional wrestling.

Going double or nothing

In the early days of AEW, former WWE World Champion Chris Jericho joined the company. The first official AEW PPV event, held on May 25, 2019, was titled *Double or Nothing*. The main event was a follow-up to a hugely popular match (which you can read about in the sidebar "The match before the match" in this chapter). The show featured a cornucopia of international stars, topped off by:

- » A main event that featured former New Japan star Kenny Omega versus Chris Jericho
- » Jon Moxley (who formerly wrestled as Dean Ambrose for WWE) showing up after the main event to attack both competitors

REMEMBER

THE MATCH BEFORE THE MATCH

Crowning a new world champion is a big deal in and of itself. The importance of this is magnified a hundred fold when it's the crowning of the very first champion in the company's existence. It's poetic that Chris Jericho, formerly a WWE figure (but then a free agent), and Kenny Omega, of New Japan Pro-Wrestling (NJPW), headlined the first-ever AEW PPV event (see the section "Going double or nothing" in this chapter). They had already had a very famous NJPW match that took place on January 4, 2018, at the Tokyo Dome in Tokyo.

Jericho's long-time friend Don Callis, who was doing color commentary for New Japan, thought a Jericho-versus-Omega Tokyo Dome match would do big business. But Callis figured that Jericho would turn down the offer, having always said that he would never work for any promotion other than WWE. But Jericho didn't immediately turn it down. After Jericho cleared the match with WWE head Vince McMahon (which he did out of his great respect for McMahon even though he wasn't working for McMahon at the time), he signed for the match.

The bout ended up being so much bigger than anyone imagined. Ticket sales for the Dome exploded. The NJPW streaming service signed up more than 35,000 new fans for the show. Thousands of fans flew in from North America for the event, the largest fly-in crowd for a Dome show ever. Tony Khan saw the success of this show as indicating a market for an alternative to WWE. In this business, timing is everything — and the timing was perfect.

Returning weekly wrestling to networks

AEW made a big splash when its flagship weekly two-hour event, *Dynamite,* debuted on the cable TV channel Turner Network Television (TNT), on October 2, 2019. Not only did this premiere kick off a new era for wrestling on Wednesday nights, but it also returned pro wrestling to Turner Networks after nearly a two decade absence. (We talk about the role of Ted Turner in professional wrestling in Chapter 6.)

More than 1.4 million viewers tuned in, marking the largest non-WWE wrestling viewing audience in North America in at least a decade. AEW had a variety of other broadcast events, including the following:

- ***Dark and Dark Elevation:*** In 2019 and 2021 respectively, the company debuted these two recurring events exclusively on YouTube.
- ***Rampage:*** On August 13, 2021, AEW launched *Rampage,* an hour-long second weekly televised event on Friday nights. *Rampage* survived until December 2024.
- ***Collision:*** This second two-hour show debuted on TNT on June 17, 2023, on Saturday night.

AEW shows feature a style that is reminiscent of the hard-hitting style of NJPW, a heavier focus on in-ring performances akin to ROH, and often the frenetic pace of ECW.

REMEMBER

Many fans who had abandoned pro wrestling in the latter part of the 2010s, not pleased with the presentation of WWE television, became AEW fans. Detractors of AEW quickly took to the internet to let the world know their displeasure. Whether they loved the promotion or hated it, people were talking about AEW.

Many AEW matches featured the same standard rules as most other North American promotions. However, the company featured many matches exclusive to AEW:

- **Blood & Guts:** A variation of the old-school classic WCW War Games, where two teams of four or more people did battle inside of two rings surrounded by a cage.
- **Continental Classic:** A nod to New Japan's G1 Climax Tournament.
- **Stadium Stampede:** Two teams of five or more brawl all throughout a sports stadium; the fight can go anywhere, and wrestlers can use anything as a weapon.

AEW paid tribute to the history of wrestling on Turner Networks by naming two of their secondary belts the TBS and TNT Titles.

Changing of the guard

WARNING

Many of the original players eventually departed from AEW. The biggest and most industry-changing exit involved co-founder Cody Rhodes and his wife Brandi. Cody's jump from AEW to WWE in 2022, the first major switch since AEW was founded, ignited WWE business and led to their biggest boom period financially in company history. (We talk about this exodus in the section "Paving the way for Cody Rhodes" later in this chapter.)

New talent also came in:

- **Adam Cole:** Former NXT (WWE's developmental league) World Champion
- **Bryan Danielson:** ROH and WWE World Champion
- **CM Punk:** A former top star and multiple time World Champion who had been gone from the entire wrestling business for seven years

The August 21, 2021, episode of AEW *Rampage* opened with the worst-kept secret in the industry at the time, Punk's AEW debut. AEW didn't advertise his appearance, but it so heavily and obviously teased it that the show completely sold out 15,000-plus seats at the United Center in Chicago and drew a whopping 1.13 million TV viewers for *Rampage,* that show's highest number ever.

Hitting a bump in the road

AEW wrestlers CM Punk and the Young Bucks had legitimate issues with each other backstage that turned into a PR nightmare. The media scrum after the *All Out* PPV show had Punk venting on camera, next to AEW President Tony Khan, about backstage frustrations with wrestlers Matt and Nick Jackson (known as the Young Bucks), and "Hangman" Adam Page. After the press conference, the Young Bucks went to Punk's locker room to talk to him, and a legitimate fight broke out. Khan immediately suspended everyone involved — multiple people and a dog were all in the room at the time of the fight (but the dog wasn't suspended).

The Bucks returned two months later; it would be almost a year before Punk returned because he suffered a torn triceps muscle in his main event match that night.

For a variety of reasons, AEW business went into a decline:

- **Unscripted fights:** The backstage drama and Khan's response to it (he refused to speak of it at all publicly, and no one made mention of it on television — multiple big stars just outright vanished and were never mentioned again until they returned).

WARNING

Things got worse for AEW when Punk returned and only a few months later got into another backstage fight with wrestler and son of actor Luke Perry, Jack Perry, at the *All In* PPV event at Wembley Stadium. Khan fired Punk the following week.

- **Poached viewers:** WWE programming was beginning to heat up around the return of Cody Rhodes and the replacement of McMahon by his son-in-law Paul Levesque (who had wrestled as Triple H). Some fans who had switched from WWE to AEW in 2019 became very disillusioned with AEW programming around the time of *Brawl Out* and switched back to the significantly improved WWE programming.

At the time of writing, AEW has working relationships with several promotions around the world:

- **Japan:** New Japan, Stardom, and Tokyo Joshi Pro
- **Mexico:** *Consejo Mundial de Lucha Libre* (CMLL; World Wrestling Council)
- **United Kingdom:** Revolution Pro Wrestling (RevPro)

AEW regularly promotes ROH events as well (see the section "Entering the Ring of Honor [ROH]" earlier in this chapter), a company Tony Khan acquired in 2022.

TIP

PRO WRESTLING IS WORLDWIDE

Professional wrestling champions or championships from other promotions appear up and down AEW programming. AEW has done one thing from its beginnings that WWE didn't until very recently: acknowledge other promotions outside of their own company. Pro wrestling is a sport in which athletes from around the world can compete to see who's the best (or who puts on the best show).

Acknowledging those other promotions acknowledges the wider world and all the other great wrestlers and promotions out there. Recognizing and working with other promotions provides a good definition of "a rising tide lifts all ships." From ticket sales to social media traffic, and even huge increases in wrestler salaries, AEW has proved that — much like WCW did before it — you get a much better wrestling landscape, for both the performers and the fans, when you have healthy competition.

Struggling at the Top: World Wrestling Entertainment (WWE)

World Wrestling Entertainment (WWE) monopolized mainstream professional wrestling from the beginning of the 21st century after it destroyed all of its viable competition in 2001. (You can read the whole story in Chapter 6.) Not only were WWE's main competitors (who pushed WWE to produce a better product) put out of business, but two of the biggest stars the industry had ever seen ("Stone Cold" Steve Austin and "The Rock") were winding down or pivoting to other career endeavors. So a rocky road lay ahead for WWE.

Producing the same thing over and over

Even though the WWE was the top dog, over the first two decades of the 21st century, the presentation got stale.

REMEMBER

If you watched WWE programming in 2018, the only difference that you really saw from 2002 was the particular wrestlers in each program and who was the top star in the company at that moment. But so much of it remained exactly the same:

- **Shows:** They ran the same two major TV shows, *RAW,* and *SmackDown.*
- **Boss:** The same guy was in charge the entire time — Vince McMahon, Jr. — and he kept the stories all the same, just with different players.
- **Staging:** The matches in 2018 looked largely the same as the matches in 2002. The producers lit and filmed shows in the exact same way, and the scripted interviews used the same verbiage. It all just felt exactly the same.

Because the early 2000s didn't have a real viable number two promotion in the United States, instead of wrestlers jumping ship from one to the other, wrestlers such as Randy Orton, John Cena, or Charlotte Flair started their career in WWE and just remained there forever. Shortly after WCW died in 2001, the WWE *RAW* weekly TV show had around 5 million viewers per week. By 2019, the average *RAW* audience had fallen to around 2.4 million. (Of course, some of this drop-off related to the overall decline in TV viewership.)

Relying on big personalities

Two of the big stars of the modern era of WWE, John Cena and Roman Reigns, had the most longevity at the top of WWE billing — and aside from completely different starts, both had somewhat similar trajectories.

Both were targeted as top stars almost immediately:

- **A wrestling fan's dream:** Rick Bassman, who had discovered both late '80s phenomenon, Ultimate Warrior, and perennial WCW top babyface, Sting, years earlier, saw Cena in a gym and recruited him to start training as a pro wrestler. Cena's entire family were huge wrestling fans, so he didn't take much convincing. Within two weeks, WWE had heard about this good-looking kid who had a fantastic physique and good promo ability (meaning an ability to effectively talk in front of the crowd and gain sympathy or ire depending on if they're a babyface or heel), and they signed him.

  WARNING

  Although he did great promos, his wrestling needed a little work. It took him a long time to get comfortable with the physical aspect of the business.
- **Keeping it in the family:** Reigns, the son of former pro wrestling star and tag team legend, Sika, was a college football player, and he also played pro football in the offseason before he retired from that sport in late 2008. A little more than a year later, WWE signed him and sent him to their developmental territory, Florida Championship Wrestling (FCW). He had the size and look that the company treasured (at 6 feet 3 inches tall and 270 pounds, and with attractive features). Very early on, management pegged him as a future main event player.

Although WWE recognized both Cena and Reigns for their potential early on, their road to the top was quite different, which you can read about in the following sections.

Perfecting a babyface

Paul Heyman, the head *booker* (matchmaker and head of creative) for the second WWE weekly show *SmackDown* when Cena debuted in 2002, was a huge proponent of Cena. Heyman, however, eventually fell out of favor with WWE and McMahon; as a consequence, Cena began to languish. But famously, Cena was on the tour bus one day and started freestyle rapping. Stephanie McMahon (McMahon's daughter) heard him and thought Cena could make it a great gimmick: The Doctor of Thuganomics, white rapper John Cena, was born.

Cena ended up the biggest draw in all wrestling promotions from 2007 through 2014 — except for 2008, when lucha libre sensation Mistico lit the Mexican promotion *Consejo Mundial de Lucha Libre* (CMLL; World Wrestling Council) and the entire wrestling world on fire.

But Cena got incredibly mixed reactions from fans on televised events:

- **Casual fans:** Cena drew money, selling both tickets and an incredible amount of merchandise to the large casual pro wrestling audience that consisted of families and children.
- **Old-school fans:** The hardcore audience that lived through the Monday Night Wars (refer to Chapter 6) saw this guy who really wasn't a great *worker* (in-ring talent) getting pushed ahead of legitimate all-time great in-ring workers: people such as Eddy Guerrero, Chris Benoit, and Kurt Angle. (For years, WWE put Cena on *SmackDown* because they often recorded — and therefore could edit — his matches.)

  Worse, Cena ended up top babyface, and they hated the vanilla, PG-style presentation, which for a time included a goofy blinged-out spinner logo gimmick WWE Title belt.

Cena received very different reactions, depending on the type of event:

- **Televised:** During televised events, the crowd booed Cena mightily, making him seem the most hated person on the entire show.
- **Touring:** On the road, at the multiple *house shows* (untelevised live events) that the company ran every week, Cena was universally cheered. More importantly, he sold tons of tickets and merchandise.

REMEMBER

Cena (see Figure 8-1) broke Ric Flair's record (according to WWE) by winning the World Title 17 times. (In reality, Flair won the title more than 20 times, but WWE officially recorded 16 because WWE excludes some title changes that were untelevised or unsanctioned by the NWA). When Cena retired, WWE branded him The Greatest of All Time.

Finally finding a fan base

In 2012, Roman Reigns debuted on WWE television as a member of the faction called the Shield, alongside former ROH star Seth Rollins (formerly known as Tyler Black) and former Combat Zone wrestler Dean Ambrose (who goes by Jon Moxley after he switched to wrestling for AEW in 2019). When the team broke up two years later and Reigns got a *singles push* (massively high profile solo run) by WWE, the audience quickly realized that the company wanted Reigns to be the next John Cena — and he wasn't the fans' first pick.

FIGURE 8-1: John Cena.

Photo by Wrealano@aol.com

At the time, many wrestlers had more all-around talent than Reigns, including his two former Shield teammates, Rollins and Ambrose, as well as other fan favorites such as former darling of the independent scene, Daniel Bryan (real name, Bryan Danielson). The hardcore fans, remembering the Cena era, booed Reigns vociferously for years.

Reigns became everything that the company wanted him to be in the post-COVID-19 period. He took on the moniker of the Tribal Chief. A lot of things came together at the same time:

- Reigns disappeared for an extended period when he went through his second battle with leukemia in 2018. The cancer fight humanized him in the eyes of many fans.
- He also vanished during a period when McMahon's booking abilities had cratered, and his ability to put together coherent storylines imploded weekly. Every Monday, McMahon took the *RAW* script that the writers crafted all week, ripped it up, and basically rewrote it — often while the live show was going on. Every week, *RAW* ended with a lineup of matches for the following week, but often none of them actually happened by the time the following Monday rolled around.

  Talent grew increasingly frustrated, and the lack of logic and nonsensical storytelling sent the company into a tailspin, with year-over-year double-digit business declines from about 2017 through 2019.

REMEMBER

Incidentally, like in 1995 with WCW, one of the main reasons that AEW debuted so strong right out of the gate in 2019 was because they began operations at literally the perfect time — when WWE business was at its weakest point in two decades.

Living through COVID and controversy

The post-pandemic 2020s saw a hurricane of change sweep through WWE. The biggest and most far-reaching involved the:

- Sale of WWE to TKO Group Holdings, a company that also had Ultimate Fighting Championship (UFC) under its umbrella
- Sexual misconduct allegations levied against McMahon that ultimately led to him departing the company

Both stories could fill a book of their own, but we talk about these events in Chapter 12.

TIP

When McMahon first retired, the role of head booker (officially called the Chief Content Officer) went to McMahon's son-in-law, Paul Levesque (who previously wrestled under the ring name Triple H). Levesque had successfully booked the NXT brand (development of newer talent) for years, and whatever anyone wanted to say about his style of booking, it was light years better than what McMahon had done over the past several years. Storylines became consistent, advertised matches took place, and wrestlers who managed to get themselves *over* (popular with the crowd) got *pushed* (featured more prominently and won more matches).

Following the Bloodline

The Bloodline storyline, which WWE head booker Paul Levesque (see the preceding section) built around Roman Reigns (discussed in the section "Finally finding a fan base," earlier in this chapter) and various members of his family (the Usos, Solo Sikoa, and so on) in August 2020, slowly started to turn the company around.

WWE put Sami Zayn, decidedly not a member of Reigns's family, into the group in April 2022, with the plan to have him there for a few weeks, maybe a month or two, and then have him break away. But Zayn was so outstanding in his role that the Bloodline segments became the most popular thing on television, and WWE extended his role for months and months.

In 2023, Zayn, at his all-time peak of popularity, turned babyface and challenged Reigns for the WWE Title at the 2023 Elimination Chamber in Montreal. The show drew more than 17,000 fans. Although Zayn winning the title that night would have been a perfect story in many fans' eyes, WWE had other long-term plans involving Reigns, so he defeated Zayn.

Paving the way for Cody Rhodes

Cody Rhodes (see Figure 8-2), one of the co-founders of the promotion (AEW; see the section "Going All In at a Pay-Per-View Event: All Elite Wrestling [AEW]" earlier in this chapter), jumped back to WWE in 2022. In his first run with WWE from 2006 to 2016, he'd been largely a *midcard act* (not low tier, but not main event). But as the first huge defection from AEW to WWE, fans suddenly saw him as not only a top star, but *their* top star, a person who had chosen WWE over AEW at a time when many wrestlers had been jumping ship the other way.

FIGURE 8-2: Cody Rhodes.

Photo by `Wrealano@aol.com`

He walked into WWE in 2022 an immediate megastar, and unlike both John Cena (see the section "Perfecting a babyface" earlier in this chapter) and Roman Reigns (discussed in the section "Finally finding a fan base" earlier in this chapter), he was a pure babyface that got a 100-percent positive reaction from fans. His journey toward the WWE Championship and his feud with Reigns and the Bloodline (see the preceding section) further exploded business.

REMEMBER

Within three years, WWE was financially the hottest it had ever been in history, breaking attendance, gate, and merchandise records left and right. In 2025, WWE grossed $1.71 billion in a calendar year, by far the most it ever had in its entire history, beating even the $1.5 billion generated by sister company Ultimate Fighting Championship (UFC) in that year.

LEAVING THE RING FOR HOLLYWOOD

Throughout history, many wrestlers have landed roles in Hollywood films. Sometimes they were smaller, one-time roles, like Harold Sakata playing the role of Odd Job in the James Bond film *Goldfinger* in 1964 or Hulk Hogan playing Thunderlips in *Rocky III* in 1982. Other times, the wrestler was the star that the film was built around, such as Roddy Piper playing the role of Nada in the 1988 cult classic *They Live*, which actually debuted number one at the box office.

But some wrestlers transcended pro wrestling and became as big or bigger stars on the silver screen. El Santo is one of the most famous Mexican wrestlers in history, a legitimate cultural icon in Mexico, based on both his professional wrestling persona and also his prolific acting career. From 1958 until shortly before his death in 1984, he starred in more than 50 films, usually campy sci-fi outings where he battled zombies, vampires, and assorted bad guys. During his peak, he was among the biggest mainstream celebrities in Mexico, and a few of his films were dubbed into English for the U.S. market.

The three biggest pro wrestling stars of modern cinema are "The Rock" Dwayne Johnson, John Cena, and Dave Bautista. All three have turned in excellent performances, Johnson in a variety of different roles, Cena best known for his comedy, and Bautista lauded by critics as perhaps the best actor of the three. All are former WWE Champions, and at one point "The Rock" and Cena were the biggest stars in professional wrestling. In fact, Johnson holds a unique distinction —he's the only human being in history who was at one time in his life both the single biggest star in the entire professional wrestling business (the late 1990s) and the number-one A-list star in all of Hollywood (the late 2010s).

4

Wrestling Around the World

IN THIS PART . . .

Explore life behind the mask of Mexico's lucha libre.

Examine *puroresu* — professional wrestling in Japan.

Taste professional wrestling in other parts of the world.

IN THIS CHAPTER

» Marveling at the history of wrestling in Mexico

» Appreciating lucha libre's unique style

» Meeting the major promotions in Mexico

» Glimpsing the top stars of lucha libre

Chapter 9

Going South of the Border — Lucha Libre

You can often tell what part of the world you're in based on the culture surrounding professional wrestling. The peoples of different regions have different languages and dialects, and they use different styles to communicate in the ring to their fans. Some places, such as Europe, featured professional wrestling before the United States did. Others, such as Japan, started professional wrestling long after the craze took hold in the United States. This chapter focuses on Mexico, which began featuring pro wrestling right around the same time as the United States.

Examining the Roots of Mexican Freestyle Wrestling

The origins of Mexican *lucha libre* (literally translated as "free fighting"), a particular type of freestyle wrestling, trace back to the time of the U.S. Civil War in 1863. Historians believe that Enrique Ugartechea came up with the idea for lucha libre. Inspired by the 19th century Italian strongman known as Romulus, who was renowned for incredible feats of strength, Ugartechea became known as Mexico's Strongest Man. Ugartechea started with a foundation of Greco-Roman wrestling to create his own type of wrestling, and lucha libre so impressed Spalding (the sporting goods company) that it offered to sponsor him.

Like pro wrestling in the United States, a wrestler could end a lucha libre match in one of three ways:

- **Pinfall:** A *luchador* their opponent's shoulders to the mat until the count of three.
- **Submission:** A *luchador* utilizes a wrenching hold until their opponent submits.
- **Disqualification:** If a *luchador* is outside the ring for too long, their opponent is awarded the win.

Match stipulations, such as competing under best-of-three-falls rules, like Pioneer Era catch-as-catch-can style (which you can read about in Chapter 11) were commonplace. However, *countouts* (see Chapter 2) outside of the ring occurred after a 20-count in Mexico, as opposed to the 10-count used in most of the United States.

TIP

In the 21st century, the only remaining major league promotion in the world that still regularly features best-of-three-falls matches is CMLL in Mexico. Flip to the section "*Consejo Mundial de Lucha Libre* (CMLL)" later in this chapter for more about this promotion.

Discovering the evolution of masked wrestlers

Although wrestling fans associate wrestling masks with *luchadores*, the first really famous masked pro wrestler was, in fact, French.

The birth of masked wrestlers in Mexico really took place in the early 1930s with *Ciclon* (Cyclone) Mackey (born Corbin James Massey), who was, ironically, an American. Competing as both *"La Maravilla Enmascarada"* (Masked Marvel) and "*Ciclon* Mackey," Massey began to influence lucha libre shortly after the birth of EMLL, Mexico's first lucha libre promotion. (We talk about this promotion in the section "*Empresa Mexicana de Lucha Libre* [EMLL]" later in this chapter.)

He inspired other athletes, such as Murciélago Velázquez, to kick off the first generation of masked wrestlers. Velázquez later went on to become an actor, appearing in several mainstream films throughout the 1950s and 1960s. We really can't overstate the crossover/mainstream appeal of these athletes in Mexico. Several luminaries in the world of lucha libre remain national icons in Mexico outside of wrestling to this day; we discuss these *luchadores* in the section "Identifying *los Mejores Luchadores* (the Best Wrestlers)" in this chapter.

Over time, particularly in the aftermath of the explosion in popularity of the original El Santo character in the early 1940s, masked wrestlers became synonymous with lucha libre. It helped that Mexico had a rich history of Aztec and Mayan folklore, which wrestlers used to design intricate and unique personal masks.

Many, but certainly not all *luchadores* begin their careers nowadays under a mask. The mask is considered sacred, and to remove an opponent's mask during a bout is grounds for disqualification. Most lose the mask at some point during their careers, perhaps because they enjoy the fame of being an unmasked *luchador*, or perhaps because they end up hard-up for cash and can make a quick buck losing their hood in "mascara contra mascara" matches. Some famous masked wrestlers lose their mask at the very end of their careers to take home a final gigantic payday for retirement.

Some of the most famous *luchadores* in history, including El Santo, Mil Mascaras, Blue Demon, and Mistico, never lost their masks.

THE MASK'S BEGINNINGS

The earliest records anyone can find detailing a person wrestling under a mask date back to 1847. We don't, however, know the name of the person under the mask, and historian Phil Lyons believes he was a local student who legitimately didn't want anyone to know who he was, so he wore a "hood."

There are a few records of other hooded wrestlers in the following years, but the man who made the concept famous was Thiebaud Bauer.

Bauer debuted his character at the 1865 World's Fair in Paris. Unlike the previous masked wrestlers, who likely wore masks out of a legitimate desire to stay anonymous for whatever reason, Bauer played up the anonymity aspect of the gimmick and his popularity exploded. Newspaper stories claimed this masked figure would arrive in a blacked-out horse-drawn carriage, driven by a deaf-mute (can't have the driver know his real identity), change in secret in the locker room, and then sneak out after the show. The anonymity was part of the draw — who was this guy? He was clearly rich and famous and thus had to hide behind his black velvet hood. Was it, perhaps, (this was real speculation) Otto Von Bismarck? Nobody knew, they only knew his wrestling name, L'Homme Masque — The Masked Man. The gimmick was a sensation and generated huge business at the Athletic Arena in Paris. It was decades before the Terrible Turks debuted and broke the old records.

FAN IS SHORT FOR FANATIC

Lucha audiences are just as raucous — often more so, in fact — than crowds north of the border. Mexican fans take lucha libre quite seriously to this day. In 2025, CMLL sold out Arena Mexico, a 16,000-seat building, three times in one week over the Christmas-week holiday. It's very rare for even major promotions like AEW or WWE to sell out the same building three times in a week in the modern era.

Rudos and *técnicos*

Luchadores generally fall into two camps, the good guys and the bad guys — similar to pro wrestling in the United States and around the world. But instead of referring to the bad guys as *heels* and the good guys as *babyfaces,* as U.S. pro wrestling does (see Chapter 2), lucha libre has the following two:

- ***Rudos:*** The bad guys, lucha libre's version of heels. *Rudos* are, as the word suggests, the roughnecks. They're rude (what *rudo* means in Spanish), underhanded, and often ugly bad guys who use underhanded tactics, (distracting the referee), and even carry hidden weapons to get an advantage.
- ***Técnicos:*** Fair fighters (lucha libre's version of babyfaces). These honor-bound heroes rely on technique and use either superb mat wrestling or dazzling aerial offense to try to overcome their ruthless opponents.

TIP

In lucha libre, *técnicos* fight fair; *rudos* don't.

Understanding the significance of masks

The once-simple designs of *luchador* masks have become very complex, detailed and emblazoned with iconography uniquely tied to each performer's character. Many stars of lucha libre utilize personas and masks drenched in Aztec and Mayan supernatural elements. The masked stars come across as larger than life while they enact battles in the ring that could rival any U.S. superhero comic book or manga from Japan.

According to the rules of lucha libre (although, especially in pro wrestling, rules are meant to be broken), a wrestler isn't allowed to remove their opponent's mask or face penalties:

- **The mask stays on.** The mask is a vital component of a *luchador*'s persona. For that reason, fans of lucha libre see attempting to remove an opponent's mask as the ultimate sign of disrespect. Many stipulation matches (called *luchas de apuestas* in Spanish) feature top stars putting their masks on the line — the loser must remove their mask.

» **If you take your mask off, you can't get it back.** After you lose your mask, you're never allowed to put another mask on again. Some wrestlers agree to lose their mask in a stipulation match at the end of their career for a huge payoff (from a wrestling promoter), and typically in a packed arena a *luchador* can lose their mask for anywhere from hundreds to tens of thousands of dollars, depending on the level of fame of that *luchador*. Other *luchadores* retire without removing their masks. And sometimes, they even have themselves buried in their masks. (See the section "El Santo" later in this chapter for one famous example.)

Exploring How Lucha Libre Differs from Other Wrestling Styles

Despite various styles of wrestling all over the world, with the U.K. having a more technical bend to it and Japan having a perceived harder hitting style, lucha libre is unique in a few different ways, which we discuss here.

Using different rules

Besides the use of certain paraphernalia (masks), here are a couple more differences in lucha libre:

» **Working the right side:** Lucha libre is the only pro wrestling style where wrestlers often work the right side. *Working a side* means doing all the maneuvers (such as leg attacks or holds) by using a particular side (right or left) of their or their opponent's body. Everywhere except Mexico in the world of pro wrestling, wrestlers learn to work the left side. Therefore, if a *luchador* had a match with a wrestler from any other wrestling style, the two wrestlers had to decide before the match started which side to work so that they could avoid confusion. Nowadays, most *luchadores* work the left side as well.

» **No need to tag:** In many lucha libre matches, you don't need a tag if you want to replace someone in the ring during a tag team match. If the wrestler legally identified by the referee as participating in the match leaves the ring, another member of that team can just replace them.

Enforcing rules

Although lucha libre rule enforcement happens less today than it did in the early-to-mid 20th century, Mexico does have wrestling commissions that enforce certain rules as if the sport wasn't predetermined.

In comparison, some U.S. states have commissions similar to Mexico's wrestling commissions, but those U.S. commissions largely govern pro wrestling event elements such as whether the wrestlers need:

- To have a doctor or ambulance at the show (provided by the event planner)
- Can bleed during a match (fines could be levied against a promotion if unsanctioned bleeding occurs in a match)
- To undergo a physical for cardiovascular, neurological, and orthopedic evaluations
- Get a license to compete from the state commission

REMEMBER

In Mexico, the commissions oversee things such as the weight limits in championship matches. If you're booked to wrestle for a welterweight title in lucha libre, you have to legitimately weigh in at welterweight; otherwise, the commission for whichever region that promotion is in doesn't allow the match to happen (although nowadays this is rarely enforced). A weight rule for pro wrestling in the United States doesn't make sense for multiple reasons — not the least of which is that everyone lies about their weight.

Recognizing the Premier Lucha Libre Promotions

Although dozens and perhaps hundreds of small promotions present lucha libre events throughout Mexico, few specific promotions have competed for gigantic television ratings and live gates as aggressively as World Wrestling Federation (WWF) and World Championship Wrestling (WCW) did at the height of the Monday Night Wars in the United States. (You can read about these ratings battles in Chapter 6.)

The following sections discuss the two big Mexican promotions — *Consejo Mundial de Lucha Libre* (CMLL; World Free Wrestling Council) and *Asistencia, Asesoría y*

Administración de Espectáculos (AAA; which translates as Assistance, Consulting, and Management of Entertainment Events). We also identify the precursor to CMLL, *Empresa Mexicana de Lucha Libre* (EMLL; Wrestling Enterprise of Mexico). And we talk about other promotions such as Lucha Underground, The Crash, and others.

Empresa Mexicana de Lucha Libre (EMLL)

Salvador Lutteroth González and Francisco Ahumada founded the precursor to CMLL, EMLL, in 1933. Lutteroth, a former soldier who fought against the forces of Pancho Villa during the Mexican Revolution (1910–1917), became a property inspector in 1924. His business trips to West Texas exposed him to pro wrestling, which he found intriguing.

After convincing an acquaintance, wealthy businessman, and financier Francisco Ahumada to financially back his plan, they created EMLL and held their first show on September 21, 1933, at Arena Modelo in Mexico City. The notable luminaries at the show included *Ciclon* (Cyclone) Mackey (discussed in the section "Discovering the evolution of masked wrestlers" earlier in this chapter), as well as the Hawaiian star who beat him, Chino Achiu. Many fans often refer to this show as The Birth of Lucha Libre.

By the early 1950s, EMLL got on the radar of one of the most prestigious governing bodies in the history of professional wrestling, the National Wrestling Alliance (NWA). (You can find the history of the NWA in Chapter 5.) EMLL benefited from becoming the official NWA territory for Mexico, including getting a television deal. Unfortunately, they couldn't host weekly TV events at their home arena, Arena Modelo, because it was too small and run-down. But by the fortune of the wrestling gods, Lutteroth won the Mexican lottery — twice:

- **1934:** Lutteroth won 40,000 pesos (the equivalent to several thousand U.S. dollars) and invested those winnings into renovations for Arena Modelo.
- **1950s:** His second win came when he and the workers at an arena he owned, Arena Coliseo, pooled their money to buy a lottery ticket. Lutteroth used a portion of his 5 million peso earnings (about U.S. $286,000) to tear down Arena Modelo and build Arena Mexico, which is still in use today.

When Lutteroth retired, he left the day-to-day operations to his son, Chavo. EMLL stayed in the family — Chavo bequeathed it to his son, Chavo Lutteroth II, and then Lutteroth II passed it on to his son, Paco Alonso.

Consejo Mundial de Lucha Libre (CMLL)

Paco Alonso's reign as head of EMLL (see the preceding section) in the 1980s saw major changes to the promotion. They split from the NWA and changed their name from EMLL to CMLL. This period also saw shakeups to the top promotion in Mexico in the form of the conflict between its two head bookers:

- **Juan Herrera:** Had an old-school wrestling mindset and wanted to push the older, larger-than-life heavyweights.
- **Antonio Peña:** Sought to focus on the younger athletes performing in faster-paced matches.

CMLL decided to follow Herrera's philosophy, creating a show that would appeal to traditionalists, but not one that appealed to the younger generation.

Asistencia, Asesoría y Administración de Espectáculos (AAA)

Peña, after having his recommendations ignored at CMLL (see the preceding section), ultimately took some of the younger and hungrier members of the roster who didn't get the push that they felt they deserved from CMLL and started his own rival promotion in 1992. He called this promotion *Asistencia, Asesoría y Administración de Espectáculos* (AAA; Assistance, Consulting, and Management of Entertainment Events).

AAA featured younger high-fliers in more intense physical matches than CMLL, and it had more outlandish storytelling than what was featured on Mexican television at the time. Televisa, at the time by far the biggest television network in all of Mexico, backed AAA.

Peña wanted to make his mark in sports entertainment and made several moves in the early years of AAA to ensure its reach extended far outside the country of Mexico:

- **Working with the WCW:** In 1994, AAA developed a working relationship with WCW. They co-promoted a joint pay-per-view event known as *When Worlds Collide.*
- **Going in with WWF:** Just three years later, AAA began working with WWF. The Mexican promotion had a noticeable presence in the 1997 *Royal Rumble* WWF event.

The 1990s also saw Peña buy out parent company Televisa's ownership, making him the sole owner of AAA.

After Peña's death in 2006, the structure of AAA management shifted with his sister Marisela taking over as head manager. Former AAA, WCW, and Total Non-stop Action (TNA) wrestling star Charles Ashenoff (who went by the ring name Konnan) was named head of creative while Dorian and Joaquin Roldan, Peña's nephew and brother-in-law were in charge of business operations.

In the 2000s,the promotion forged another partnership, this time with TNA, a promotion that went back and forth between working with AAA and CMLL.

Lucha Libre AAA Worldwide

In 2015, AAA (see the section "*Asistencia, Asesoría y Administración de Espectáculos* [AAA]" earlier in this chapter) officially rebranded to Lucha Libre AAA Worldwide because they wanted even the most casual fans to know what the company was about.

Although the 2020s saw short lived working relationships with All Elite Wrestling (AEW, discussed in Chapter 8) and later the National Wrestling Alliance (NWA; see Chapter 5), everything changed in 2025. In August of that year, AAA went into business with World Wrestling Entertainment (WWE), formerly known as WWF. WWE's parent company, TKO Group Holdings, bought a controlling stake in AAA.

Lucha Underground

In 2014, at the dawn of what many consider the modern golden age of independent wrestling, television got Lucha Underground, a joint production between:

- Television producer Mark Burnett and his production company One Three Media
- Filmmaker Robert Rodriguez's genre-leaning television venture, El Rey Network
- AAA

The weekly show utilized AAA *luchadores* and wrestlers from around the world and was recorded in front of a live crowd at The Temple, an "arena" (warehouse set) in the Boyle Heights section of Los Angeles, California.

Lucha Underground gained a cult-like following during its four seasons on El Rey Network because of its:

- *Telenovela* (Mexican soap opera)-style storytelling
- A sprinkling of supernatural elements
- Violence on par with late 1990s Extreme Championship Wrestling (ECW; see Chapter 7)

One of its keys to success involved signing talent familiar to the wrestling audience in the United States, such as Johnny Mundo (known as Johnny Nitro in WWE), Jake Strong (Jack Swagger in WWE), and multiple-time WWE champion Rey Mysterio (Óscar Gutiérrez Rubio, whom we discuss in the section "Rey Mysterio" later in this chapter).

The problems for Lucha Underground came from two fronts:

- **The talent:** The wrestlers enjoyed quite a bit of freedom in the ring and with their characters, but the business side of their deals with Lucha Underground restricted their professional options.

  In February of 2019, Jorge Luis Alcantar, who wrestled as King Cuerno in Lucha Underground, filed a lawsuit that challenged Lucha Underground's contracts, which locked talent into five-year exclusive deals, blocking them from working in any other promotion, regardless of whether Lucha Underground was currently taping a season. Lucha Underground settled the case, allowing wrestlers to start working elsewhere. Alcantar ended up in WWE as Santos Escobar.
- **The budget:** On November 7, 2018, Lucha Underground executive producer Eric Van Wagenen appeared on the podcast *Masks, Mats & Mayhem* and made it publicly known that Lucha Underground faced budgetary concerns at the end of Season 4. Because of these concerns, Lucha Underground stopped recording shows in late 2018 (part of the motivation behind Alcantar's 2019 lawsuit).

Lucha Underground died in 2018, and a year later, the business partners of El Rey, Univision, sold its stake, ending its run as an over-the-air broadcast network. Today, Lucha Underground lives on in storyline as part of the American based-promotion, Major League Wrestling (MLW).

Exploring Smaller Lucha Libre Promotions

Not every wrestling promotion has the capital, connections, or social footprint to compete with the top promotions in a territory. This is the same in the United States, Japan, and even Mexico. That being said, some of the following smaller companies provided strong alternatives to what the premier wrestling promotions had to offer.

International Wrestling Revolution Group

Former wrestler Adolfo Moreno founded the International Wrestling Revolution Group (IWRG) in 1996, working with the TV Azteca network to provide an alternative to CMLL and AAA.

Beginning as a partner to Universal Wrestling Association, Moreno provided a place where many independent wrestlers in Mexico could find work on a per-appearance basis. Unlike AAA and CMLL, whose shows aired largely from Mexico City, IWRG aired from Naucalpan, a municipality just northwest of the city, in the Arena Naucalpan (formerly Arena KO Al Gusto).

After Moreno passed away in 2007, his sons, Alfredo and Marco, took over operations. They didn't as adamantly demand sticking to strictly independent performers; the company worked with CMLL in the early 2000s and with AAA in 2010.

REMEMBER

However, the majority of IWRG's working relationships involve promotions under the Toryumon Mexico umbrella, as well as with the Japanese promotion Pro Wrestling NOAH (see Chapter 10). Although their shows do feature wrestlers considered regulars, they don't have any actual full-time stars working for them, and the roster often changes from month to month. IWRG still operates like a true independent promotion.

The Crash Lucha Libre

A man named Nacho de la O founded The Crash in 2011, a promotion that operates primarily out of the Mexican cities of Tijuana and Monterrey, with the majority of their shows taking place at Auditorio de Tijuana. Whereas companies such as IWRG (see the preceding section) have partnerships with promotions across Mexico and Japan, The Crash has a much more global reach.

The Crash has boasted partnerships with other promotions based in:

- **Mexico** (discussed in the preceding sections) including AAA, CMLL, and IWRG.
- **China:** Oriental Wrestling Entertainment (OWE).
- **Japan** (see Chapter 10) including New Japan Pro Wrestling and Pro Wrestling NOAH.
- **United States** (covered in Chapter 8) including DEFY Wrestling, Major League Wrestling (MLW), Pacific Coast Wrestling (PCW) Ultra, Pro Wrestling Guerilla, Ring of Honor, and TNA.

Although The Crash Lucha Libre company doesn't have the financial footing or the mainstream acceptance of AAA and CMLL, The Crash is still going strong even today.

Identifying *los Mejores Luchadores* (the Best Wrestlers)

Stars of various shapes and sizes, masked and unmasked, have entertained millions of fans in Mexico and worldwide over the last 100 years of lucha libre's existence. Several of these *luchadores* (and female *luchadoras*) were crossover sensations, making a mark in the entertainment industry as well as wrestling; and a small handful became global icons. These sections name some of the best.

El Santo

One of the first lucha libre megastars, Rodolfo Guzmán Huerta, began wrestling as El Santo (see Figure 9-1): The Man in the Silver Mask in the 1940s. Although considered the greatest *técnico luchador* in history, he actually started his career as a *rudo*. Working primarily for EMLL, which you can read about in the section "*Empresa Mexicana de Lucha Libre* (EMLL)," earlier in this chapter, Santo won several prestigious titles, such as the Mexican National Middleweight Championship and the National Wrestling Alliance (NWA) World Welterweight Championship. His wrestling career was legendary, but his film career was iconic.

Between 1952 and 1982, Santo appeared in 53 films, many of them lucha-themed and featuring fantastical elements, such as vampires or zombies. He always wore his mask, whether battling in wrestling attire or conducting business in a three-piece suit. He also appeared in comic books, cartoons, and other media throughout his lifetime.

FIGURE 9-1: El Santo.

Photo by Wrealano@aol.com

Many lucha fans consider El Santo one of the most famous Mexicans of the 20th century. He remains a cultural icon:

- His funeral, in 1984, was attended by more than 10,000 people (among the largest turnout for a funeral in the history of Mexico). And he was buried in his mask.
- Local authorities and community groups in Mexico have erected statues in his honor.
- Many mainstream top-ten lists of most famous people in Mexico reference him.

He ranks among the most famous pro wrestling stars in world history, surpassing the likes of even Hulk Hogan, and on par only with genuine mainstream icons like Dwayne "The Rock" Johnson (also most famous for his movie roles).

Negro Casas

José Casas Ruiz, who wrestled under the name Negro Casas, began his wrestling career in 1979, at age 19. Casas, like many *luchadores* throughout history, was part of a large wrestling family and had numerous relatives all working in the business. Casas performed in CMLL for the majority of his career, opting to work for AAA in the 2020s. And if you do the math, yes, he still wrestles professionally in his 60s at the time of writing. Though he wasn't the only one, Casas is one of the few *luchadores* that chose to not wear a mask when performing.

Casas's versatility in the ring and his high work rate, even in his advanced years, has earned him more than a dozen championships and landed him on many Greatest *Luchadores* lists.

Rey Mysterio

Starting out as Rey Mysterio, Jr. (see Figure 9-2), Óscar Gutiérrez Rubio began wrestling in 1989 at the tender age of 14. After a few years of learning the ropes, he began wrestling for AAA, feuding with the likes of Juventud Guerrera and Psicosis. His agility in the ring was only matched by the sympathy that he garnered from the fans watching his matches because of how well he sells an injury.

FIGURE 9-2: A young Rey Mysterio, Jr.

Photo by `Wrealano@aol.com`

Rey was first brought to the United States wrestling world by ECW, but his career took off in WCW, where his rivalry with the charismatic Eddie Guerrero became the stuff of legend.

In 2002, he debuted for WWE as Rey Mysterio. The constant underdog — standing at only 5 feet 2 inches tall — Mysterio fought his way to several WWE championships. Because of his worldwide fame over decades in WWE, Mysterio is arguably the *luchador* most famous specifically for his role as a *luchador*.

Noting *Las Mejores Luchadoras* (the Best Female Wrestlers)

As in every culture around the world, women have played an important role in the history of professional wrestling in Mexico as well. Here are a few:

- **Irma González:** Debuting in 1955, Irma Morales Muñoz (who wrestled as Irma González) was a trailblazer in women's wrestling in Mexico and one of the first *luchadoras* (female wrestlers) in Mexico. González competed for more than four decades, wrestling primarily in EMLL and the Universal Wrestling Association (UWA). She operated while wearing a mask at times and without a mask at others.

  Her longtime rivalry with *La Dama Enmascarada* ("The Masked Woman") led to one of the first *mask-versus-mask matches,* where *La Dama* lost to González and had to unmask. After this match, González came out on top in several stipulation matches.

- **Lola González:** Very few women's wrestlers in the 1980s reached the level of stardom that Lola González did. The wrestling boom of that decade saw González featured on the covers of several Mexican magazines, such as *Box y Lucha, El Halcón,* and *Super Luchas,* among others.

  She racked up several championships in her matches around the world. Lola's long career and international success made her one of the most respected *luchadoras* of the 20th century.

- **Fabi Apache:** Fabiola Balbuena Torres, better known by her ring name Fabi (or Faby) Apache, is one of the greatest *luchadoras* in the history of AAA. She trained not only in Mexico, but also in the dojos of Japan. After nearly two years overseas, Apache returned to Mexico to have a successful career with AAA that has been going for more than two decades at the time we write this book.

  Embroiled in storylines with her father and trainer, Gran Apache, her sister Mari Apache, and her husband Billy Boy, the fact that they all were family made her storylines feel authentic to fans in attendance.

  She has gained even more fans by appearing on shows for the U.S. promotions TNA, AEW, and even WWE.

IN THIS CHAPTER

» Discovering Japanese *puroresu*

» Checking out the top men's and women's promotions in Japan

» Exploring the origins of Japanese mixed martial arts

Chapter 10

Surveying *Puroresu* — Japanese Professional Wrestling

Professional wrestling has been a staple in Japan since Matsuda Sorakichi transitioned from sumo in the late 1800s. Although some Japanese promotions embrace the same tropes as Western promotions, others take a markedly different approach to the action and presentation in the ring. Whichever method they choose to tell stories, some of these wrestling promotions have broken through to mainstream status in Japan and around the world.

This chapter focuses on arguably the biggest traditional professional wrestling promotions (*puroresu*) in Japan — New Japan Pro-Wrestling (NJPW), All Japan Pro-Wrestling (AJPW), Pro Wrestling NOAH, All Japan Women's (AJW), and Stardom. It also features a rundown of MMA promotions like Pride and the UWF.

Examining How *Puroresu* Compares to Western Pro Wrestling

Puroresu is Japan's answer to North America's style of professional wrestling. The sport started in the 1950s, spearheaded by sumo wrestler-turned-promoter, Rikidōzan (see Figure 10-1).

FIGURE 10-1: Rikidōzan.

Jim Melby photos from Dr Mike Lano's Collection

Japan's presentation of professional wrestling has some similarities to the North American presentation, including the following:

- The wrestling takes place in the same type of ring.
- The match can end with a pinfall, submission, countout, disqualification or referee stoppage (see Chapter 2) just like any other form of traditional pro wrestling.
- *Babyfaces* (wrestlers with a good guy persona) and *heels* (the bad guys) populate the roster.

Here are the significant differences that set Japanese wrestling apart:

- In many cases, the matches are put together to appear less like a performance and more like a combat sport.
- Because many promotions don't have North American–style episodic weekly television, the events don't focus on week-to-week storylines as much as in North American pro wrestling.
- Countouts occur upon a referee's 20-count, instead of a 10-count.

REMEMBER

Other minutiae can vary from promotion to promotion. However, one thing that unifies them is the term *strong style*, which describes a harder hitting, stiffer style of working in a match. The masters of strong style don't hit anyone any harder than anyone else; they just perfect their technique so that it looks more like real striking than the sometimes-hokey punching and kicking you might see in North America. But it is, like everything else, just an illusion. Check out the section "Delving Deeper into Strong Style" later in this chapter for more information.

Recognizing Japan's Most Prominent Pro Wrestling Promotions

New Japan Pro-Wrestling (NJPW) and All Japan Pro-Wrestling (AJPW) are the longest-surviving wrestling promotions in Japan, both being founded in 1972. But other major promotions, featuring both male and even exclusively female wrestlers, have sprung up over the years.

New Japan Pro-Wrestling (NJPW)

The most successful wrestling promotion in Japan, New Japan Pro-Wrestling's (NJPW) popularity has reached global proportions over the last 10 to 15 years. One of the biggest reasons for this is what made them stand out in their early years, their willingness to utilize international talent in high profile angles and matches.

Renowned wrestling performer Antonio Inoki (see Figure 10-2) founded NJPW after he was fired from the Japanese Wrestling Association (JWA; essentially, the first major professional wrestling promotion in Japan), where he had been one of their biggest stars. He allegedly planned to take over the promotion.

FIGURE 10-2: Antonio Inoki (left) with the legendary Lou Thesz.

Photo by Wrealano@aol.com

Relying on international stars

The newly formed promotion's very first live event was called *Opening Series*, which started on March 6, 1972, from Ota Ward Gymnasium in Tokyo, Japan. The show featured talent from all over the world, including:

- Argentina's legendary El Furioso, who became prolific in the 1950s-1970s.
- Germany's Karl Gotch, who was not only a great performer, but also helped to train an entire generation of greats.
- Japan's Tatsumi Fujinami who started wrestling at age 17 and is renowned for his lengthy run in NJPW, winning six world championships.
- American performers such as Jim Durango (who would go on to become the iconic "Bullet" Bob Armstrong; a staple of the National Wrestling Alliance whose career spanned five decades).

TIP

The first six months of NJPW events were so successful and did such big TV ratings that the Japanese broadcasting network NET (now TV Asahi) gave them a weekly Friday night prime-time show called *World Pro Wrestling.*

In fact, utilizing top foreign stars was the bread and butter for New Japan in its earliest years. Luminaries such as Bob Backlund, "Superstar" Billy Graham, and Stan "The Lariat" Hansen had stints in NJPW. Even today, many top stars from around the world in every major American promotion either made their names or had meaningful runs in New Japan.

Watching the big shows

Because NJPW's governing body is known as the International Wrestling Grand Prix (IWGP), NJPW's championships are all referred to as IWGP titles. The first IWGP Championship was awarded in the event called the IWGP League, which later became the G1 (for Grade One) Climax Tournament.

The winner of that first tournament in 1983 was Hulk Hogan prior to his most famous run in World Wrestling Federation (WWF), with subsequent winners being renowned figures such as Antonio Inoki and later the Eighth Wonder of the World, André the Giant. Hogan was awarded a championship belt for his win.

In 1987, the IWGP Championship became your typical regularly defended World Title belt. The IWGP world champion often competes in the G1 tournament. Whereas if a challenger wins, they get a title shot against the world champion at the biggest show of the year, *Wrestle Kingdom*; if the world champ wins, they get to decide who their opponent is.

REMEMBER

Their biggest show of the year, *Wrestle Kingdom*, typically occurs on January 4 from the Tokyo Dome, and Japanese sports fans see it as one of the most important sporting events of the year. Much like *WrestleMania* (which we talk about in Chapter 6), many of the major feuds throughout the year and celebrity appearances usually occur at *Wrestle Kingdom.*

The road to *Wrestle Kingdom* is typically paved throughout the year, primarily at the G1 Climax Tournament:

- A round-robin tournament held every summer
- Lasts several weeks
- Features a block system (often A and B blocks, but sometimes more)

The winners of each block are determined by using a points system:

- Two points for a victory (pin, submission, countout, or disqualification, which we talk about in the section "Examining How *Puroresu* Compares to Western Pro Wrestling" earlier in this chapter)
- One point for a draw
- Zero points for the loser or for both wrestlers if the match ends in a *no contest* (both competitors counted out or disqualified)

WARNING

Though some of the best matches of the year occur during this tournament, the grueling schedule opens up the possibility for injuries far more than the rest of the yearly schedule does.

At press time, the rise in popularity of NJPW has placed them in a dead heat with Mexico's promotion *Consejo Mundial de Lucha Libre* (CMLL; World Wrestling Council, see Chapter 9) as the third-largest wrestling promotion in the world, behind only the U.S. promotions World Wrestling Entertainment (WWE) and All Elite Wrestling (AEW). (Flip to Chapter 8 for more about these promotions.) NJPW is still seeking to expand its television programming to other countries, including the United States.

All Japan Pro-Wrestling (AJPW)

The year 1972 saw the founding of both NJPW, discussed in the section "New Japan Pro-Wrestling (NJPW)" earlier in this chapter, and another popular Japanese professional wrestling organization, All Japan Pro-Wrestling (AJPW). Legendary wrestler Shohei "Giant" Baba (see Figure 10-3) left the JWA of his own accord because he wanted to start his own promotion: AJPW.

FIGURE 10-3: Shohei "Giant" Baba.

Photo by Wrealano@aol.com

Getting TV on AJPW's side

Prior to the split, JWA had two television deals, one with the broadcasting network Nippon Educational Television (NET) and one with Nippon Television (NTV) for Friday and Monday nights. Inoki (who started NJPW) and Baba were the two big stars of the JWA, and Inoki's matches would usually air on NET and Baba's on NTV.

When Baba split to form All Japan, NTV sided with him for the television rights over NJPW, making AJPW a force right out of the gate. Mitsuo and Yoshihiro Momota, the sons of JWA founder Mitsuhiro Momota (who went by the ring name Rikidōzan), helped Baba's dream come to life.

REMEMBER

The promotion leaned into Rikidōzan's booking philosophy of bringing in larger Americans to work as heels in programs against the top Japanese babyfaces in the company, playing off still simmering World War II tension.

Their inaugural live event occurred at Machida City Gym in Tokyo on October 21, 1972. Although the *card* (list of matches for a show) presented Japanese stars such as former sumo wrestler and tag team specialist Motoshi Okuma, Akio Sato who also had a prolific run in the United States with the NWA, as well as amateur and freestyle wrestler Thunder Sugiyama, it also featured wildly popular foreign performers such as "Classy" Freddy Blassie, Terry Funk, and the legendary Bruno Sammartino (see Chapter 5).

Setting up a governing body

Baba set up the Pacific Wrestling Federation (PWF) as the governing body for AJPW. Its premier championship, the PWF World Heavyweight Title, was first held by Baba, who did battle for the title against "The Destroyer" Dick Beyer, Abdullah The Butcher, Bobo Brazil, Pat O'Connor, and several other luminaries.

The belt's importance has fluctuated over time, thanks in no small part to AJPW joining the National Wrestling Alliance (NWA), the major governing body that ruled many wrestling promotions around the world, in 1973.

Since 1973, AJPW has presented their annual tournament, the *Champion Carnival,* otherwise known as Haru no Saiten (Spring Festival). The tournament provided a valuable tool to promote AJPW's biggest stars and elevate new people to main event status. Stars of yesteryear, such as Toshiaki Kawada, Mitsuharu Misawa, and Keiji Muto, and modern talent, such as Kento Miyahara, Rei Saito, and Minoru Suzuki, have all had excellent outings in the tournament.

TECHNICAL STUFF

Both the *Champion Carnival* and the NJPW G1 Climax Tournament (discussed in the section "Watching the big shows" earlier in this chapter) have their roots in the old JWA World Big League Tournament, which began in 1959.

At All Japan's Champion Carnival Tour on April 18, 1989, Jumbo Tsuruta defeated Stan Hansen in an unprecedented title unification match where three belts, the NWA International Heavyweight Championship, the NWA United National Championship, and the PWF Heavyweight Championship were merged to form a new primary championship: the AJPW Triple Crown. The title holder possessed all three belts during their reign until August 2013, when AJPW introduced one unified title belt, incorporating elements from all three belts.

Identifying All Japan's style

All Japan's style is referred to as *King's Road* (the idea of a pure royal path to the top of professional wrestling), which includes the following:

- The promotion leans heavily into storytelling (or, more accurately, long-term rivalries), with fewer *promos* (long-form interview segments) and week-to-week *angles* (big moments that change the direction of a story). Chapter 2 provides more details.
- The matches themselves tell intricate stories, so over the course of a series of matches, a satisfying narrative unfolds.
- Angles often go on for many months (and, in some special cases, years).
- Their unique storytelling style make wins and losses seem important, and when a *lower to mid-card talent* (meaning lower ranked) gets an upset victory, the fans feel very invested.

Struggling with leadership

One of the more controversial periods in All Japan's history was the mass exodus of wrestling talent at the start of the millennium. Like with many Japanese wrestling promotions, the company leaned on four superstar wrestlers as their main event players. For AJPW, those performers were Mitsuharu Misawa, Toshiaki Kawada, Kenta Kobashi, and Akira Taue, otherwise known as the Four Pillars of Heaven.

When Baba passed away in January 1999, 18-year AJPW veteran and former world champion, Mitsuharu Misawa took over as company president. However, he and the widow of Baba, Motoko (majority owner of the company), butted heads, leading to disagreements about:

- Different booking philosophies causing the product to stagnate under Motoko's dated booking style
- Misawa getting stonewalled when trying to push younger talent

» Motoko diverting merchandise sales to a separate company she set up without Misawa's knowledge

Ultimately, the executive board forced Misawa to vacate the seat of president. Not long after that, Misawa held a press conference to announce that he and 24 All Japan wrestlers (out of a total of 26 on the roster) were leaving to start their own promotion, Pro Wrestling NOAH, which we discuss in the following section.

Pro Wrestling NOAH

Misawa founded *Puroresuringu Noa* (Pro Wrestling NOAH) in 2000 after his split from All Japan Pro Wrestling (see the previous section). The product gained fame as a solid alternative to the big two, NJPW, which we talk about in the section "New Japan Pro-Wrestling (NJPW)," and AJPW, discussed in the section "All Japan Pro-Wrestling (AJPW)" both earlier in this chapter.

The dynamic is similar to how the U.S.-based promotions Total Nonstop Action (TNA) and Ring of Honor (ROH) became alternatives to World Wrestling Entertainment (WWE); flip to Chapters 7 and 8 for talk about those promotions. Although Pro Wrestling NOAH had a period of extraordinary growth and popularity in the mid-2000s, the company faced difficult challenges.

Death of the founder

Misawa himself passed away at the age of 46 following a tag team match on June 13, 2009, at the Hiroshima Green Arena. He was paired with Go Shiozaki to take on the team of Akitoshi Saito and Bison Smith. Aside from his roles as booker and promoter, Misawa was renowned as one of the greatest professional wrestlers to ever live, but his style involved a lot of legitimately dangerous bumps on his head and neck. There was always concern about the style, but no matter what crazy high-angle bump he took, Misawa always got up — until, unfortunately, he didn't.

WARNING

Years past his prime, he took a *high-angle back suplex* (wrapping arms around opponent's waist from behind, lifting them and driving their neck and shoulders to the mat) from Smith, which turned out to be fatal because of the years of back and neck trauma Misawa had suffered.

Working with the wrong crowd

NOAH, which many considered the best pro wrestling promotion in the world in the mid-2000s, had fallen considerably by the time Misawa passed away in 2009 (see the preceding section).

POTENTIAL CRIMINAL TIES IN SPORTS & ENTERTAINMENT

Japanese pro wrestling and the Yakuza have had ties dating back to the inception of Japanese promotions in the 1950s. In reality, the Yakuza has ties to essentially every sports and entertainment business in Japan from the early 1950s through today. It's an open secret, but issues always arise if news of these connections becomes public.

Three years later, information leaked that NOAH upper management had connections to the *Yakuza* (the Japanese mafia). In fact, a Yakuza member stabbed renowned wrestler Rikidōzan in 1963, which led to the wrestler's death. NOAH General Manager Ryu Nakata and Haruka Eigen were specifically named, and both were demoted.

But the damage ran far deeper. Several wrestlers quit the company to avoid being associated with the scandal, and NTV canceled NOAH's weekly television show. Although NOAH survived the scandal, they never rose to anywhere near their greatest heights again.

REMEMBER

Over the next decade, the struggling company was purchased multiple times. Through the various sales, members within NOAH created and dissolved partnerships, some for the benefit of the company and others not. The biggest blow was the loss of their relationship with New Japan (discussed in the section "New Japan Pro-Wrestling [NJPW]" earlier in this chapter) in 2016, which badly hurt business.

However, following the sale of NOAH to CyberAgent in 2020 (which then merged NOAH and another Japanese wrestling promotion known as DDT into the company CyberFight), NOAH rekindled the relationship with NJPW.

Focusing on Women's Wrestling in Japan

Venues in Japan featured women's wrestling for American occupational troops as early as the late 1940s. Although the presentation wasn't earnestly trying to make the female wrestlers stars, that all changed with the rise in popularity of foreign women's stars, such as Mildred Burke (a dominant multiple-time champion), June Byers (a ten-year Women's World Champion), Ida Mae Martinez (who juggled wrestling with a professional yodeling career and obtaining a master's degree in nursing), and Marva Scott (one of the first Black female professional wrestlers in the United States), from the 1930s through the 1960s. It was only a matter of time before *joshi* (which means *woman* in Japanese) *puroresu* promotions sprouted up all over the country.

REMEMBER

Women's promotions in Japan lay a lot of attention and focus on physical attractiveness — so much so that calendars and model photobooks provide promotions with high-revenue merchandise.

The following sections identify two of the top promotions that focus on Japanese women's wrestling.

All Japan Women's Pro-Wrestling (AJW)

All Japan Women's Pro-Wrestling (AJW), formed in 1968 by four brothers — Takashi, Kenji, Kunimatsu, and Toshikuni Matsunaga — was the first major and financially viable women's promotion in Japan. Much like the men's promotions (which you can read about in the section "Recognizing Japan's Most Prominent Pro Wrestling Promotions" earlier in this chapter), AJW at first utilized talent from promotions outside of Japan and employed the foreign heel storylines in their bookings.

Getting women in on the action

In the mid-1970s, a young wrestler named Mach Fumiake won the top prize, the World Women's Wrestling Association (WWWA) Title — allegedly the same belt made famous by Burke — at the age of just 15. Women's wrestling promotions started to heavily push beautiful and athletic teenage women as top stars.

In February of 1976, the Matsunagas teamed up 16-year-old Maki Ueda with 18-year-old Jackie Sato to form The Beauty Pair, who:

- Exploded business for AJW
- Shot to superstardom as rock stars, their biggest album selling just under 1 million copies in the late 1970s
- Got the Fuji TV Network to give AJW weekly prime-time television spots, giving Japanese women's professional wrestling more visibility than any men's promotion in the entire country

REMEMBER

The Beauty Pair had a two-year run of popularity as enormous mainstream superstars, gracing magazine covers and performing in both concerts and wrestling matches on television. At one point, they worked more than 250 wrestling shows in a single year and sold out virtually every single one of them (legitimately, unlike the fuzzy numbers some American promotions used, which we talk about in Chapter 8).

By the late 1970s, the first boom had slowed down, but AJW remained a popular organization. It had its share of controversies, including:

- A mandatory retirement age of 25, with the argument that after that age, a wrestler was no longer relatable to the teenage audience
- Many women getting fired for breaking any of the three rules ("No smoking, no drinking, no men")

Continuing the girl power

The company saw two huge boom periods after the initial massive popularity of the Beauty Pair (see the preceding section):

- **Early to mid-1980s:** The Crush Gals (wrestlers Chigusa Nagayo and Lioness Asuka) had a run that eclipsed the Beauty Pair boom. During this peak, TV ratings regularly climbed to the 14.0 range, and the Crush Gals even made the front page of the U.S. newspaper *The Wall Street Journal*. (Chapter 13 identifies one of the Crush Gals battles.) The boom ended when their greatest rival, Dump Matsumoto (one of the top women in AJW), retired, proving that you can't have good without evil.
- **Mid-1990s:** A generation of young girls who had grown up watching AJW wanted to become idols like their own idols. A wave of incredible talent rose up. The best women of this era were better in the ring than the best male wrestlers anywhere on Earth.

Putting on a show

Arguably the pinnacle of AJW — and perhaps women's pro wrestling, in general — took place on November 20, 1994, when the company ran the *Big Egg Wrestling Universe* event at the Tokyo Dome, drawing 42,000 fans and generating $8 million in revenue (including ticket sales, merchandise, videotapes, TV and sponsorship fees, and so on). The show featured 23 matches (no joke) and lasted 10 full hours (also no joke).

It was an incredible spectacle, said to be the most elaborate wrestling show of all time, comparable to a National Football League (NFL) Super Bowl, with more than $1 million spent on production for ring entrances and related razzle-dazzle. But, as incredible as the show was, it was the last time the Tokyo Dome ever hosted a women's wrestling event; and, in fact, it was the last time women wrestled a match at the Dome for more than 25 years.

Making bad business decisions

WARNING

The death of All Japan Women was more related to the collapse of the real estate market in Japan. During the second boom period, the Matsunaga Brothers heavily invested their profits into real estate. The collapse of the market, combined with the loss of popularity in professional wrestling, led to the company declaring bankruptcy in 1997. But they continued to struggle for nearly another decade, until they had $30 million in debt because of tax, real estate, and pro wrestling debts, at which point, they closed shop permanently.

AJW during its peak periods was an incredible cultural phenomenon. Although many other women's promotions would come along, they probably wouldn't enjoy the success that they do if All Japan Women's Pro-Wrestling hadn't paved the way.

Stardom

Several wrestling promotions (including women's promotions) popped up in the 2010s, with some of them becoming hits and others being no longer of this world. Some of those victims were Global Force Wrestling, Lucha Underground, and What Culture Pro Wrestling.

One promotion who not only survived, but whose popularity has exploded over the last decade is Stardom. World Wonder Ring Stardom (just Stardom for short), founded in September 2010, was the brainchild of pro wrestling booker and producer Rossy Ogawa, mixed martial arts (MMA) star and model Fuka Kakimoto, and professional wrestler Nanae Takahashi. Ogawa started out at the age of 18 as a photographer for AJW, which we talk about in the section "All Japan Women's Pro-Wrestling (AJW)" earlier in this chapter. He ultimately worked his way into the office there. When AJW collapsed, Ogawa left and formed a new group, Arsion, which lasted only a few years before it folded in 2003. He then disappeared from the business until forming Stardom.

Starting small

They held their first event as Stardom's *dojo* (training school), Shin-Kiba 1st Ring, in Tokyo. The arena holds 290 people, so it was a bit of a slow start. Several top acts from other promotions, such as Miho Wakizawa (AJW, who was known for working in several promotions at any given time), as well as wrestler and MMA star Mika Nagano (Ice Ribbon) were joined by non-exclusive talents such as Io Shirai (competing in WWE as Iyo Sky), as well as young up-and-comers, such as Arisa Hoshiki and Mayu Iwatani.

Here are a few aspects of Stardom that make it unique:

TIP

- **It books its touring schedule like seasons of a real sport.** A season lasts roughly 60 to 90 days. This type of schedule allows Stardom to better utilize foreign talent because it can fly women in for the entire three-month season and have them all live in an apartment together. This scheduling saves money by not having to fly talent in and out regularly like promotions do with a more standard pro wrestling travel schedule.
- **Performers don't work other promotions unless they get a special exception.** This requirement is similar to the World Wrestling Entertainment (WWE; see Chapter 8).
- **They expanded quickly.** They went from having shows at their small base of operations, Shin-Kiba 1st Ring, to a larger facility, out of which DDT and Pro Wrestling Zero1 also operated. They also began to promote shows at Korakuen Hall, an arena in Tokyo, on a regular basis, which signaled an uptick in business.

Stardom championships

The promotion currently features five main roster championships (excluding developmental leagues or training promotions and titles from other promotions):

- World of Stardom (world title)
- Wonder of Stardom (secondary title)
- Goddesses of Stardom (tag team title)
- Artist of Stardom (trios title)
- High Speed Championship (similar to a cruiserweight or X-Division Title, meaning faster-paced matches featuring wrestlers with more aerial offense)

Rather than having one giant spectacle of a show each year, like WWE's *Wrestle-Mania* (flip to Chapter 6 for info on this show), the promotion holds big seasonal shows, such as *All Star Grand Queendom* in the spring and *New Year Dream* in the winter. The promotion also holds several tournaments throughout the year.

REMEMBER

Their most famous tournament, the 5 Star Grand Prix, has gained popularity much like the NJPW G1 Climax Tournament (see the section "Watching the big shows" earlier in this chapter). The best Stardom matches of the year (some would say best matches historically) occur in this tournament. Fans talk of one match, the 2016 bout between Mayu Iwatani and Io Shirai, in the same rarified air as Hiroshi Tanahashi versus Tetsuya Naito from 2017's G1 Climax match (mentioned in Chapter 13).

Stardom has developed working relationships with several noteworthy promotions, from Sendai Girls' Pro Wrestling, a promotion founded by wrestler and trainer Meiko Satomura (and a promotion where some epic interpromotional matches and title changes took place) to Mexico's *Consejo Mundial de Lucha Libre* (CMLL; World Wrestling Council).

Joining the guys

In 2019, Bushiroad Inc. — the parent company of NJPW — purchased Stardom. Although men's and women's promotions in Japan historically operated separately, that all changed in 2020, when NJPW booked a women's tag team match as a *dark match* (an untelevised match only for the crowd in attendance) at *Wrestle Kingdom XIV* in the Tokyo Dome.

The purchase by Bushiroad, like everything in life, came with positives and negatives:

- Early on, business increased to the point that Stardom became the number-two promotion in all of Japan and the top women's organization worldwide.
- Stardom founder Ogawa became increasingly frustrated with decisions made by Bushiroad management (similar to how TKO management made changes to *WrestleMania* plans in 2026, which frustrated fans and people working inside WWE).

Ogawa, who worked as Stardom's executive producer, had signed a no-compete agreement when Bushiroad bought Stardom, but it was no secret that he planned to leave Stardom and start his own promotion at some point.

WARNING

He gave notice in November of 2023. However, on February 4, 2024, immediately following an in-ring celebration to conclude Stardom's 13th anniversary show, management told Ogawa that they were canceling his contract, effective immediately. They then proceeded to bury him in the Japanese press, saying he was fired because he was trying to poach talent from Stardom to create his own company.

Creating a new promotion

In reality, Ogawa and Stardom had talked about him leaving to form his own group and had even discussed potentially doing an interpromotional feud down the road.

After leaving Stardom, Ogawa did start his own company, Dream Star Fighting Marigold (more popularly known as just Marigold). And he didn't really have to poach talent because many of Stardom's top stars, including Utami Hayashita,

Giulia, Nanae Takahashi, Mai Sakurai, and Mirai were loyal to him and eager to follow. Marigold immediately set up a working agreement with WWE. They ran their first show, *Marigold Fields Forever,* on May 20, 2024, at the Tokyo arena Korakuen Hall.

Delving Deeper into Strong Style

Strong style professional wrestling is a style that, while popularized in Japan, has become a fixture in many promotions around the world. The emphasis is on realistic martial arts techniques, more realistic-looking striking (like you'd see in kickboxing or boxing),and realistic submission holds to make the match look as real as possible.

The following sections focus not on one singular promotion, but rather a string of promotions and a genre that they helped create.

Pro wrestling and mixed martial arts (MMA) in Japan share the same common ancestors, and although pro wrestling is *worked* (staged) while MMA is (for the most part) legitimate, the Japanese sports media treated them both alike. In no other country in the world have the two sports been so intertwined through history.

Hisashi Shinma, who was the mastermind and *booker* (who puts matches together) during New Japan Pro-Wrestling (NJPW)'s hot period of the early 1980s (see the section "Watching the big shows" earlier in this chapter), was forced out of NJPW because he took the fall for financial scandal connected to Antonio Inoki. He decided to start his own promotion, built around Akira Maeda, whom he believed could be the biggest post-Antonio Inoki wrestling star in all of Japan.

REMEMBER

Maeda had a new concept in mind. He had worked terrible matches with over-the-hill wrestlers during a tour of the U.S. promotion World Wrestling Federation (WWF). Because he was a fan of European technical wrestling, he created the concept of *shoot-style wrestling* — essentially, a style composed of only the legitimate-looking elements of pro wrestling:

- **Suplexes:** A wrestling throw where the attacker lifts their opponent and throws them overhead
- **Submissions:** Holds or stretches used to immobilize an opponent and (if possible) make them *tap out* (surrender)
- **Strikes:** Examples include boxing- and kickboxing-style punches and kicks (meaning no corny movie-style *haymakers* [wild semicircular punches])

Universal Wrestling Federation (UWF)

Shinma and Maeda created the Universal Wrestling Federation (UWF) to put Maeda's shoot-style wrestling into practice. He pushed it as real professional wrestling, distinct from the theatrics of New Japan, and used notable wrestlers in Japan such as Yoshiaki Fujiwara, Kazuo Yamazaki, and Satoru Sayama. Of course, it was just as predetermined as any other pro wrestling promotion. But fans in Tokyo chose to believe it was the real deal, and it very quickly became very hot.

Unfortunately, it was hot only in Tokyo, and because of the lack of a reliable television deal, as well as the more realistic style appealing only to the most niche audience, within a few years UWF died its first death. All the wrestlers who had left New Japan for UWF returned to New Japan, and they did an *invasion angle* (where wrestlers from one promotion show up in another promotion to disrupt the show), New Japan versus UWF. The feud was a big business success.

But Maeda grew increasingly frustrated that traditionalists weren't properly respecting his new style (which the UWF wrestlers continued to work in New Japan). Plus, he once again had to participate in bad matches that included wrestlers doing a style that he hated.

WARNING

So, during a six-man tag team match, while wrestler Riki Choshu put his opponent Osamu Kido in a *Scorpion deathlock* (attacker hooks opponent's legs, flips them over and applies pressure to their knees and back), which tied up both his hands and left his face wide open, Maeda legitimately kicked him full force in the face and shattered his eye socket. He was, of course, immediately suspended.

UWF, take two

After his suspension, Maeda quit New Japan, and because of his immense popularity, was able to raise funding without having to rely on other financial backers, and the UWF was reborn in 1988. The second UWF was a much bigger success than the first because now it had a compelling story — a rebellious group of young wrestlers were sick of this fake professional wrestling and wanted to fight for real.

TIP

They got two years of exposure on New Japan television prior to the reemergence of UWF, and even without their own TV deal, they began selling out events left and right. UWF became the cool thing, and in fact became the first-ever professional wrestling show to sell out the Tokyo Dome, on November 29, 1989.

But because of financial mismanagement, the UWF died again in 1990.

Strong-style promotions after UWF

Three new promotions sprung up from the ashes of UWF. All three are pivotal to the history of combat sports in Japan because they all in one way or another led to the rise of Japanese mixed martial arts (MMA):

- **Fighting Network Rings (RINGS):** Headed by the original head of UWF, Akira Maeda. The only promotion in history that began as a worked promotion and ultimately morphed into a legitimate MMA promotion.
- **Pro Wrestling Fujiwara Gumi (PWFG)/Pancrase:** Headed by Yoshiaki Fujiwara, and featuring UFC and WWF star Ken Shamrock, Masakatsu Funaki, and New Japan stalwart Minoru Suzuki. Although it began as PWFG, it eventually morphed into Pancrase (named after the Greek sport of pankration, a mixed martial art featured in the original Olympic Games). Pancrase was the first professional wrestling promotion in history to feature almost exclusively legitimate matches (although for various reasons, worked matches occasionally occurred).

  REMEMBER

  Shamrock became a huge star when he came to America and was one of the earliest faces of Ultimate Fighting Championship (UFC), which debuted in 1993.
- **Universal Wrestling Federation International (UWFi):** Headed by and built around wrestler Nobuhiko Takada; had the biggest lasting impact on shoot-style wrestling (see the following section).

Universal Wrestling Federation International (UWFi)

Wrestler Nobuhiko Takada, like Inoki in the 1970s, made his name by beating either big and scary (Vader, Koji Kitao) or real-life combat sports opponents (Jamaican professional boxer Trevor Berbick) in allegedly real fights (they weren't). To many Japanese fans, the toughest guy in Japan was Takada.

However, during the height of UWFi, UFC was exploding in North America. Royce Gracie (son of the legendary mixed martial artist Helio Gracie) was a multi-time UFC tournament winner, and his bigger brother Rickson had won similar tournaments in Japan for PRIDE and Vale Tudo Japan. Unlike UWFi, these tournaments involved real competition between fighters, not predetermined matches.

Those within UWFi saw the threat that legitimate MMA organizations posed if they revealed that UWFi wasn't actually as legitimate as advertised. So, on

December 7, 1994, UWFi's Yoji Anjo, who had legitimate submission training, flew to California with a plan to show up at Rickson's dojo with Japanese magazine photographers and writers, and then issue an impromptu challenge. He thought that, because Rickson wouldn't have any time to prepare, Rickson would either:

- **Turn down the challenge:** If Rickson declined to fight, it would be a victory for UWFi because they would've used the opportunity to make it seem that Rickson was afraid of their fighters.
- **Lose in a fight:** Anjo thought he would surely beat Rickson because he outweighed him by 40 pounds and had trained hard in preparation.

WARNING

Rickson got the call about Anjo's challenge while at his house. He drove to the dojo while taping his fists in the car and proceeded to beat Anjo within an inch of his life. Anjo returned to Japan in disgrace; and worse, when the story hit the press, people started asking questions about why Rickson's tournament fights looked so different from UWFi matches. Fans also expected Takada to challenge Rickson and teach him a lesson, but, in fact, Takada was dead silent about the issue.

UWFi business collapsed to the point that, a year later, they had to make a deal with New Japan to do a New Japan versus UWFi feud — which, of course, New Japan dominated. UWFi was dead.

PRIDE Fighting Championships

Gracie versus Takada was the main event of PRIDE 1. PRIDE Fighting Championships, during its heyday, was Japan's answer to North America's UFC — except in those days, it was far bigger, far more outrageous, drew far bigger crowds, and was an MMA promotion unrivaled in history for many reasons. Their biggest event ever, *Shockwave* in August of 2002, drew an announced 91,107 fans, still the largest crowd to ever witness an MMA event.

RETIRING WITH A PAYDAY

After UWFi's end (in large part at the hands of Rickson Gracie, which you can read about in the section "Universal Wrestling Federation International [UWFi]," in this chapter), with UWFi's founder Nobuhiko Takada nearing retirement, he had one more option for a big payday: another Rickson match. On October 11, 1997, Rickson beat Takada in less than five minutes by using an *armbar* (submission hold attacking the arm) in a match that Rickson almost certainly allowed to go about four minutes longer than he needed to defeat Takada.

From 1997 to 2007, they ran more than 60 events, drew gigantic numbers on broadcast and PPV television, and made stars of the likes of Fedor Emelianenko, Kazushi Sakuraba, Antonio Rodrigo Nogueira, Mirko Crocop, Wanderlei Silva, Rampage Jackson, Alisteir Overeem, and Shogun Rua. Unlike UFC (which featured fights inside of a caged octagon), PRIDE promoted matches inside a wrestling/boxing-style ring; and with no drug testing to speak of, it was the Wild West of MMA.

WARNING

But it was a shooting star. In 2006, the press revealed PRIDE's ties to the *Yakuza*, and Japanese television networks canceled all PRIDE's lucrative broadcast deals. In March of 2007, Lorenzo Fertitta and Frank Fertitta III, owners of the UFC, purchased the company, and the glory days of the original PRIDE officially came to an end.

IN THIS CHAPTER

- Diving into the European wrestling scene
- Working catch wrestling promotions
- Meeting major catch wrestling figures
- Seeing how wrestling developed in Canada
- Understanding the roles of the top Canadian wrestlers

Chapter 11

Touring Pro Wrestling in Europe and Canada

Really good professional wrestling has a science to it. Beyond just the basics of the sport, a certain skill set is required, whether it's for the more theatrical U.S. style of wrestling or the more perceived physical style of Japan and even the more graceful and agile style of Mexico. Wrestling in Europe, mostly the United Kingdom and Canada, leans heavily into mat-based technical wrestling.

Exploring Catch Wrestling in Europe

In Europe, professional wrestling was real before it was fake. When you watch modern pro wrestling anywhere in the world today, you're watching the evolution of an art form that rose to prominence as a sport in Europe hundreds of years ago.

Of course, wrestling probably began as soon as animals had limbs (not even hominids, in fact — just watch two cats grappling). Humans have wrestled all over the world for millennia — from the very beginning of humanity, through the original Olympic Games, up through today — in every culture on Earth.

THE STYLES BEFORE CATCH-AS-CATCH-CAN

The catch-as-catch-can wrestling style has its roots in several wrestling styles that came before it:

- **Bolton:** Sometimes referred to as *Lancashire*, the county in Northwest England where it originated almost 1,000 years ago. Renowned for being very rough, competitors were allowed to punch, kick, wrestle and strangle, and a competitor won by throttling their opponent unconscious or making them give up.
- **Westmorland:** Also named for where it originated, a form of wrestling where two wrestlers grip each other and try to force the other to the ground through throws or trips; a wrestler can also win by breaking their opponent's grip.
- **Cornwall:** Also named for the county in which it originated, wrestlers wore durable jackets that allowed them to grip their opponents better, and all grips needed to be taken on the jacket.
- **Indian Pehlwani:** Along with strict diet and spiritual concepts, this form of wrestling leaned heavily into shoulder throws and strangle pins.

But you can trace the roots of modern-day professional wrestling most directly to Europe in the 19th century. The following sections walk you through the history of catch wrestling.

Creating catch wrestling

The *catch-as-catch-can* wrestling style was characterized by its somewhat anything-goes nature; the goal was to *catch* (grab) your opponent however you could in order to pin their shoulders to the mat or make them give up. This style exploded in popularity in the early 1800s.

Around the 1820s, the term *catch-as-catch-can* or *catch* for short (used in relation to that specific wrestling style) had emigrated to the United States.

REMEMBER

Catch-as-catch-can wrestling evolved as a safer version of The Bolton Method in the early 1800s. So many people had been badly injured or killed that the Bolton Method was outlawed. A new, safer style came into vogue, variously called Lancashire or catch-as-catch-can. Within a few decades several local organizations codified an official set of rules:

» **Falls:** Bouts could now end via a *fall,* which happened when a wrestler's two shoulders touched the mat, either because the winner threw the loser, who landed on their back, or the winner maneuvered the loser into position with a wrestling hold. Matches were usually best-of-three or best-of-five falls.

» **Submissions:** Bouts could end via submission, which involved one wrestler giving up.

» **Allowed techniques:** Any wrestling hold, throw, joint lock to any limb, and neck cranks were all legal.

» **Banned techniques:** Striking, such as punching or kicking, grabbing an opponent's clothing, "small digit manipulation" (attacking fingers), and choking and gouging were all outlawed.

Many of these rules remain in professional wrestling today.

With the new rules, catch-as-catch-can wrestling gained popularity over the ensuing decades, to the point that a version of it became an Olympic sport in 1904 and appeared in the Olympics on and off through 1936. In the early 1900s, catch wrestling basically featured the same ruleset as modern-day freestyle wrestling.

Renaming to freestyle wrestling

In 1921, *Fédération Internationale des Luttes Associées* (FILA; International Federation of Associated Wrestling Styles), the world governing body for amateur wrestling, chose to rename catch wrestling as *freestyle wrestling* in an attempt to distance itself from any connotations associating amateur and professional wrestling (see the sidebar "Making wrestling a spectacle" in this chapter for why). Freestyle wrestling (as well as Greco-Roman wrestling) remain Olympic sports to this day.

TECHNICAL STUFF

Ironically, *freestyle wrestling* was a rough translation of the French term *lutte libre,* which itself was a rough translation of — you guessed it —*catch-as-catch-can.*

MAKING WRESTLING A SPECTACLE

In the early 1900s, professional wrestling was a full-on entertainment spectacle and didn't have the best reputation. In 1919, for example, a riot broke out in Sioux City, Iowa, following a match between Wladek Zbyszko and Joe Stecher, with fans screaming "Fake!" The wrestlers needed police protection to even make it back to the dressing room.

Legitimate catch wrestling didn't die out with the name change, and a quarter-century later, Karl Gotch began teaching catch to Japanese pro wrestlers, some of whom went on to become all-time greats. One of them, Antonio Inoki, had a very famous boxer-versus-wrestler mixed match with legendary boxer Muhammad Ali in 1976, which some point to as the birthplace of both Japanese and later worldwide mixed martial arts (MMA). (You can read more about this matchup in Chapter 16.)

Seeing catch-as-catch-can live on

Today, many *worked* (performance) pro wrestling promotions in Europe carry on the heritage by using the term *catch* in their promotion name; these organizations present predetermined performance wrestling the same as World Wrestling Entertainment (WWE) and All Elite Wrestling (AEW) in the States, or New Japan Pro-Wrestling (NJPW).

However, catch wrestling lives on as a legitimate grappling style, practiced by champion mixed martial arts (MMA) competitors such as Josh Barnett, Randy Couture, Demetrious Johnson, Kazushi Sakuraba, and the Shamrock brothers, Ken and Frank.

THE TRUTH ABOUT CATCH-AS-CATCH-CAN IN THE UNITED STATES

WARNING

Although you may find information online saying that catch-as-catch-can wrestling, particularly in the United States, stayed legitimate up through the 1920s, that information is false. Here are the facts:

- Nearly every wrestler in the 1800s had a legitimate background.
- These wrestlers were almost certainly capable of defending themselves against an untrained opponent.
- Legitimate matches certainly existed at that time.

But a large percentage of matches were *worked* (scripted or preplanned), probably from the very beginning of catch-as-catch-can's arrival in the States in the early 19th century.

Identifying Catch-Themed Promotions

You can find a staggering number of promotions in Europe throughout the years that utilized the phrase *catch wrestling.* Many of those promotions took the base tenets of catch wrestling and evolved the style into something wholly unique. The following sections look at some of these companies.

Catch Wrestling Association

What became the Catch Wrestling Association (CWA, not to be confused with the Continental Wrestling Association, also called the CWA) was originally known as the *Internationaler Berufsringer-Verband* (IBV; International Professional Wrestler's Association), founded in 1973 by German promoter Nico Selenkowitsch. In 1978, one of Selenkowitsch's top stars, Otto Wanz, won a World Title that didn't exist. Wanz got the rights to the Canadian Wrestling Association (a fictional promotion) World Title belt from South African wrestler Jan Wilkens. Wanz then set up legendary American wrestler Don Leo Jonathan to lose it to him so that he could promote himself as the CWA World Champion.

Wanz took over IBV from Selenkowitsch in 1987 and renamed the promotion Catch Wrestling Association, so the CWA belt became the Catch Wrestling Association World Title belt. Wanz, a former American Wrestling Association (AWA) world champion, set up a working arrangement between the CWA and AWA, as well as NJPW.

TIP

The Austria-based CWA promotion was unique among its fellow modern catch promotions in several ways:

- **Showing off strength:** In addition to pro wrestling (under the blanket term *catch,* not referring to any specific style of wrestling), the company also featured Strong Man competitions, which were unregulated, theatrical exhibitions held in circuses, music halls, and more often than not coincided with wrestling shows.
- **Going for rounds:** Matches followed European rules, meaning that instead of one fall leading to a finish, the promotion divided bouts into three-minute rounds, in which referees could determine the winner via multiple falls, countouts, knockouts, or referee decisions.

CWA's biggest annual event through the 1990s was the Euro Catch Festival, held twice yearly — July in Graz, Austria, and December in Bremen, Germany. The promotion closed (due to the market no longer supporting this type of old school wrestling) after the 1999 tournament.

International Catch Wrestling Alliance

The International Catch Wrestling Alliance (ICWA), a French promotion, debuted in 2003. Former professional wrestler Pierre "Booster" Fontaine co-created ICWA with French commentator Christophe Agius, and Fontaine is the booker for the promotion. This company is:

TIP

- Not just a wrestling promotion, but also a wrestling school. Here, students learned the fundamentals of catch wrestling as well as the basics of modern professional wrestling.
- Connected with the famed American organization National Wrestling Alliance (NWA), which gives ICWA legitimacy in the eyes of longtime wrestling fans.
- Involved in edgy events, such as Hellfest Open Air music festival, which features heavy metal, hardcore, and punk music acts. These associations make ICWA more North American wrestling-like than other Western European promotions.

The Snake Pit

The Snake Pit, a wrestling facility in Wigan, England, promotes competitions including the Catch Wrestling World Championships. Old school aficionados describe it as the modern home of catch wrestling.

Founded by professional wrestler Billy Riley in 1948 and originally named Riley's Gym, the facility taught freestyle, professional (what many call *show wrestling*), and old-school Lancashire catch-as-catch-can wrestling. Wrestlers from Europe, Asia, and North America trained here and became among the toughest wrestlers of the mid-20th century.

Although professional wrestling was 100 percent a worked sport in the 1940s, you still needed the ability to legitimately grapple if you wanted to be under consideration for the world championship. Within a few decades, that vestige of the old days of pro wrestling was gone. Essentially, anyone could be a world champion if they looked and acted the part. And as a result, Riley made the decision to close his gym in the early 1970s.

REMEMBER

One of his students, Roy Wood, later revived the facility and shifted the training to focus on freestyle wrestling. Riley agreed to return to coach. When the facility was becoming too rundown to maintain, two Japanese pro wrestlers, Kazuo Sakurada and K.Y. Wakamatsu, visited from Japan. They saw the dilapidated gym as the spiritual home of catch wrestling and ultimately helped to finance a renovation; the organization rose like a phoenix once more, reopening in 2012.

Riley's Gym, and later the Snake Pit, turned out many greats:

- **The first generation:** Riley's Gym turned out several all-time pro wrestling greats, including Karl Gotch (no relation to Frank Gotch who we discuss later in this chapter in the section by the same name) and Billy Robinson.
- **The second-generation:** Alumni include Tatsumi Fujinami, Osamu Nishimura, and the Dynamite Kid.
- **Modern names that trace back to Riley's:** Mixed martial arts (MMA) legends Frank and Ken Shamrock, Bas Rutten, Kazushi Sakuraba, Brock Lesnar, Josh Barnett and Demetrious Johnson, and trainers Erik Paulson and Matt Hume.
- **Japanese wrestlers:** Gotch and Robinson also helped train a generation of major Japanese pro wrestling icons, including Antonio Inoki, Akira Maeda, Minoru Suzuki, Tatsumi Fujinami, and Yoshiaki Fujiwara.

World of Sport

A staple of professional sports in the United Kingdom, *World of Sport* began on ITV in January 1965 as a sports news program. Hosted by Irish sports commentator Eamonn Andrews, *World of Sport* covered everything from soccer to tennis to motor racing to professional wrestling. The program ran for 20 years before ITV cancelled it in September 1985.

Pro wrestling was always among the most popular segments in *World of Sport*, with the biggest matches drawing millions of viewers. Two short revivals, along with attempts to air other wrestling programming (such as All Star Wrestling [ASW] and World Championship Wrestling [WCW]), showed that the British audience still had a thirst for action in the squared circle.

REMEMBER

Because wrestling aired on *World of Sport* alongside other, you know, actual sports, the show presented the pro wrestling competitions as real. As a result, they didn't go overboard with the gimmicks and pageantry; it was mostly mat-based technical matches performed under — we're not making this up — Admiral-Lord Mountevans rules. This serious-sounding ruleset included that:

- Matches feature six 5-minute rounds.
- Winning usually comes from a best-of-three-falls (see Chapter 2 for more discussion about falls).
- Referees use a verbal warning system.

The matches still had *babyfaces* (wrestlers who took on good-guy personas) and *heels* (the bad guys), and the heels tried to cheat — but the interactions weren't nearly as overdone as you see in any pro wrestling organization today.

In October 2016, ITV brought wrestling back under the *World of Sport* banner. Jeff Jarrett of Impact Wrestling helped to produce the show, and the incomparable wrestling commentator Jim Ross helped call the matches on the first episode. The show mostly featured independent wrestlers such as "British Bulldog" Davey Boy Smith, Jr., Dave Mastiff, *El Ligero* (The Lightweight), and Grado.

Recognizing Top-Level Catch Wrestlers

Great technical wrestling has a formula: The blending of holds and submissions that includes enough showmanship to keep a crowd enthralled. Those wrestlers who did most assuredly etched their names into the wall of all-time greats. The following sections talk about a few of the most notable catch wrestlers.

The Great Gama

Born in what is today Punjab, India, in May 1878, Ghulam Mohammad Baksh Butt was a strongman who won his first competition at age 10. The Maharaja of Datia (ruler of the Bundelkhand region of Madhya Pradesh, India) took Butt to train in the sport of Pehlwani (similar to catch-as-catch-can wrestling, discussed in the section "Exploring catch wrestling in Europe" earlier in this chapter, and one of the precursors to modern mixed martial arts [MMA]). Butt trained at several of the most grueling *akharas* (wrestling gymnasiums) in the Punjab region. This training regimen included an incredibly strict dietary plan and pushup and squat workouts numbering in the thousands.

Gama's career went through the stratosphere, proving himself to be a force to be reckoned with (and an attraction that many fans would go out of their way to see):

- **Drawing his first match:** At age 17, Butt challenged one of the top champions in the sport, Raheem Bakhsh Sultani Wala, to a match that ended in a draw. This match put Butt on the map in a major way.
- **Competing as "The Great Gama":** After adopting his ring name, "The Great Gama," he competed against the best wrestlers from around the world, defeating world champions from Sweden and Switzerland.
- **Becoming "The Great Wrestler of India":** After he defeated former world champion Stanislav Zbyszko of Poland and received the royal Silver Mace from Prince Edward VIII of Wales, Gama became known as "The Great Wrestler of India."

REMEMBER

Some of his matches had controversial aspects — including his second match with Zbyszko in 1928 that ended in less than a minute (some believe Zbyszko took a secret payoff to lose, unbeknownst to Gama). But despite these potential issues, many wrestling historians believe that Gama was one of the greatest legitimate wrestlers of all time.

Organizations like the National Wrestling Hall of Fame maintain that, in his 52-year career, no one ever beat him. And although the make-believe world of professional wrestling has all kinds of questionable undefeated records, no one has any actual evidence to the contrary in Gama's case. He was an enormous bull of a man, heavily muscled in a time before anabolic steroids, and his training and diet regimen influenced many generations of fitness buffs, including the famous martial artist and actor Bruce Lee.

Frank Gotch

A native of Humboldt, Iowa, Frank Gotch (see Figure 11-1) was born on April 27, 1878. Although he grew up on a farm, Gotch wanted to wrestle when he was just a teenager.

FIGURE 11-1: Frank Gotch.

Jim Melby photos from Dr Mike Lano's Collection

Although he had setbacks, Gotch became arguably the greatest North American wrestler of the 20th century, and among the most influential:

- **Early defeats:** When he was 21, Gotch began competing around Iowa. In one of his earliest matches, he nearly defeated Dan McLeod, a former heavyweight champion. His next major bout was against another champion, Martin "Farmer" Burns.
- **Great training:** Although Gotch lost to Burns, his effort made a lasting impression, and Burns took him under his wing to train in catch and technical wrestling. In January 1904, just a few years after completing his training with Burns, Gotch beat the American wrestling champion Tom Jenkins.
- **World champion:** After this momentous accomplishment, Gotch sought to compete against the world heavyweight champion, George Hackenschmidt (who we talk about in the next section) whom he eventually defeated. He himself had a five-year run as world champion.
- **Going out on top:** Gotch went undefeated during the last seven years of his career before retiring in 1913.

TIP

Although he had many professional rivalries during his career, his most famous was with the legendary George Hackenschmidt (see the following section).

Frank Gotch was arguably the most important American professional wrestler of the 20th century. His matches were front-page news stories worldwide, and in the early part of the 20th century, he was as big of a mainstream sports superstar as the boxers John L. Sullivan and Jack Dempsey, and the baseball legend Babe Ruth. Professional wrestling became respectable, and amateur wrestling became a staple of public schools and colleges nationwide.

George Hackenschmidt

Born in what is now Tartu, Estonia, Georg Karl Julius Hackenschmidt (see Figure 11-2) was a jack-of-all-trades athlete as a young man. He excelled at cycling, gymnastics, running, swimming, and weightlifting. (Fun fact: The *hack squat*, where you do squats on an angled machine or with a barbell, is named after him!)

TIP

Hackenschmidt worked in blue-collar jobs during his young adulthood, and he kept in top shape, particularly in strength training. Like Gama (see the section "The Great Gama" earlier in this chapter), Hackenschmidt had an incredible physique long before athletes had such things as anabolic steroids to help build muscle mass.

FIGURE 11-2: George Hackenschmidt.

Jim Melby photos from Dr Mike Lano's Collection

His pro wrestling career took many twists and turns:

- **A lucky physician:** Hackenschmidt began making a name for himself as a strongman and wrestler until he injured his hand at his day job, as a blacksmith's apprentice. In an epic stroke of serendipity, one of Hackenschmidt's physicians also worked for Tsar Nicolas II, the Emperor of Russia. This physician, Dr. Vladislav von Krajewski, funded Hackenschmidt's wrestling training.
- **Training and the army:** Hackenschmidt personally felt that his mat game wasn't up to par and that he leaned too much on his immense strength. After continued training, followed by a stint in the Russian army, Hackenschmidt returned to wrestling, now brandishing the nickname "The Russian Lion."
- **European victories:** In 1904, after winning several tournaments around Europe, Hackenschmidt beat Ahmed Madrali to be recognized as the World Heavyweight Champion.

» **Going to the States:** He then came to the United States, where he defeated American Heavyweight Champion Tom Jenkins, which gained him recognition in America as the World Champion.

REMEMBER

He held the title for four years before the first of two all-time legendary matches between himself and Frank Gotch (see the preceding section). We discuss the two Gotch-versus-Hackenschmidt matches in detail in Chapter 4.

Billy Robinson

William Alfred Robinson was born September 18, 1938, in Manchester, England. Coming from a family of boxers, Robinson seemed destined for combat sports. But an unfortunate eye injury in his childhood prevented him from pursuing boxing.

He began amateur wrestling at age 14, underwent rigorous catch wrestling training at The Snake Pit (flip to the section "The Snake Pit" earlier in this chapter, for more about this facility), which laid the foundation for him to win the 1957 British Senior Championships (a legitimate freestyle title).

The following year, he debuted as a professional wrestler. He went on to compete against top talent from around the world, from Billy Joyce in London, to Antonio Inoki in Japan, and even Dory Funk, Jr., for the National Wrestling Alliance (NWA) World Heavyweight Championship.

TIP

In 1999, the Universal Wrestling Federation opened a new Snake Pit in Japan. Robinson (who transitioned to training) became a coach, teaching both catch wrestling and MMA. One of his students, Kazushi Sakuraba, went on to become one of the greatest MMA fighters in history.

Ed "Strangler" Lewis

Ed "Strangler" Lewis (whose real name was Robert Herman Julius Friedrich) was born in Nekoosa, Wisconsin, on June 30, 1891. Lewis trained in many sports as a youth but fell in love with wrestling. At the age of 14, he competed under his ring name, instead of using his birth name, because he didn't want his parents to find out about what he was doing.

REMEMBER

Working with Billy Sandow and Raymond "Toots" Mondt as "The Gold Dust Trio" in the 1920s, Lewis helped to craft some of the earliest pro wrestling concepts and storylines, paving the way for the modern version of professional wrestling that fans see today. One of Lewis's most heated rivalries — both on and off the mat — was with Joe Stecher, whose brother Tony also ran a rival promotion. The Lewis-Stecher rivalry included one of the most famous double-crosses in wrestling history:

» **A non-wrestler is given the World Championship.** On January 8, 1925, Lewis, Sandow, and Mondt, in a very controversial decision at the time, put the World Title on Wayne Munn (a college football player from the University of Nebraska who had no legitimate wrestling background).

» **The title is stolen in the ring.** Polish wrestler Stanislaus Zbyszko, one of the Gold Dust Trio's top wrestlers, so disagreed with this philosophy that when asked by the Trio to lose to Munn on April 15, 1925, Zbyszko instead double-crossed Munn, legitimately humiliated him in the ring, and beat him for the title. He then defected and joined up with Stecher's promotion. Stecher's group had stolen the World Title.

Lewis and Zbyszko eventually came to an agreement, and Stecher lost the title in a match against Lewis three years later.

Lewis, like Gotch (see the section "Frank Gotch" earlier in this chapter), was a feared *shooter* (legitimate wrestler) and one of the most famous mainstream American sports stars of the early 20th century, on par with the greatest icons of any other sport. He continued to wrestle through 1948, despite being nearly blind. Post-retirement, he worked as a manager for one of the biggest stars of the mid-20th century, and one of the last great pro wrestling World Champion shooters, Lou Thesz, who we discuss in Chapter 5.

Examining Professional Wrestling in Canada

Like in the United States and the United Kingdom, wrestling in Canada began at carnivals and local fairs. Also, in the same way that the U.K. adopted some of the styles it used in wrestling from India, many Canadian wrestlers of the early 1900s borrowed grappling techniques from First Nations peoples. But, outside of the short-lived Carl Berch Promotions, Canada didn't have many organized professional wrestling promotions until the 1930s and 1940s.

Over the ensuing decades, four major National Wrestling Alliance (NWA) promotions ran events in Montreal, Toronto, Calgary, and Vancouver. Vince McMahon, Jr., during his national (and international) expansion of WWF in the mid-1980s, purchased the Montreal, Toronto, and Calgary territories. The Vancouver wrestling territory, along with all the remaining territories in the United States, largely died out by the early 1990s.

Though Canadian wrestling territories worked with each other, the great distances between them meant that it wasn't on a frequent basis. This did allow companies to develop strong and unique identities among the wrestling landscape in the Great White North. The following sections examine the Toronto, Calgary, and Montreal markets.

Maple Leaf Wrestling

Founded in 1930 by Jack Corcoran and purchased in 1939 by Frank and John Tunney, the Toronto-based promotion was originally called the Queensbury Athletic Club. It became known as Maple Leaf Wrestling because they ran events at the Maple Leaf Gardens for more than 60 years. Queensbury Athletic Club promoted pro wrestling and other combat sports, including boxing. The promotion joined the NWA in 1949, setting the stage for it to become the premier Canadian pro wrestling promotion.

Some of the most renowned athletes to come out of Maple Leaf were Hall of Fame NWA Champion "Whipper" Billy Watson (see the section "'Whipper' Billy Watson" later in this chapter), Tiger Jeet Singh, and Rocky Johnson (father of Dwayne "The Rock" Johnson).

In 1984, Maple Leaf broke away from the NWA and entered a business relationship with WWF. The co-head of the company at that time, Jack Tunney (who was the son of John, who purchased the promotion in 1939), was put in charge of Titan Sports Canada (WWF's Canadian wing) and given an on-air figurehead role as WWF President Jack Tunney.

TECHNICAL STUFF

Although the promotion ran occasional shows until 1995, many viewers didn't consider it its own entity for about a decade because the content it aired was primarily rebranded WWF television shows with some additional (required by the Canadian Radio-television and Telecommunications Commission) Canadian content.

Stampede Wrestling

Stu Hart and Al Oeming founded what would become Stampede Wrestling in Calgary, Alberta in 1948. The company would go through three different names:

- **Klondike Wrestling:** Before becoming Stampede, Klondike Wrestling had its first show in September 1948. They ran shows for decades in Calgary at venues such as the Victoria Pavilion and Stampede Corral. These shows weren't just under the Klondike name.

» **Big Time Wrestling:** The company's name was changed to Big Time Wrestling in 1958 to give the promotion a larger-than-life feel.

» **Wildcat Wrestling:** In 1965, the promotion underwent another rebrand.

» **Stampede Wrestling:** Hart settled on this name in 1967.

WARNING

The infamous Stampede Dungeon was Hart's training facility, where he both taught wrestlers and beat up local tough guys (football players and so on), gleefully *stretching* them (trapping them in painful submission holds) in an effort to convince them that wrestling was no joke.

Top stars came up through Stampede, including the Dynamite Kid, "British Bulldog" Davey Boy Smith, Brian Pillman, and Bret and Owen Hart (two of Stu's sons), performers whose work still resonates today.

McMahon bought out the promotion in the mid-1980s and gave wrestling jobs to Bret Hart, Dynamite Kid, and Davey Boy Smith. Vince reneged his promised payments to the Hart family following the sale, and they regained control of Stampede Wrestling a few years later. Stu's son Bruce Hart ran shows for the promotion until 1990, due to creative differences with Stu and ultimately, the WWF expansion, which made it impossible for smaller promotions like Stampede to compete. And then in 1999, Bruce and Ross Hart (another one of Stu's kids — he had a lot) reopened the promotion until they lost their TV deal a few years later.

Lutte Internationale

Canadian wrestlers Gino Brito and Frank Valois, along with French wrestler André the Giant (André Roussimoff) founded the Montreal, Quebec-based promotion Lutte Internationale. It operated from 1980 to 1987 and competed as one of the top three promotions in Canada (along with Maple Leaf Wrestling and Stampede Wrestling, discussed in the preceding sections). It filled a gap left by the end of All Star Wrestling (a smaller Vancouver-based promotion) and Grand Prix Wrestling (an independent promotion that toured Nova Scotia, New Brunswick, and Prince Edward Island), both of which had promoted shows in Quebec for years.

Brito and Valois convinced André, one of the biggest stars in the history of professional wrestling and a worldwide top draw, to help bring wrestling to a city that was like a second home to him. Through connections André made during his time with the American Wrestling Association (AWA) and later the WWF, Lutte International brought in many big names to the promotion, including Hulk Hogan (before *Hulkamania*, the rise of popularity of Hulk Hogan, explained in Chapter 5), who faced André in the main event of Lutte International's first show at the Paul Sauve Centre.

Lutte Internationale had many Canadian and international wrestlers in their shows:

- **French-Canadian stars:** Including Dino Bravo, "Rugged" Ronnie Garvin, "The Model" Rick Martel, and Jacques and Raymond Rougeau.
- **Stars from around the world:** Such as former WWF Champion Bob Backlund, Butch Reed, Billy Robinson, Kendo Nagasaki, and Ricky "the Dragon" Steamboat — all had runs in the territory, as well.
- **Puerto Rico:** Lutte International got an influx of talent through a working relationship with Puerto Rican promotion World Wrestling Council (WWC).

WARNING

As in many other territories across North America, a nasty promotional war and talent raids by the WWF led to a decline in business, and in 1987, Lutte Internationale closed its doors. The promotion has come back several times, as recently as 2011, but never had the staying power it did in that initial run.

Naming Notable Grapplers from the Great White North

Highlighting all of the fantastic wrestlers from Canada would require an entire book (which, in fact, you can find in Greg Oliver and Steven Johnson's Pro Wrestling Hall of Fame series). In the following sections, we focus on a few wrestlers who laid the foundation for Canada's great technical wrestling.

TIP

Many of these Canadian wrestlers worked with the big promotions, including the NWA, AWA, — and, of course, the WWF.

George Gordienko

One of the earliest pro wrestlers in Canada was George Gordienko. Friends convinced Gordienko, who was born in Winnipeg, Manitoba, on January 7, 1928, to pursue wrestling. He trained at the same facility as Olympic wrestler Jimmy Trifunov.

Gordienko connected with promoter Tony Stecher, who got Gordienko booked in several cities across the United States. Although he bowed out of the pro wrestling business to pursue his other passion, art, in 1953, professional wrestling lured him back (or more accurately, wrestling provided him with the financial freedom to continue traveling and developing his career as an artist).

Gordienko wasn't afraid to take on challengers. From the U.K. to South Africa, and from the Middle East to Australia, Gordienko wrestled and was a worldwide star. Lou Thesz (see Chapter 5) often cited him as one of the greatest legitimate wrestlers of his generation.

TECHNICAL STUFF

He was mostly a big star internationally because the United States suspected him of being a Communist in the late 1940s, and so he couldn't work in the United States during his heyday. Other countries gave him a platform to ply his trade, so he put on incredible wrestling matches for crowds all over Europe.

Gene Kiniski

Eugene Nicholas Kiniski went by many names in his pro wrestling career:

- Blue Destroyer
- Crimson Knight II
- Masked Marauder #2

Born in Edmonton, Alberta, on November 23, 1928, the nearly 6-foot-4-inch athlete competed in wrestling, boxing, and American football (eventually playing for the Edmonton Eskimos) until a torn kneecap ended his gridiron career. Under the tutelage of Tony Morelli and Dory Funk, Sr., Kiniski trained to become a professional wrestler:

- **Making it in the States:** He made his televised debut in the United States in 1954, winning the International TV Tag Titles with John Tolos and competing for the NWA World Championship against Lou Thesz.
- **Back to Canada:** After competing in territories in Southern California and Texas, Kiniski went back north, where he competed for Maple Leaf Wrestling (see the section "Maple Leaf Wrestling" earlier in this chapter) and the AWA, forging alliances with Buddy Rogers and engaging in iconic feuds with the likes of "Whipper" Billy Watson (discussed in the section "'Whipper' Billy Watson" later in this chapter).

  TIP

  His highest-profile matches were his wins against AWA World Champion Verne Gagne, his series of matches with Bruno Sammartino in the World Wide Wrestling Federation (WWWF; the precursor to WWF), and his win over Thesz for the NWA World Championship.

- **Going independent:** Kiniski wrestled even into the 1990s for the independent promotion West Four Wrestling Alliance (WFWA), teaming with Sudden Impact (future Hall of Famers Lance Storm and Chris Jericho) against "Bulldog" Bob Brown, Jerry Morrow, and "The Natural" (Don Callis, a manager for All Elite Wrestling [AEW] at the time of writing).

Although Kiniski dabbled in acting, his passion was always professional wrestling, and his charisma and work ethic earned him more than two dozen championships throughout his career.

Abdullah The Butcher

Lawrence Robert Shreve, who used the ring name Abdullah The Butcher, was born in Windsor, Ontario, on January 11, 1941. Shreve was an amateur martial artist, learning judo and karate as a kid. Jack Britton, a promoter in Windsor, got wind of the large athlete and gave Shreve his first break in professional wrestling.

Abdullah's claim to fame was his love of bleeding and violence (he once remarked that his favorite hold in wrestling involved using a fork — really, a piece of cutlery seemingly jabbed into an opponent). His forehead was a roadmap of scars running every which way, but mostly from back to front and so deep that he could stick coins inside them.

His hardcore wrestling style led to some of the bloodiest and most gruesome matches on several continents, against the likes of The Sheik, the Funk family, Carlos Colon, Giant Baba, and Dusty Rhodes (all of whom had something in common — they loved to bleed). Abdullah won championships in multiple promotions, across various countries and regions:

- **Japan:** All Japan Pro-Wrestling (AJPW)
- **United States:** Georgia Championship Wrestling (GCW) and the NWA
- **Canada:** Stampede Wrestling (see the section "Stampede Wrestling" earlier in this chapter)
- **Puerto Rico:** World Wrestling Council (WWC)

Because of his wrestling persona (in his storylines, he didn't speak English), he needed a manager. A who's who of greats fulfilled that role, from Gary Hart to Paul Jones to J.J. Dillon — and even Ed "Bearcat" Wright. Many wrestlers, from Mick Foley in the 1990s to Nick Gage today, took inspiration from the "Madman from Sudan."

TECHNICAL STUFF

As a sidenote, your co-author Bryan Alvarez once interviewed Abdullah in person for a *shoot interview* DVD (meaning an interview that exposes things from behind the curtain). We met at his home and later visited his famous Abdullah The Butcher's House of Ribs restaurant near his home in Atlanta. Abdullah, unlike his horrifying "Madman from Sudan" persona, was very sweet and gracious with his time.

"Rowdy" Roddy Piper

The man who would become one of the best talkers in the history of professional wrestling, Roderick George Toombs (better known by his ring name "Rowdy" Roddy Piper), was born in Saskatoon, Saskatchewan, on April 17, 1954.

WARNING

Piper said that a troubled childhood led him to run away from home at around 12 or 13 years old (although Piper told many versions of his life story throughout his career, and some aspects were flat-out made up). He worked at local gyms by running errands for athletes. Starting as an amateur boxer in his early teens, Toombs pivoted to professional wrestling in 1969 when he began training under wrestler and promoter Al Tomko.

Although his first major exposure was in the AWA, Piper became a marquee attraction in the NWA Hollywood Wrestling promotion and the Pacific Northwest territory promotion.

REMEMBER

His time in WWF made "Rowdy" Roddy Piper a household name. Piper became regularly involved in the most high-profile angles for the most high-profile promotion in North America:

- **Piper's Pit:** *Heat magnet segments* (meant to get Piper mega-booed as a bad guy) that set up numerous momentous feuds, such as his legendary sit-down with Bruno Sammartino.
- ***WrestleMania:*** Matches and angles involving luminaries such as Hulk Hogan, superstar actor Mr. T, and even pop singer Cyndi Lauper when she was one of the biggest stars in the world.

During his run in the WWF and later World Championship Wrestling (WCW), Piper also dipped his toe in the acting pool. He appeared in several movies, most notably the 1988 cult classic sci-fi film *They Live.*

Although he may never have been the WWF World Champion, he is one of the most memorable performers to have ever worked for the company.

Bret Hart

Few wrestlers did more to legitimize professional wrestling as a sport than Bret "The Hitman" Hart. Hart was born in Calgary, Alberta, on July 2, 1957. He was one of 12 siblings, which meant he also had a small hand in his father's pro wrestling business, handing out fliers for events that Stu Hart promoted (see the section "Stampede Wrestling" earlier in this chapter, for more about dad's business).

Bret Hart's pro wrestling career took many turns, putting him on a journey through several territories across multiple countries:

- **Starting out in Texas:** Interestingly, Hart didn't train as a wrestler with his family; instead, he trained in Texas and had his first match with Dennis Stamp.
- **Wrestling for Stampede:** He returned to Calgary and had his first match for the family business, Stampede Wrestling, in 1978. The wrestler scheduled for the card didn't show up, so Stu asked Bret to step into the ring as the replacement (interestingly, a lot of wrestling careers began as last-minute substitutions).
- **Training with Japanese wrestlers:** His matches against talent from Japan, such as Kazuo Sakurada and Mr. Ito, led to Hart becoming a student of theirs, which added to his repertoire.
- **Running with the WWF:** He then had a 13-year run with the WWF, seeing much success as a tag team wrestler with his brother-in-law Jim "The Anvil" Neidhart, as well as in factions such as The Hart Foundation with another brother-in-law, the "British Bulldog" Davey Boy Smith, and his brother Owen Hart (one of the most gifted and underrated performers in wrestling history, according to fans and journalists).

  WARNING

  Bret was a multiple-time champion, but one of those world championships was at the center of the most infamous incident of the 1990s and one of the most famous finishes of all time, the Montreal Screwjob (which we talk about in Chapter 6).
- **Getting hurt at the WCW:** After leaving the WWF, Bret had a short run in World Championship Wrestling (WCW), which ended when multiple concussions made it impossible for him to continue wrestling.

He also had success outside of the ring, appearing on TV shows such as *The Simpsons* and *Mad TV*.

Many wrestlers in the current era cite Bret Hart as their biggest influence. And many modern-day fans see him as the most iconic Canadian professional wrestler of all time — although long-time wrestling historians would give that honor to "Whipper" Billy Watson (see the following section).

"Whipper" Billy Watson

TIP

If you don't focus on only recent wrestlers, the most famous and beloved wrestler to ever come out of Canada was "Whipper" Billy Watson, whose real name was William John Potts. Born in East York, Ontario, Canada, on July 25, 1917, Watson was both a beloved professional wrestler inside the ring and a beloved human being outside of it. He:

- Worked with numerous charities designed to help both handicapped kids and adults (including Easterseals, a nonprofit that helps the disabled, seniors, and veterans)
- Lent his name (for a fee) to everything from barbells to soda pop
- Was inducted into the Ontario Sports Hall of Fame in 1995
- Was named the number-one wrestler in Canadian history by historian Greg Oliver
- Had a school named after him, W.J. Watson Public School, in Keswick, Ontario.

In the ring, he was a multi-time World Champion, once beating the great Lou Thesz, and did years of incredible business through his feud with Gene Kiniski. Watson was the babyface to Kiniski's heel, the greatest Canadian rivalry of all time (according to outlets such as the *Pro Wrestling Post*), which spanned the late 1950s through the mid-1960s.

His career ended in 1971 after he was hit by a car and almost had to have his leg amputated. The injury caused him to balloon up to 350 pounds, which ultimately led him to shift focus in his charitable work to include weight loss. He died in 1990 and remains a celebrated figure to this day.

5

Meeting the Superstars of Yesterday and Today

IN THIS PART . . .

Appreciate the top wrestlers of all time — what they did and how they impacted professional wrestling.

Stand in awe of the greatest bookers and managers in the business.

Find out more about some of the top matches throughout history.

IN THIS CHAPTER

» Meeting the most important promoters in pro wrestling

» Identifying some other non-wrestling Hall of Famers

Chapter 12

Supporting Wrestling Outside the Ring

A ton of thankless work goes into professional wrestling behind the scenes. From the *bookers* (the people who determine the match results) to the *ring crew* (the backstage staff that assembles the ring before a show and breaks it down after) to the camera operators, everyone has a role to play. But professional wrestling as we know it today wouldn't exist without promoters.

As we note in Chapter 4, pro wrestling had its Wild West days during, in fact, the actual Wild West; and the transition to the modern pro wrestling business kicked off with the Gold Dust Trio in the 1920s. Those three promoters — Ed "Strangler" Lewis, Joseph "Toots" Mondt, and Billy Sandow — worked together to develop most of the concepts used today in pro wrestling, from longer-term storylines that feature contracted wrestlers to traditional booking concepts and storylines designed to sell tickets to events.

Throughout the next 100 years, many Hall of Fame promoters built their companies from the ground up. Others acquired them through savvy business dealings. This chapter highlights some of the most successful wrestling promoters, as well as some other notable non-wrestlers in the pro wrestling business. Chapter 10 highlights Japanese promoters who were as well known or better known as wrestlers, such as Antonio Inoki and Giant Baba.

Naming the Hall of Fame Promoters

Running the business side or the creative side of the wrestling business is a thankless and, seemingly, never-ending job. Booking venues, managing and scouting talent, marketing, and dealing with the financials were all tasks that very few were able to successfully juggle. The following sections identify a handful of the most notable promoters.

Wrestling with the McMahon family

If you use the word *dynasty* to describe one family in professional wrestling, you're probably talking about the McMahons. However, that story doesn't start with the Vince McMahon most modern fans think of. McMahon, Jr. — or, as he was often called by other promoters, Junior (a moniker he hated) — was actually a third-generation promoter, following in the footsteps of both his father and grandfather.

Laying the foundation: The elder McMahons

Jess McMahon was a boxing, wrestling, and concert promoter whose son Vince James McMahon was born in Harlem, New York, on July 6, 1914. Vince McMahon (yet to get his "Senior" status) got his start working for his father in promotions.

In 1952, "Toots" Mondt, one of the most influential men in wrestling history, and McMahon, Sr., took control of New York City wrestling, forming the Capitol Wrestling Corporation (CWC), the precursor to the WWWF (World Wide Wrestling Federation, which lost the "Wide" when Junior took over, which we talk about in Chapter 6).

TIP

McMahon, Sr., was generally regarded as a fair promoter:

- **Sharing income:** He often split the *gates* (revenue from ticket sales) with the wrestlers.
- **Playing fair:** As often happened in the mid-20th century, he had handshake deals with other promotions and territories to not *raid rosters* (lure wrestlers from other promotions) or try to put each other out of business.
- **Staying out of the ring:** He didn't want the bookers and promoters to become part of the show.
- **Sticking to wrestling:** He felt that the wrestlers should stick to their trade to maintain *kayfabe* (see Chapter 2) and avoid entering other forms of entertainment, such as movies.

Riding the McMahon, Jr., rollercoaster

Because Vince McMahon, Sr., and Victoria Elizabeth Hanner divorced very early in his life, Vince McMahon, Jr. never even met his father until he was 12 years old. When he did get to spend time with Senior, he was entranced by professional wrestling and was soon accompanying his father to events.

His father didn't like the idea of his son becoming a wrestler himself, and in 1969, Vince, Jr., made his debut as the company's ring announcer. Although he maintained the humble public-facing jobs of ring announcer and commentator, behind the scenes, his power continued to grow, and soon he was helping to promote cities.

Shortly before his death, McMahon, Sr., sold the company to his son, who proceeded to pay back his father with company profits. After Senior died, Junior literally did everything that his father had frowned upon:

- He invaded other territories and stole their talent.
- He pushed hard for his wrestlers to get involved in outside projects to boost their mainstream appeal.
- He made himself not only a professional wrestler at the age of 50 but also booked himself to win the World Wrestling Federation (WWF) Championship.

REMEMBER

McMahon, Jr., wanted to make pro wrestling an expansive entertainment empire with the following tactics:

- Cross-promoted to get wrestlers visibility in as much other media as possible. One example of this is Sgt. Slaughter appearing as a character in the cartoon *G.I. Joe*.
- Referred to his wrestlers as superstars
- Called pro wrestling itself *sports entertainment* (a name that didn't stick, despite his pushing it for decades — as far as we know, no one has ever asked a friend whether they watched the "sports entertainment" last night)
- Marketed T-shirts, action figures, title belts, teddy bears, and everything you can imagine (including ice cream bars!), which sold by the millions
- Created the event known as *WrestleMania,* by far the biggest wrestling event every year for the better part of four decades

During his reign as head of the company, Vince's wife, Linda McMahon, became president and CEO. His son Shane and his daughter Stephanie both became on-screen characters (and occasional wrestlers!) and also worked behind the scenes.

In the aftermath of the legendary *Survivor Series 1997* event finish called the Montreal Screwjob (see Chapter 6) and in the lead-up to the company's transformation into the publicly traded World Wrestling Entertainment (WWE; a name change after the World Wildlife Fund brought a lawsuit — check out the whole crazy story in Chapter 7), McMahon became a primary antagonist on WWE programming.

Evaluating the failings

WARNING

For all the success Vince McMahon, Jr., brought to WWE, he had just as many failures. He was constantly mired in controversy:

- **Rumors of covering up illegal activities:** In one case, a murder by WWF wrestler Jimmy Snuka in the 1980s.
- **Steroid trials:** He was exonerated after being indicted for allegedly being part of the conspiracy to distribute steroids to his performers, although solely because of a jurisdictional issue.
- **The ring boy sex scandal:** Accusations that certain employees in the WWF groomed and sexually abused teenage boys. Knowledge of this surfaced in the 1990s (and is still in litigation at the time of writing).
- **Multiple sexual assault allegations:** Multiple women accused him of sexual assault allegations, first in the 1980s through the 2020s.

Exiting the ring

McMahon, Jr., ultimately fell out of favor with the WWE Board of Directors because of allegations of sexual trafficking and assault by former employee Janel Grant:

- In April 2022, the Board began investigating McMahon over an alleged $3 million hush-money payment (one of many, it turned out), and McMahon announced his retirement.
- Six months later, McMahon pulled a power play and returned to facilitate a sale of WWE to TKO Group Holdings, which he hoped would guarantee him a job for life because it was assumed that he'd be kept on in some creative capacity (CEO Ari Emanuel also promised him he'd help him deal with his ongoing legal issues).
- After the sale went through, Grant filed a lawsuit. The final straw was when the WWE lost sponsorship from the Slim Jim brand (a long-time sponsor forever associated with wrestler "Macho Man" Randy Savage) because of the lawsuit accusations.

REMEMBER

- McMahon stepped down from the TKO Board of Directors the following day (in reality, the Board ousted him), ending the decades-long run of McMahons running the biggest wrestling company in history. (But the decades-long run of Slim Jim sponsorship was saved because they immediately returned after McMahon left).

Vince, Linda, Stephanie, and Shane all departed WWE by 2024. But Stephanie's husband, Paul Levesque (who wrestled under the ring name Triple H), maintains the Vince McMahon role in the TKO-owned WWE as far as being the head of creative decisions with the company.

Creating Tony Khan's All Elite Wrestling

Tony Khan, a business executive — and the son of a man who owns an American football team (the Jacksonville Jaguars) and a British soccer team (Fulham Football Club) — grew up a fan of pro wrestling from the 1980s and 1990s. Growing up in Champaign, Illinois, he spent much of his youth online trolling fans during his junior high years on message boards, most famously `deathvalleydriver.com`, which started as an ezine and tape trading hub, and evolved to a popular wrestling message board. As an adult, when the timing, money, and business partners all aligned, he started a pro wrestling promotion, All Elite Wrestling (AEW).

In 2018, Khan saw an opportunity for a second major national wrestling promotion when the pro wrestling juggernaut WWE began seeing double-digit year-over-year business declines. (Check out Chapter 6 for the WWE's story.) Khan felt the time was right and, with the financial backing of his father, he launched AEW in January 2019:

- **Big stars:** Khan built AEW on the backs of Nick and Matt Jackson (The Young Bucks), Kenny Omega, Cody Rhodes, (these four competed just prior in Ring of Honor and New Japan Pro Wrestling and were the founding fathers of AEW) and its biggest star of the original era, a star who worked in Extreme Championship Wrestling (ECW), World Championship Wrestling (WCW), and the WWE, Chris Jericho.
- **Big deals:** AEW quickly signed a deal with Turner Network Television (TNT) — the old home of WCW, the only promotion in history to beat then-World Wrestling Federation (WWF) in business in the 1990s (you can find the whole story in Chapter 6). AEW's first weekly wrestling show, *Dynamite,* was an immediate success.
- **Big records:** Since its debut, AEW has broken several records, including the largest verified legitimate paid attendance for a pro wrestling show in history (*All In* at Wembley Stadium in 2023, with 81,035 paid fans in attendance).

TIP

With the launch of AEW, the pay structure for pro wrestlers changed drastically for the first time in 20 years. Because of competition between WWE and AEW, wrestlers could command much higher contracts for far fewer dates than ever before. AEW almost never ran live untelevised events, and WWE soon essentially eliminated non-televised house shows, as well.

In 2024, AEW and the mass media giant Warner Brothers Discovery (WBD) signed a multi-year television deal valued at more than $185 million per year, making AEW in just five years the second most successful wrestling promotion to ever exist.

Promoting in the 1800s — Harry Hill

Harry Hill, who was born in Epsom, England in 1827, worked as a jockey and a horse trainer, and he wrestled. He continued wrestling when he came to the United States in 1852 and was one of the first American Collar & Elbow Champions (a belt won by champions who compete in an older traditional form of Irish wrestling) of the Civil War era. But among those who know his name, he was most importantly the first true promoter of professional wrestling matches.

In Manhattan, New York, Hill converted a grocery store into Harry Hill's Variety Theatre.

TIP

Hill, with his background in horseracing and betting, began promoting prize fights, both boxing and wrestling, at his saloon on a regular basis (people buy more liquor when they're watching fights, he discovered). He was soon drawing a very eclectic crowd to the fights, spectators from every class, all the way up through New York politicians.

Hill made significant money as a boxing and wrestling promoter, and at one point, rumors floated around that his worth was between 500,000 and 1 million dollars (the equivalent of 32 million dollars today; although Hill always claimed his real worth was half that value). He promoted matches amongst some of the biggest wrestling names of the period, including William Muldoon and John McMahon, and fights between the biggest boxing stars of the era, including John L. Sullivan and Nell Saunders (the first female boxing champion).

REMEMBER

Harry Hill's Variety Theatre was literally the birthplace of organized professional wrestling in the United States. In 1880, Hill expanded out of the saloon and promoted the Muldoon versus Thiebaud Bauer match, which drew 4,000 spectators to Madison Square Garden. Hill at his peak was one of the most well-known sportsmen in the United States.

HARRY HILL FALLS ON HARD TIMES

In 1886, everything went south for Harry Hill. He accused two police officers of extortion, saying that they forced him to pay hundreds of dollars per week for protection, and after those accusations, a New York State Senate committee ruled that Harry Hill's Variety Theatre had to close at 1 a.m., a big change from remaining open until sunrise as they did previously. This schedule change drastically hurt business because most of the action happened between midnight and dawn.

Hill eventually shut the theatre down in 1886 because of money losses. Hill's other investments went south because of mismanagement, and he largely lost his fortune. In 1890, he used what little he had left to open a hotel, which burned down three years later.

He was stricken with illness in the summer of 1896, and not only passed away, but largely passed out of history.

Creating the world's oldest pro wrestling promotion: The Lutteroth family

The Mexican promotion *Consejo Mundial de Lucha Libre* (CMLL; World Wrestling Council), founded as *Empresa Mexicana de Lucha Libre* (EMLL; Wrestling Enterprise of Mexico) by Salvador Lutteroth in 1933, remains the oldest still-existing professional wrestling promotion in the world, and still remains hugely popular. See Chapter 9 for more information on Lutteroth.

Watching Antonio Peña start AAA

Antonio Peña, the wunderkind behind Lucha Libre AAA (originally *Asistencia, Asesoría y Administración de Espectáculos;* which translates to Assistance, Consulting, and Management of Entertainment Events), was born in Mexico City, Mexico, on June 13, 1951. In Chapter 9, we go into detail about his history in the ring and in the creative chair.

REMEMBER

Peña's legacy survives today in a style of wrestling that dates back to the mid-1990s, when many of his top stars — smaller, high-flying *luchadores* (Mexican wrestlers) like Rey Mysterio Jr., Juventud Guerrero, La Parka, and Psicosis — left for the United States. They first went to ECW, then to WCW, and in the case of Mysterio, finally to WWE. (We talk about these big U.S. promotions in Chapter 7.) You can trace the roots of the lighter-weight high-speed, high-flying, spectacular dive-oriented style of modern promotions such as Ring of Honor, Total Nonstop Action (TNA), AEW, and even sometimes WWE, in part to Peña's vision.

In 2025, WWE acquired AAA after remaining in the Peña family since its inception through a partnership with Mexican sports and entertainment holding company, Fillip (WWE owns 51 percent and Fillip owns 49 percent). WWE announced a media rights deal with Fox Corporation in Mexico later that year, leading to a weekly one-hour television show that features AAA and WWE wrestlers.

Noting the Crockett family

Long before Ted Turner bought Jim Crockett Promotions (JCP) to use as the foundation to build WCW, which we talk about in Chapter 5, the Crocketts carved out a respectable corner of the professional wrestling landscape.

Jim Crockett, Sr., born in Bristol, Virginia, on June 2, 1908, was a wrestling fan from his youth, watching stars such as Ed "Strangler" Lewis. Crockett became a wrestling promoter in his mid-20s, building a strong territory in the Carolinas that he called Jim Crockett Promotions. Under the promotion's Eastern States Championship Wrestling (ESCW) banner, Crockett became one of the most influential members of the National Wrestling Alliance (NWA).

When Jim, Sr., died in 1973, his son Jim Crockett, Jr., inherited Senior's assets. Junior took over the day-to-day operations of JCP and eventually served as the NWA's president on three separate occasions. ESCW was newly christened Mid-Atlantic Championship Wrestling. Jim Jr.'s brother, David, became an in-ring competitor and later a commentator with the company.

The then-WWF under Vince McMahon, Jr., (see the section "Riding the McMahon, Jr., rollercoaster" earlier in this chapter) began its national expansion in the 1980s, scooping up talent and killing territories left and right. Crockett, one of the only people able to aggressively compete against McMahon, acquired:

- Mid-South Wrestling (accounting for Arkansas, Louisiana, Mississippi, and Oklahoma)
- The Florida, Georgia, Kansas City, and St. Louis territories

WARNING

This rapid expansion soon backfired. Increased spending, combined with McMahon's predatory tactics, had JCP on its deathbed by 1988. Ultimately, Crockett sold JCP to Turner Broadcasting in November of that year for $9 million, paving the way for WCW's rise to power in the mid-1990s.

REMEMBER

The Crockett family was the first to battle the behemoth now known as WWE on an even footing, and their successor, WCW, was the first promotion in history to beat McMahon at his own game. Although the Crocketts ultimately flamed out, WCW would remain the most successful number-two promotion in America until the rise of AEW in the 2020s.

Noting Professional Wrestling's Non-Wrestlers

When casual fans think of professional wrestling, they almost always first name an actual wrestler. Sometimes they may even mention a promoter. Very rarely does a casual viewer bring up a manager, or a commentator. Nevertheless, those roles are some of the most vital parts of the presentation of professional wrestling and the shows would suffer without them. The following sections look at a few non-wrestlers and their impact on professional wrestling.

A BRIEF HISTORY OF TV BROADCASTING IN PROFESSIONAL WRESTLING

Although *studio wrestling shows* (events broadcast from a small-time local television studio) date back to 1942, professional wrestling exploded onto the scene in 1948 when the Dumont Television Network decided to broadcast shows. Dumont gave wrestling wide exposure in the Northeast at a time when television was beginning to become commonplace in the United States. By the early 1950s, every major national network aired a pro wrestling show — both more and less impressive than it sounds because the United States had only three major national stations at the time, but if you owned a television in 1954, you couldn't easily avoid running into professional wrestling on it. During this first golden era of televised pro wrestling, stars such as Gorgeous George (who had his extravagant robes and Georgie pins) became household names.

Early pioneers of wrestling commentary included Jack Brickhouse (we're astounded nobody has stolen that for a wrestling name), Dennis James, and Ray Morgan. Morgan did commentary for shows promoted by Vince McMahon, Sr., up through the early 1970s. When McMahon, Sr., relocated his television operations from Washington, D.C., to Hamburg, Pennsylvania, instead of raising Morgan's salary because of the drive involved, McMahon, Sr., replaced Morgan with a new commentator — his son, Vince McMahon, Jr.

From the late 1950s through the mid-1980s, most wrestling territories gained some sort of local television outlet. Often, the person calling the action worked at the television station, also doing news or weather. Other times, the promoter himself would call the action.

Announcing the bouts — Commentators

The *commentators* (who fans usually call the *announcers*) call the action of the event on TV. (A *ring announcer* is someone different — it's the person who stands in the middle of the ring before the match and introduces the participants and who announces the winner when the match is over.) The following sections examine what characteristics are important for a commentator to be exemplary and recognizes who some of the greatest of all time are.

Understanding what makes a great commentator

A commentator needs to not just call the action in the ring: A great one possesses the most important characteristic — credibility — when it comes to selling the product to the viewer. Here are several traits that make a great commentator:

- **Engagement:** They engage the viewer, tell the story of who the wrestlers are, why they're wrestling each other, the ramifications of the match, the history of the wrestlers, and more.
- **Sales:** They convince you to buy tickets to the next house show or pay-per-view (PPV) event because you see them as credible. A commentator needs to express seemingly genuine delight when something great happens, or outrage or disgust when a heel does something dastardly. Without credibility, an announcer just becomes a talking head in the background of a show.
- **Storytelling:** They attempt to make each match meaningful. Not only do they explain what's happening in a story, why it happened, and where it might go in the future, they also give details about events during the match, identifying a move, explaining the execution, and detailing how it affected the opponent.

REMEMBER

Vince McMahon, Jr., who did commentary for his own promotion, World Wrestling Federation (WWF), from the 1970s through the 1990s, succeeded at the story aspect (he himself created all the storylines). But, for the most part, he had absolutely no idea how to call a match, and would constantly shout only, "What a devastating maneuver!"

Naming some of the greatest commentators

Some of the greatest commentators of all time include the following:

- **Howard Finkle:** Ring announcing legend whose mannerisms and trademark lines — including, "And still!" — continue to be used by other ring announcers to this day
- **Jimmy Lennon:** Los Angeles territory ring announcer during its heyday in the mid-20th century

RECOGNIZING JIM ROSS'S MANY ROLES

Few people in this chapter have worn more hats than James William Ross, born January 3, 1952. Though he was born in Fort Bragg, California, he grew up in Westville, Oklahoma. In his youth, Ross involved himself in everything from baseball and football to agriculture and politics. He dipped his toe into the world of professional wrestling as a referee with the Universal Wrestling Federation (UWF).

Ross found his calling in professional wrestling as a broadcaster. He has a resume featuring work with the UWF, Mid-South Wrestling, JCP, WCW, Smoky Mountain Wrestling, WWE, New Japan Pro Wrestling, and AEW. During his career, he also served as the:

- Head of Broadcasting and part of the booking committee in WCW (from 1991 to 1993)
- Head of Talent Relations in WWE (from 1997 to 2004)
- English commentator for New Japan's weekly broadcast (from 2015 to 2018)

Ross has faced battles both internal (multiple bouts of *Bell's palsy*) and external (accusations of racism, which he vehemently denies). For all of his feats and all of his foibles, Ross has worked harder than nearly anyone in both backstage and on-screen roles and stands as one of the greatest voices in the history of professional wrestling.

REMEMBER

- **Alfonso Morales:** An announcer for the Mexican promotions *Consejo Mundial de Lucha Libre* (CMLL) and *Asistencia, Asesoría y Administración de Espectáculos* (AAA), who was so good that many fans loved his commentary, even if they didn't understand Spanish
- **Gene Okerlund:** WWF icon of the 1980s; one of the greatest interviewers of all time, who sometimes would literally do the promos for the wrestlers because he could do a better job
- **Lance Russell:** The voice of the promotion Memphis Wrestling for decades, including the peak period in the 1970s when it regularly drew 11,000 fans weekly to the Mid-South Coliseum in Memphis, Tennessee
- **Jim Ross:** The voice of the *Attitude Era* (mid-to-late 1990s); see the nearby sidebar
- **Gordon Solie:** All-time legend of the promotions National Wrestling Alliance (NWA) and WCW; see the nearby sidebar for more on Solie
- **Kent Walton:** Host of the TV show *World of Sport* in the United Kingdom from the 1950s through the 1980s.

HAVING GORDON SOLIE CALL THE MATCHES

REMEMBER

Though he's gone by many names throughout his life (including Francis Jonard Labiak and Jonard Pierre), the name *Gordon Solie* commands immediate attention and respect from longtime wrestling fans.

Born in Minneapolis, Minnesota, on January 29, 1929, Solie got into radio production at a very early age, working at it in high school. After a stint in the military and a move to Tampa, Florida, Solie began his career as a broadcaster — in stock car racing. Shortly thereafter, he pivoted to professional wrestling, where he began as a ring announcer while also picking the brains of great bookers and promoters such as Eddie Graham.

Solie earned the respect of many in the pro wrestling world through many traits he exhibited (largely due to his more serious journalistic approach to the sport):

- **Showing respect:** Solie's grounded and respectful commentary earned him the nickname "The Dean." Solie was so respectful of the business that he had wrestlers legitimately put submission holds on him backstage so that when he was calling the action, he could explain to the audience how those holds felt.
- **Working the territories:** He called matches in some of the most prolific territories, including Championship Wrestling from Florida (CWF), Georgia Championship Wrestling (GCW), Continental Wrestling Federation (also CWF), and USA Championship Wrestling (USACW), to name a few.
- **Elevating the stars:** His commentary elevated matches with top stars such as Dory Funk Jr. and Dusty Rhodes to must-see status.

Solie was a great voice whose career and later life were sadly taken by throat cancer. He passed away on July 27, 2000, at the age of 71.

Authority figures — in and out of the ring

Every professional wrestling promotion has someone who's in charge of the business (usually the owner) and someone in charge of the make-believe universe of professional wrestling. The *business authority figure* and *show authority figure* can sometimes be the same person, or they can be different people. See the sidebar "Taking on both roles of authority" in this chapter for examples of how adopting both roles can work for or against a promotion.

Doing business

The owner of any wrestling company is the real-life authority figure. Sometimes the owner is an individual. Tony Khan today owns AEW. He makes all the final decisions and also is in charge of all the storytelling; what he says goes.

In some cases, the owner assigns someone else to oversee the operation. For example, Ted Turner and Turner Broadcasting owned WCW from 1998 through its demise in 2001, but Turner himself never really had much to do with the day-to-day operations of the company. He hired one person after another to be the boss — most famously Eric Bischoff, who both rocketed WCW to its greatest success, and also was instrumental in crashing it into oblivion shortly thereafter. (We talk about the history of WCW in Chapter 6.)

Today, TKO Group Holdings owns WWE, and Endeavor is TKO's parent company. The head of Endeavor is Ari Emanuel, and even though he could make the final call in anything involving WWE, he doesn't have a hand in the day-to-day operations. WWE employs hundreds of people, and currently Nick Khan (no relation to Tony Khan) and Paul Levesque (former wrestler Triple H) are the President and Chief Content Officer and make most of the final business decisions.

Assuming the authority figure persona

In a pro wrestling storyline, the *authority figure* is someone in charge of making matches, putting together *cards* (who is wrestling who), and laying down the law. They go by many names — president, general manager, director of authority, or simply the boss. Usually a former wrestler takes on the boss persona on television. Among the things an authority figure must do include the following:

- **Setting up retaliation matches:** Determining the proper format in which to avenge a storyline slight. For example, if Swerve Strickland attacks Kenny Omega during an interview at the AEW *Dynamite* event, someone must rule that they have to face off in a one-on-one match at next month's PPV event.
- **Handing out suspensions:** When a storyline has a wrestler do something against the rules. If Bron Breakker starts throwing things around ringside in a fit of rage and accidentally (supposedly) injures one of the commentators, someone must rule that he gets suspended for 30 days.

TAKING ON BOTH ROLES OF AUTHORITY

When people take on both authority figure roles — acting as both the real-life boss and on-screen boss — you get mixed results. This concept worked for Vince McMahon, Jr., in WWF in the late 1990s. He went from being an on-screen commentator (while everyone knew he was the boss of the business) to the actual on-screen boss, the heel McMahon. At the time, "Stone Cold" Steve Austin was rising to superstardom, and the McMahon versus Austin feud — evil boss versus working man — was one of the most successful programs in WWF history.

McMahon could play both roles because he had assembled a team that could handle the day-to-day operations of the company, including a booking team responsible for putting together the storylines. Everyone else did all of the legwork, and then he simply had to either approve the plans or suggest changes. It was a very taxing job, but he pulled it off.

Eric Bischoff, however, couldn't juggle both roles as the head of WCW. Even though he also had a team that helped him with booking, he still considered himself the boss of the business — everything needed to go through him. As a person who watched every episode of *Monday Nitro* from its debut in 1995 through its season finale in 2001 twice, co-author Bryan Alvarez can state that the quality of the television show declined dramatically right around the time that Bischoff made himself an on-screen heel character. His attention shifted from creating the best TV product possible to worrying more about his own storylines on television; at that point, things slowly began to unravel for WCW.

Identifying the most famous authority figures

McMahon is, by far, the most famous authority figure in wrestling history. His daughter Stephanie, his wife Linda, and his son Shane also played the role in the late 90s and early 2000s. WWE also placed numerous wrestlers and non-wrestlers in the role over the years. Famous wrestling authority figures included Roddy Piper, Shawn Michaels, Mick Foley, William Regal, and Ric Flair. Non-wrestling authority figures included Teddy Long (former manager), and Vickie Guerrero (the late Eddy Guerrero's wife). Today, Adam Pearce and Nick Aldis are the GMs of *RAW* and *SmackDown* respectively. Interestingly, both had long wrestling careers, but never in WWE.

WCW's on-screen authority figures were mostly storyline, former wrestlers such as Nick Bockwinkel, JJ Dillon, Terry Funk, Ric Flair, Sting, and Kevin Nash. But sometimes, whoever was booking at the time would also essentially play the role, as was the case with Bischoff, Vince Russo, and to a much smaller degree Jim Herd, Bill Watts, and Bill Busch.

AEW's authority figures are all the real-life authority figures. The main on-screen boss is the real-life boss, Tony Khan. Kenny Omega, the Young Bucks, and Cody Rhodes all had executive vice president titles in real life, and those carried on into TV storylines as well.

Outside of Dixie Carter, who was president of TNA when her father's Panda Energy owned the company, most of the on-screen TNA authority figures have been purely storyline, including Don Callis, Vince Russo, Dusty Rhodes, and Santino Marella.

Handling wrestlers' affairs — Managers

Managers manage the affairs of their wrestlers and are on-screen characters. With a few exceptions (perhaps the most famous being Miss Elizabeth for Randy Savage), most managers are heels.

Laying out what a manager does

The manager had a multifaceted role in pro wrestling:

REMEMBER

- **Creating characters:** One of the most important aspects of professional wrestling is the ability to cut a promo. Bland, boring wrestlers generally don't make it too far in this business. A wrestler needs to be able to get their personality across through their verbal abilities, the way they connect to the fans during interviews, the way they trash-talk their rival ahead of their next big match. But realistically, not everyone has the gift of gab. In that case, the manager handles the hype.

  REMEMBER

  The greatest managers in history were also among the best promoters and most colorful characters.

- **Generating heat:** A manager needs to *generate heat* (rile up the crowd). Managers interfere in matches to cost the babyface the win. Sometimes, they hit the babyface with a weapon behind the referee's back or pass a weapon to the heel. Using a manager also helps protect the babyface from being seen as weak during a loss because not only did they get cheated, but they got cheated two-on-one.

- **Taking bumps:** Managers have to know how to take *bumps* (falls) because, in the end, the manager usually gets foiled in some way. Sometimes, the babyface just gets in a clean shot. Other times, the manager gets forced into a match with a wrestler. Some managers take a bump on every show. Others bump very infrequently, so when the time finally comes for them to get their comeuppance, it becomes more meaningful.

Recognizing some of the greatest managers

Some of the greatest managers include:

- **Bobby "The Brain" Heenan:** A former wrestler who also played the role of heel commentator for years alongside Gorilla Monsoon and others (see the nearby sidebar for more about Heenan).
- **Jim Cornette:** One of the greatest managers in history, as well as a former promoter and booker.
- **Paul Heyman:** Owned and promoted ECW when that promotion helped redefine the business in the 1990s. Still one of the greatest managers in wrestling today, most notably as the advocate for Brock Lesnar and Roman Reigns during WWE's recent boom period.
- **Jimmy Hart:** Hulk Hogan's long-time manager, a living cartoon character that fit in perfectly in the 1980s. Hart, like Paul Ellering with the Road Warriors, was also one of the rare managers who actually worked as a legitimate real-life business manager for his clients.
- **"Classy" Freddie Blassie:** A multi-time WWA Heavyweight Champion before becoming a manager.
- **"Captain" Lou Albano:** Also a former wrestler, whose pairing with Cyndi Lauper helped explode the WWF into the mainstream in the early 1980s (refer to Chapter 16 for more on Lauper).

DOING IT ALL WITH BOBBY HEENAN

Although a number of people find success as a professional wrestler, others as a wrestling manager, and still others as a great commentator, only a rarified few make a prolific career doing all three: And Raymond Louis Heenan, known as Bobby "The Brain" Heenan, was one of them. Heenan was born in Chicago, Illinois, on November 1, 1944, and started wrestling in 1965. His career took many turns, taking him from a pretty boy rookie to one of the greatest managers and commentators of all time:

- **Wrestling:** He never received formal wrestling training but got his first bookings in the Indianapolis, Indiana territory. Although he wrestled well, his physical comedy, microphone skills, and (most importantly) his ability to draw heat led him to become a manager as well.
- **Managing:** Working as a manager, Heenan helped elevate to stardom wrestlers such as Blackjack Lanza in the World Wrestling Association (WWA), Nick Bockwinkel and "The Crippler" Ray Stevens in the American Wrestling Association (AWA), Ernie Ladd in Georgia Championship Wrestling (GCW), and a veritable who's who in the WWF, such as André the Giant, Big John Studd, Paul Orndorff, Mr. Perfect, and Rick Rude. His biggest managerial fame came in WWF as the perennial heel manager always trying to get one over on WWF Champion Hulk Hogan (refer to Chapter 6 for more on Hogan).
- **Commentating:** Not too long after the first *WrestleMania* event in 1985, Heenan transitioned again, this time to the role of color commentator, a role he excelled at for nine years in the WWF, then six more years in WCW.

He made sporadic appearances in the 2000s until his health began to decline following a throat cancer diagnosis. He ultimately lost that battle in 2017. Heenan is subjectively (and many circles say, objectively) the greatest wrestling manager of all time.

IN THIS CHAPTER

» Being awed by some of the greatest matches of all time

» Discovering who was elevated to superstardom

» Marveling at the promotions putting on these stellar matches

Chapter 13
Emphasizing the Most Memorable Wrestling Encounters

Professional wrestling has many moving parts and components that help it stay a well-oiled machine that's been functioning for a century. One of the key components that makes wrestling work is *the big fight* — the long-awaited confrontation between two rivals.

In the same way that characters, gimmicks, and storylines can transcend and memorably stand the test of time, individual matches can also leave an indelible mark on fans and on the sport in general. When athleticism, intensity, psychology, and technical prowess all coalesce to create an elite-level match, magic happens. This chapter identifies some examples of matches that have helped make professional wrestling what it is.

Exploring Some of the Greatest One-on-One Matches

The most famous matches in history have been *one-on-one matches* — two wrestlers facing off to determine who is the best, often with a major championship at stake. Here we discuss a few.

Switching sides: A Canadian Hitman and a Texas rattlesnake

The term "double turn" hadn't been something ingrained in the audience's minds yet. That being said, seeing a hated bad guy gaining sympathy from the audience, while a beloved hero turns to the dark side, can make for absolute cinema in the ring.

Straight-laced family man and national hero Bret "The Hitman" Hart and the beer-swilling, foul-mouthed anti-authority figure "Stone Cold" Steve Austin couldn't be more different. That dichotomy provided the core of a feud which culminated at:

- **Event:** *WrestleMania XIII*
- **Venue:** Rosemont Horizon arena
- **Location:** Rosemont, Illinois
- **Date:** March 23, 1997

The technical savant, Hart, seemed like he would have the edge against the brawler, Austin, given that this would be a *submission match* (the only way to win is to make your opponent tap out). Former UFC fighter and then-current WWF performer, "The World's Most Dangerous Man," Ken Shamrock, acted as the guest referee to keep both competitors in line:

- **Austin rides high:** Austin won the 1996 King of the Ring tournament that gives a career boost to the winner, and since that win was coming closer and closer to becoming the top heel act in the company.

WARNING

- **Hart recuperates:** Hart, however, was on hiatus during much of 1996, recovering from a knee injury and contemplating his future with the company. Austin saw this as the perfect opportunity to get some heat by taunting Hart.

The two met in the ring several times leading up to the *WrestleMania XIII* match:

- At *Survivor Series* at the end of 1996, Hart emerged the victor over Austin.
- They confronted each other again at the *Royal Rumble* in January 1996, where, because of a referee's distraction, Austin eliminated Hart.
- A title match at *In Your House 23: Final Four* between Hart and Sycho Sid led to interference by Austin, causing Hart to lose the match.

Because this submission match was also *no disqualification* (anything goes), the wrestlers could use chairs, ring steps, basically any weapons they wanted to:

- Like with many "Stone Cold" matches during this period, Austin attacked Hart during his entrance to the ring.
- Ever the tactical genius, Hart launched Austin into the guardrail, making him bleed. Hart then worked over Austin's leg, setting up his submission finisher, the Sharpshooter.
- When Hart locked in the submission, a bloody and battered Austin scratched and clawed the mat, screaming while he refused to tap out.

REMEMBER

Something interesting occurred during this spot: The crowd began to boo Hart and cheer Austin. The men recognized the fans' vibe and committed to following the crowd's lead, with Hart acting more villainous and Austin trying to overcome all odds like a hero.

Austin finally passed out due to blood loss (part of the storyline) giving Hart the victory. The match gave both wrestlers new directions for their careers:

- **Going to heel:** Hart went on to become the top heel in the company, rebuilding his former tag team, the Hart Foundation, as a Canadian heel faction.
- **Cleaning up:** Austin became one of the highest-grossing babyface acts in the history of professional wrestling.

Watching the Ungovernable defeat the Ace

Hiroshi Tanahashi remained at the top of the card for much of his run in New Japan Pro-Wrestling (NJPW). He was as much the face of NJPW as John Cena was for WWE. Many people tried to knock him off from his top spot. Very few accomplished this. Yet one match at the 2017 G1 Climax proved that one other had Tanahashi's number.

The most intense tournament in all of professional wrestling is the G1 Climax from NJPW, which lasts for several weeks, with the winner earning a shot at the World Title at New Japan's biggest show of the year, January's *Wrestle Kingdom*:

- **Event:** G1 Climax rubber match
- **Venue:** Ryogoku Kokugikan stadium
- **Location:** Tokyo
- **Date:** August 11, 2017

REMEMBER

No two competitors could be more opposite than the fan favorite top babyface in New Japan, the "Ace" Tanahashi, and the aloof leader of the heel faction *Los Ingobernables de Japon* (The Ungovernables of Japan), Tetsuya Naito.

These two competitors met several times after this match, but it remains possibly their greatest encounter because of the intensity of the match, the elevation of a new top star, and the fact that it stood out at the G1, an event which any given year may have 25 "match of the year" candidates. The match opened with a deliberate and methodical pace by the two men, which made sense given their many prior encounters:

- **Showing no respect:** The cool and collected Naito, who usually slaps his opponents in the face (and sometimes spits at them), had to deal with back-to-back slaps from Tanahashi.
- **Causing injury:** A *chop* (open handed strike to the chest) exchange led to Naito focusing his offense on his opponent's arm and bicep, making Tanahashi rely on the chop less.

While the match escalated, they attempted big moves:

- **Trying neckbreakers:** Tanahashi countered Naito's *spinning neckbreake*r (a throw or slam focusing on the opponent's neck) with his own Twist and Shout neckbreaker.
- **Working the injury:** Naito then countered a *crossbody* (a maneuver in which a wrestler jumps onto his opponent and lands horizontally across the opponent's torso) by delivering a *dropkick* (leaping into a double footed kick to the chest) to Tanahashi's shoulder. Every time Tanahashi tried to build up a head of steam (a somersault senton wrestler leaps forward, performs a 360-degree front flip, and lands back-first across a laid out opponent, for example), Naito would evade it and go back to working over Tanahashi's injury.

WARNING

At one point, while Naito was on the floor outside the ring, Tanahashi delivered his *frog splash finisher* (wrestler leaps from the top turnbuckle, extends their body horizontally, and tucks their arms and legs in just before crashing down onto a grounded opponent), called the high fly flow, doing more damage to his own arm in the process.

- **Going for finishers:** After a flurry of elbows to each other, Naito attempted his finisher known as the Destino (a move where you slam your opponent's head into the mat). He hit one Destino and went for the pin, but Tanahashi *kicked out* (he got his shoulder up).
- **Pitting a finisher against a neckbreaker:** After Tanahashi connected with three twist and shouts against Naito, Naito countered a fourth one by performing a second Destino. He picked up Tanahashi and hit a third one for good measure.

Because of that well-timed counter, Naito picked up the pinfall victory over Tanahashi.

Going to the extreme

In a *rubber match* (the final match of a tied series), the hard-hitting Bryan Danielson (Ring of Honor World Champion, meaning the top champion in the company) and the technical wizard Nigel McGuinness (Ring of Honor Pure Champion, which was the top belt within the Pure division of Ring of Honor) had a feud throughout 2006 to see who was truly the best:

- At Ring of Honor (ROH)'s *Weekend of Champions* event in April of that year, the men competed in a title unification match that ended with McGuinness winning by countout, meaning no titles changed hands.
- Their next encounter was in July at ROH *Generation Now,* with only Danielson's title on the line, where the champion prevailed.

The rematch that fans clamored for as they wanted to see two technical wizards once again do battle:

- **Event:** *ROH Unified*
- **Venue:** Liverpool Olympia
- **Location:** Liverpool, England
- **Date:** August 12, 2006

The match, a *Pure rules* bout, meant:

- Each wrestler could use only three *rope breaks* (grab the ropes) to break submission holds.
- Opponents couldn't throw closed-fist punches to the face.
- The title could change hands on a disqualification (DQ) or countout.
- ROH would fire anyone interfering in the match.
- If the match ended in a draw, a panel of three judges would determine the winner.

This bout had to be one of the hardest-hitting matches under Pure rules in ROH's history:

- The wrestlers started with a feeling-out process early in the match, exchanging twisting each other's arms, *back elbows* (rear strikes with elbow to opponent's head), and *European uppercuts* (an upper forearm strike to opponent's chest or chin).
- Because McGuinness was the hometown hero, Danielson was more than happy to play the heel. For example, he teased a *surfboard stretch* (trapping the opponent's legs and pulling back on their arms while shoving their foot into the opponent's back), but then just stomped McGuinness's knees.
- Danielson dropped McGuinness onto a table, then stood on his opponent's throat, choking McGuinness to the point he was bleeding from the mouth. The men then headbutted each other so hard that it was difficult to believe the bout was still a work.
- Danielson attempted his submission finisher, the *Cattle Mutilation* (which involved a grounded bridging double chicken wing submission) several times, but McGuinness countered each time.
- Danielson then hit McGuinness repeatedly with his elbows. McGuinness had a massive shiner and was effectively knocked out, prompting the referee to stop the match and award the victory to Danielson.

Putting a mask on the line

When Mexican wrestling, lucha libre, first made waves in the United States in the mid-1990s, it had a rabid cult-like audience. Unfortunately, the only semi-national exposure to lucha libre in the United States came from the relatively small Extreme Championship Wrestling (ECW).

TIP

Then along came World Championship Wrestling (WCW) in 1988, a promotion that, unlike the World Wrestling Federation (WWF), sought to provide a large platform for Mexican *luchadores* (wrestlers) to ply their trade. Climbing the ranks of the cruiserweight division were the ever-calculating heel Eddie Guerrero and the masked super-heroic babyface Rey Mysterio, Jr.

Guerrero refused to give Mysterio a title shot unless Mysterio put something on the line — one of the most sacred possessions to a *luchador*, his mask. Mysterio agreed, so WCW booked a mask-versus-title match:

- **Event:** *Halloween Havoc*
- **Venue:** MGM Grand Garden Arena
- **Location:** Paradise, Nevada
- **Date:** October 26, 1997

This was a grudge match to see who the top *luchador* in WCW was:

- Despite all of Guerrero's bragging in the early moments of the match about ripping Mysterio's mask off, Mysterio tossed him around with lucha-style *arm drags* (hooks opponent's arm and flips them over and onto the mat), *monkey flips* (using feet to catapult opponent overhead and behind them), and a *flying crossbody* (hitting your opponent with your body), which launched Guerrero out of the ring.
- Guerrero pulled Mysterio off the apron and slammed his back into the ring stairs. Heading back into the ring, Guerrero began to focus on Mysterio's back and ribs, hitting a *tilt-a-whirl backbreaker* (spinning opponent in mid-air before dropping them, spine first, onto the attacker's knee) and locking in an *abdominal stretch* (a submission move that stretches the opponent's torso and obliques).
- Mysterio attempted to counter, but Guerrero seamlessly transitioned into a *pumphandle backbreaker* (hook opponent's arm behind their back, lift them upside down, and slam their back onto the attacker's knee) and then tried a *camel clutch submission* (a back stretch); however, his repeated attempts to rip off Mysterio's mask allowed the challenger to make comeback after comeback.
- The opponents unleashed punches and kicks to each other in the corner of the ring, which led to Mysterio getting hung in a *tree of woe position* (a wrestler hung upside down).

- Guerrero attempted a *baseball slide* (sliding dropkick), but Mysterio dodged, causing the champion to slide his crotch into the ring post.
- Mysterio proceeded to unleash a flurry of aerial maneuvers, from *corkscrew moonsaults* (twisting version of the moonsault where a wrestler backflips from the top rope, landing on an opponent) to *springboard moonsaults* (a flip off the ropes), and even attempted his finisher, a *springboard huracanrana pin* (leaping onto opponent's shoulders and performing a backflip to send the opponent reeling).
- Guerrero countered and catapulted Mysterio to the top rope, looking to hit his signature *avalanche sitout crucifix powerbomb* (a slam high on the shoulders) that he called Splash Mountain.
- In one of the coolest-looking reversals in wrestling history, Mysterio countered into a huracanrana pin, where he got the pinfall and won the WCW Cruiserweight Championship.

REMEMBER

Perfecting the Three-Way Match

A *three-way match* is one where three wrestlers compete in one match that typically has no countouts or disqualifications. The phenomenon really took off in the United States in the 1990s and has become a fixture of modern professional wrestling.

The following sections identify some of the best three-way matches in professional wrestling. Everyone from ECW (Taz versus Mike Awesome versus Masato Tanaka at 1999's *Anarchy Rulz* event) to WWE (Kurt Angle versus "The Rock" versus The Undertaker at 2002's *Unforgiven* event) delivered great attempts, but TNA's was, for lack of a better word, phenomenal.

Defending against two challengers

One of the most memorable three-way matches pitted the champion, "The Fallen Angel" Christopher Daniels against both AJ Styles and Samoa Joe. Although pro wrestling had three-way matches long before the creation of the promotion Total Nonstop Action (TNA), some argue that TNA perfected the formula.

In this particular match, the champion, Daniels, had to defend his title against both wrestlers:

- **Event:** *Unbreakable* pay-per-view
- **Venue:** Impact Zone (soundstage at Universal Studios)
- **Location:** Orlando, Florida
- **Date:** September 11, 2005

TIP

In a tournament that acted as a lead-up to the match, Daniels interfered in the finals between Joe and Styles. So living legend, retired wrestler and commentator, Larry Zbyszko, who was a member of the Championship Committee, determined that Daniels had to defend his title against both Joe and Styles.

These three competitors put on a match that would serve as the blueprint for future triple-threat matches:

- **Doing the most damage:** From the opening of the championship match, Joe and Styles attempted to one-up each other by beating the tar out of Daniels, taking turns delivering escalating intensity football kicks to his spine.
- **Using enemies against each other:** After an aerial assault by Styles, Daniels sought to use each of his opponents' momentum against the other, causing some impressively planned spots that allowed the "Fallen Angel" to escape his opponents' wrath.
- **Dodging defeat:** Whenever Joe or Styles was finally on the verge of defeating Daniels, the other opponent intervened to prevent the attacker from following up with a pin attempt. For example, Joe had Daniels in a *Coquina clutch submission* (otherwise referred to as a rear naked choke, where one wraps their arms around their opponent's neck from behind to force a submission), but Styles attacked Joe to break up the hold. And when Styles was about to hit Daniels with a *superplex* (suplex off the top rope), Joe struck them both.
- **Ending with a pin:** The finish of the match saw Daniels take possession of the X Division Title belt and kick it into Joe's head, then pivot to hit Styles with the *Angel's Wings,* the name for Daniel's *double underhook facebuster* (locking opponent's arms behind their back and slamming their face into the mat). Styles countered with a *bridging pin* (wrestler arches their body and drives opponent's shoulders to the mat).

Styles won the X Division Championship for the fifth time.

Watching three women go at it

What happens when two powerhouse contenders have a heated feud and underestimate a smaller, but faster and more experienced champion? That is a story that unfolded at *WrestleMania 41:*

» **Event:** *WrestleMania 41*

» **Venue:** Allegiant Stadium

» **Location:** Paradise, Nevada

» **Date:** April 20, 2025

On Night 2 of *WrestleMania 41*, female wrestlers Bianca Belair, Rhea Ripley, and Iyo Sky faced each other in a triple-threat match, the winner of which would walk out as the WWE Women's World Champion.

The feud leading up to their championship bout saw heated exchanges between the two powerhouses, Belair and Ripley, with the smaller Sky feeling slighted because she was the Women's World Champion, but she felt like both competitors were overlooking her. Interference during contract signings and disqualifications in matches meant there was no clear dominant winner of this feud.

Despite the strength of Belair and Ripley, as well as the speed of Sky, this was truly anyone's match to win:

» Sky brought the offense early, delivering a *double blockbuster* (front flip from the top rope, catching opponents mid-flip and slamming them neck first into the mat) to both of her opponents.

» After Sky hit Ripley with a *moonsault* (refer to the section "Putting a mask on the line" earlier in this chapter for a definition), and then Belair hit her with a *clothesline* (spinning her opponent and then using their arm to strike them across the chest), Sky went for the pinfall but couldn't successfully pin Ripley.

» As the fight got out of control and spilled out of the ring, Belair hurled Ripley and Sky into the security barrier.

» Ripley later lifted Sky for a *crucifix bomb* (an attacker lifting the opponent overhead with their arms spread and drops them onto the mat), slammed her onto Belair, and went for the pinfall on both, but Sky and Belair kicked out.

» Nearly every time Sky attempted a top rope move and one of her opponents went up to stop her, the third participant hit them both with a big move.

» Belair proved that she can hang in the air with the best of them by delivering a *450 splash* (front flipping splash from the top rope) to Sky.

- For several minutes, whenever one woman went for her finisher, the opponent the move is being put on would counter it.
- Belair finally nailed Ripley with her finisher, the Kiss of Death (KOD), which involved a *torture rack* (carrying opponent on their shoulders), and then transitioning into an *Argentine facebuster* (face planting them down onto the mat).
- Sky then hit Belair with her moonsault finisher, getting the pinfall victory and overcoming huge odds to retain her championship.

Wrestling with Multiple Opponents — The Battle Royal

The *battle royal*, a match where dozens of wrestlers are all inside the ring at the same time and the last person not thrown over the top rope to the outside wins, is so famous that the term is used by non-wrestling fans for any wild brawl. The following discusses a couple classics.

Getting lessons in Aztec Warfare

When Lucha Underground aired their first *Aztec Warfare* event during season one, they presented a completely unique version of the battle royal. However, it being the first, there was room after to improve upon. The creative team learned and utilized the second *Aztec Warfare* to not only push several character storylines forward, but to also debut a new monster bad guy to the fold.

Aztec Warfare II is one of the best *battle royal* (multi-person matches, usually with a stipulation involved where wrestlers have to throw opponents over the top rope to eliminate them) matches ever put together:

- **Event:** *Aztec Warfare II*
- **Venue:** Lucha Underground Temple arena
- **Location:** Boyle Heights section of Los Angeles
- **Date:** March 23, 2016

REMEMBER

This event addressed several feuds and storylines based on lucha libre, Mexican wrestling where masked *luchadores* (wrestlers) take to the skies to do battle (refer to Chapter 9 for more details). Lucha Underground also used a *telenovela* (Mexican soap opera) approach to storylines, where supernatural elements felt like a natural part of the narrative.

Aztec Warfare II was beyond entertaining. Here's just a snapshot of what happened:

- **Falling down the stairs:** The *rudo* (the bad guy persona) *luchador* known as Drago tossed the high-flying *técnico* (good guy) Jack Evans down a flight of stairs.
- **Going flying:** King Cuerno (who had a big game hunter persona) tried to prove to the acrobatic Fenix that he was a superior high-flier to Fenix by hitting Cuerno's spear, called the Arrow from the Depths of Hell, through the ropes, sending Fenix into the first row of fans.
- **Showing off:** The large, laid-back star known as Mack and the cyborg muscle-bound machine known as Cage tried to one-up each other to prove who was the best big athlete, capable of performing aerial moves in the same way that the legit *luchadores* do.

Furthermore, the match included three huge debuts:

- **Dragon Azteca:** The young and hungry high-flying *luchador*
- **Matanza:** Translates as *Slaughter;* the huge masked monster difficult to defeat
- **Rey Mysterio Jr.:** Possibly the most recognizable new addition, a former WCW and WWE superstar (flip to Chapter 9 for more about Mysterio and Chapter 7 for the details on these promotions)

The battle was unpredictable and chaotic, yet still *well-booked* (meaning logical from a storyline standpoint). Matanza eliminated nine people in his debut and went on to win the match and the prized Lucha Underground Championship in the process.

Tag teaming, Japanese style

The year 1987 featured hundreds of matches that you could consider unique. Yet one featuring a pair of literal teen idols going up against a pair of the hardest hitting women in professional wrestling at the time, would make for arguably one of the best matches of that year.

Tag team wrestling is an art that doesn't get the respect it deserves, which goes double for women's tag team wrestling. But during a period in the mid-1980s, the promotion All Japan went out of its way to showcase two women's tag teams that had massive international exposure, including wrestling for the WWF:

- **Event:** *All Japan's Tag League: The Best*
- **Venue:** Osaka-jo Hall
- **Location:** Osaka, Japan
- **Date:** September 14, 1987

The team the Crush Gals (Chigusa Nagayo and Lioness Asuka) went to war with the Jumping Bomb Angels (Itsuki Yamazaki and Noriyo Tateno):

- Yamazaki was on the defensive early, trying to evade *roundhouse kicks* (semicircular kick to the head) and *short-arm clotheslines* (see the "Watching three women go at it" section earlier in this chapter for a definition of clothesline) from Nagayo, who then *tagged in* (refer to Chapter 2) Asuka, and they nailed Yamazaki with a double-team sandwich clothesline.
- Tateno tagged in and evaded much of Asuka's and Nagayo's offense. The Angels fired back with *double-team dropkicks* (refer to the section "Watching the Ungovernable defeat the Ace" earlier in this chapter for a definition of dropkick). However, Yamazaki couldn't get a three-count with her pin attempt on Nagayo.
- She then worked a headlock on Nagayo, followed by a *hammerlock* (pulling opponent's arm behind their back and bending it). Nagayo fought out of it.
- Nevertheless, Yamazaki used her momentum to put Nagayo in a pinning predicament, but Nagayo kicked out.
- Tateno tagged in and dropped an elbow from the top rope, followed by repeated elbows to Nagayo's back. Nagayo attempted to counter into an *armbar* (grabbing hold of opponent's arm and hyperextending their elbow), but Yamazaki quickly tagged in and cut her off.
- Nagayo caught Tateno with a *kneebreaker* (lifting opponent and dropping their knee onto her own) and made the tag to Asuka.
- Asuka went to town on Yamazaki with a clothesline from the top rope.
- When Asuka attempted to pin Yamazaki, Yamazaki got her foot on the bottom rope at the *referee's one-count,* which means the person pinning their opponent must release the pin.
- Asuka picked her opponent up for a big swing, spinning Yamazaki around nine times before dropping her and going for the pin, but her attempt at pinning Yamazaki resulted in Yamazaki kicking out at the count of two.

» In the end, Yamazaki nailed Nagayo with a *diving headbutt* (falling from the top rope and headbutting opponent), allowing Tateno to hit a *big splash* (jumping from the top rope and landing horizontally across her opponent) and get the pinfall victory for the Jumping Bomb Angels.

Exploring Series Wrestling

Very rarely is a gigantic match only wrestled one time. Rematches happen every day in professional wrestling around the world. As we discuss here, sometimes, a series of matches can become legendary.

Battling for New Japan's World Title

The mid- to late 2010s saw a resurgence in the popularity of promotion New Japan Pro-Wrestling (NJPW). The roster was bursting at the seams with star power. The World Title picture was as loaded as it had been in years, with several major names jockeying for the top spot.

REMEMBER

Two younger talents climbing the rankings battled each other for the International Wrestling Grand Prix (IWGP, the governing body of New Japan Pro-Wrestling) World Heavyweight Championship in a feud that ran throughout 2017 and 2018:

» **Kazuchika Okada:** Nicknamed "The Rainmaker." The pretty-boy member of the babyface Chaos faction.

» **Kenny Omega:** Nicknamed "The Cleaner." The leader of the heel Bullet Club.

Omega won the 2016 G1 Climax Tournament, earning himself a title shot against Okada for the IWGP World Heavyweight Championship.

The following sections discuss the four matches in which these two battled over the next 18 months, many of those were for the top belt in New Japan Pro-Wrestling.

Going for the title

The first match:

» **Event:** *Wrestle Kingdom XI*

» **Venue:** Tokyo Dome stadium

- **Location:** Tokyo
- **Date:** January 4, 2017

This was the first championship bout between Okada and Omega, a championship match that many have been itching to see. In the end Okada got the win and retained his title.

Fighting for Dominion

The second fight between Okada and Omega:

- **Event:** *Dominion*
- **Venue:** Osaka-jo Hall arena
- **Location:** Osaka, Japan
- **Date:** June 11, 2017

Wrestling fans had been waiting for this rematch, and they weren't disappointed (depending on how the finish of the match sat with them): After a long battle, the bout ended in a draw.

Proving Omega's ability

Their next encounter wouldn't feature the title on the line, but would be an important one nonetheless as Omega would show why he still deserves to be in the World Title picture:

- **Event:** 2017 G1 Climax
- **Venue:** Ryogoku Kokugikan arena
- **Location:** Tokyo
- **Date:** August 12, 2017

This bout, held on Day 18 of the G1 Climax, was a non-title tournament match. Despite not competing for the title in this match, the men fought hard. Omega connected with the One-Winged Angel and then covered Okada for the one, two, and three.

TIP

Omega now proved that he could beat Okada.

The last fight

One last match for the richest prize in NJPW, and one that is on many wrestling pundits' lists for greatest matches of all time:

- **Event:** *IWGP World Heavyweight Championship at NJPW Dominion*
- **Arena:** Osaka-jo Hall arena
- **Location:** Osaka, Japan
- **Date:** June 9, 2018

The final confrontation was a *best-two-out-of-three-falls match* (a series of three matches in one night, where the winner would be the first to get two victories), and nearly one year had passed since their most recent battle. Because of the title match format, Omega wasn't as aggressive in the early part of the match as he was last time. In the end though Omega won, reaching the top of the mountain and was crowned the new IWGP World Heavyweight Champion.

REMEMBER

This feud still rages on at the time of writing, but the quadrilogy of matches these men had in NJPW is an epic tale worth revisiting again and again.

Following the Flair/Steamboat trilogy

Lumping a series of matches together may seem odd to the casual wrestling fan. But in 1989, the National Wrestling Alliance (NWA) territories' trilogy of matches between the humble family man Ricky Steamboat and the ostentatious "dirtiest player in the game," Ric Flair, told a complete and compelling story that chronicled their feud over the NWA World Heavyweight Championship, which Flair held at the start of the first match. In the following sections, we look at what stands out about these three matches.

Changing champions

The first match between the two megastars set the scene for a multiple-match series:

- **Event:** *The Chi-Town Rumble*
- **Venue:** UIC Pavilion arena
- **Location:** Chicago, Illinois
- **Date:** February 20, 1989

In this match, Ricky Steamboat became the new NWA World Heavyweight Champion.

Putting an asterisk by this victory

Steamboat and Flair's second match was a best-two-out-of-three falls match, meaning that to win, the wrestler had to secure two pinfalls:

- **Event:** *Clash of the Champions*
- **Venue:** Superdome stadium
- **Location:** New Orleans, Louisiana
- **Date:** April 2, 1989

Flair did his level best to get into the head of his opponent, but Steamboat didn't lose his focus. In the end Steamboat once again locked in the chicken wing, leading to Flair tapping out again, ending the match.

But Steamboat's victory came with a caveat because Flair's leg was under the ropes, (means the person applying the hold has to release it); yet the referee didn't see that positioning, so he didn't force the champion to break the hold, per the rules.

Reclaiming a title

The final match of this trilogy:

- **Event:** *WrestleWar '89*
- **Venue:** Nashville Municipal Auditorium
- **Location:** Nashville, Tennessee
- **Date:** May 7, 1989

Flair got the pinfall victory and won back the NWA World Heavyweight Championship.

6
The Part of Tens

IN THIS PART . . .

Examine the pro wrestling events that had the biggest audiences.

Probe some impactful pro wrestling moments.

Look at times when celebrities got into the ring.

IN THIS CHAPTER

» Finding the pro wrestling matches that made TV-viewing history

» Seeing which matches drew the biggest crowds

Chapter 14
Ten of the Most Watched Matches of All Time

In the annals of professional wrestling history, certain moments created stars, and those stars created moments. These moments happened not only with crowds of spectators live in the arena, but also with millions of viewers watching remotely.

This chapter looks at some of the most-watched matches in wrestling history around the world. This list isn't a traditional ranked top-ten list because no one has all the records to definitively identify the ten most-watched matches worldwide in order. Furthermore, televised matches always have more viewers than non-televised matches, and television has changed dramatically since it first started appearing in homes in the 1940s.

So, in this chapter, we break down our discussion into ten of the most-watched matches in different categories — TV and otherwise.

The argument that only a small handful of fans are into wrestling tends to get numerous holes poked into it when you see the massive drawing power of many of its top stars around the world. And the massive shows that we talk about in this chapter occurred throughout the decades, from the 1950s to the 2020s. Professional wrestling, in some shape or form, always has an audience.

The Most-Watched Match in U.S. History

The most-watched match in U.S. history (at the time of writing) was Hulk Hogan versus André the Giant on February 5, 1988, from Market Square Arena in Indianapolis, Indiana. The World Wrestling Federation (WWF) was so hot in the 1980s that they aired a show several times a year in place of *Saturday Night Live.* Yes, NBC pre-empted *Saturday Night Live* for professional wrestling. This particular match actually aired on a Friday (so the producers branded it *The Main Event*, not *Saturday Night's Main Event*).

REMEMBER

This 1988 Hogan-versus-André match was actually a rematch of the famous 1987 *WrestleMania III* pay-per-view main event, a main event which the WWF made some (less-than-factual) claims:

- **Hogan slammed André for the first time in André's career.** In fact, other wrestlers had slammed André many times in his career.
- **The event occurred in front of 93,173 fans.** The WWF made up this number for entertainment purposes.
- **Hogan pinned André, ending André's 15-year undefeated streak.** Opponents had pinned André many times all over the world in the prior decade.

Their rematch on *The Main Event* drew an astounding 26.64 million viewers (often reported erroneously as 33 million by World Wrestling Entertainment — WWE — you can probably see the issue with keeping records in professional wrestling) and a 15.2 share. (A *share* means that of all the TVs turned on in the entire United States at that moment, that percentage of them — 15.2 percent — had this match on.)

When you think of that number today, a period where a great episode of WWE's second flagship show, *SmackDown* might get 1.5 million viewers, 26.64 million seems like a gigantic number. And it was. But *The Main Event* wasn't even close to the most-watched show on TV that evening — that honor went to *Dallas* on CBS.

Do you want to know what happened in *The Main Event?* Buckle up. For the finish, André gave Hogan a quite frankly horrific *sloppy suplex* (he kind of threw him), then fell on top of him. The referee dropped down to count, and Hogan raised his shoulder at the one count, which by wrestling rules meant that the referee should have stopped counting. But the ref continued counting, and when he reached three, he then rang the bell, signaling that André had won the match.

André immediately presented his newly won WWF World Championship belt (and therefore supposedly the championship itself) to Ted DiBiase. The storyline that the WWF created had DiBiase, known as the Million Dollar Man (a million dollars went a lot further in 1988), paying some fellow to have plastic surgery to make him look exactly like WWF referee Dave Hebner. This man then replaced Dave in order to screw Hogan out of the championship.

TIP

In real life, this fellow was actually Dave's identical twin brother, Earl Hebner, who had been working as a referee outside WWF. So an evil twin ultimately screwed Hogan out of a championship he had held for four years.

The storyline led to WWF President Jack Tunney ruling that one man can't give another man a championship; therefore, the WWF declared the belt vacant, and he arranged a tournament for *WrestleMania IV* to crown a new champion.

REMEMBER

Ironically, nine years later, Earl Hebner would actually deny Bret Hart the WWF Championship in what became known as the Montreal Screwjob, which we explain in Chapter 6.

The Most-Watched Match in Cable TV History

The absolute peak of U.S. cable TV viewership occurred on June 28, 1999, from the Charlotte Coliseum in Charlotte, North Carolina, when a WWF main event of "Stone Cold" Steve Austin versus the Undertaker drew a whopping 10.7 million viewers on USA Network.

By the 1990s, cable TV was widespread. Even though the networks still enjoyed ratings dominance, the top shows on cable were starting to draw big numbers. WWF and World Championship Wrestling (WCW) battled head-to-head every Monday night on the USA Network and TNT, respectively, from 1995 through WCW's crash-and-burn death in 2001 (see Chapter 7 for details about WCW's end).

For the first several years, WCW won handily. But from 1998 through 2001, WWF absolutely exploded in popularity, riding the wave of personalities such as Steve Austin, Vince McMahon, Dwayne "The Rock" Johnson, and others.

REMEMBER

If you consider the number of available television stations in 1999 and the total audience for the USA Network (about 75 million homes), not to mention the match itself aired outside of prime time (at approximately 11 p.m. Eastern Time), this is probably the most impressive rating for any match in U.S. history.

Austin won the match in the middle of the ring by using a *Stone Cold stunner* (his knockout finishing move to win the WWF Championship.

The Most-Watched Match in WCW History

The segment that popped the highest rating in the history of WCW came about in the most unorthodox of ways — with an apologetic re-airing. During the yearly WCW *Halloween Havoc* pay-per-view (PPV) event in 1998, WCW experienced some technical issues, to put it diplomatically.

The main-event match featured Diamond Dallas Page versus Bill Goldberg for the WCW World Heavyweight Championship. Unfortunately, in many markets, the PPV feed cut out during the match. In 1998, wrestling PPVs were three hours long (astonishing news to modern fans who sit through five-hour PPVs on a regular basis). WCW decided to run an extra half hour for *Halloween Havoc*. But they didn't alert the cable companies to the extended time needed, so right in the middle of the Page-versus-Goldberg match, 25 percent of the PPV buyers lost the feed. It just cut out.

Fans flooded the cable companies with complaints and demanded refunds. WCW, all in, lost more than a million dollars in refunds as a result. They also irritated the already-irritated cable companies further by airing the match in its entirety for free the following night on WCW's flagship show, *Monday Nitro* as an attempt to make good. The cable companies didn't want the match aired for free because they wanted to sell a Tuesday night replay.

Despite the disaster, the match airing for free on *Nitro* drew a 7.18 Nielsen rating, a brand new cable record. This viewership surpassed even the Bill Goldberg-versus-Hulk Hogan match that occurred at the Georgia Dome in Atlanta several months earlier. But this match was the very last time that WCW ever beat the WWF in the ratings war of the late 1990s.

The Most-Watched Match in U.K. History

The 1981 match between Big Daddy and his former tag team partner Giant Haystacks goes down as the most-watched match in British history and also holds the record for the worst match to ever draw a record number in professional wrestling history, lasting only a little more than 2 minutes.

Approximately 18 million television viewers watched the match, a ridiculously gigantic number given the entire population of the United Kingdom at the time was approximately 56 million (meaning 32 percent of the population tuned in).

The two wrestlers used to compete together as one of the most dominant and villainous tag teams in the U.K. wrestling scene. However, when Shirley Crabtree, Jr. (who went by Big Daddy) went *babyface* (good guy), his former tag team partner, Martin Austin Ruane (better known as Giant Haystacks), was none too pleased, leading to an intense rivalry that went on for several years.

Heat surrounding the feud reached fever pitch when they collided (literally — they ran into each other over and over) in their big match at the *Dale Martin Extravaganza,* which took place in Wembley Stadium on June 18, 1981. The bout included a *knock out stipulation* (meaning a wrestler could win only if they knocked out their opponent, not by getting a pinfall or submission).

The first 50 seconds consisted of both men grappling for position (basically, they were hugging). The two men knocked down the referee while they grappled, and Haystacks got some heat (getting the crowd to boo him). Big Daddy then made a comeback and knocked Haystacks out of the ring and through a ringside table, at which point the referee furiously counted to ten and declared Big Daddy the winner. The action was so fake and unbelievable that no one watching could possibly claim that professional wrestling was a legitimate sport.

TIP

If you want to watch it (which may be the only way that you can believe it), look for it on YouTube at `www.youtube.com/watch?v=9sDBd6-SGo4`.

The Highest Live Attendance for a Wrestling Event in Mexico

On April 30, 1993, Mexico's televised wrestling promotion *Asistencia Asesoría y Administración* (AAA, which translates as *Assistance, Consulting, and Administration*), only a year old at the time, held a monumental event, *TripleMania,* at Plaza de

Toros in Mexico City. This event featured matches between their most prolific stars:

- A six-person tag match included Octagon, *El Hijo del Santo* (Son of the Saint), and *Villano* (Villain) III going up against *Fuerza Guerrera* (Warrior Force), Heavy Metal, and Rambo.
- *Perro Aguayo* (Aguayo the Dog) faced Máscara del *Ano 2000* (Mask of the Year 2000; at the time, a futuristic gimmick) in a hair-versus-mask match (in which the loser lost either their mask — Máscara — or had to be shaved bald — Aquayo).
- *Cien Caras* (One Hundred Faces) and Konnan competed in the main event, a best-two-out-of-three-falls match, where the loser had to retire from AAA. Konnan lost the main event after he got into an altercation with former WWF star Jake "The Snake" Roberts at ringside and the referee counted him out of the ring.

The show drew more than 48,000 fans, which makes it the largest crowd of any modern show in Mexico as of this writing.

The Most-Attended Match

In 1995, a two-night professional wrestling event in North Korea drew a combined 315,000 people over those two nights.

WARNING

Although this event did sell tickets and make a lot of money (approximately $17 million combined over both days), the North Korean government used the shows as a propaganda event and ordered the vast majority of spectators to attend. (Rumors swirled around the show having *forced attendance*). Despite the lack of voluntary viewers, we list this event for no other reason than pro wrestling will probably never draw an in-person crowd that large again.

The event dubbed *Collision* was a combined World Championship Wrestling (WCW) and New Japan Pro-Wrestling event, taking place at the May Day Stadium in Pyongyang, North Korea on April 28 and 29, 1995. Antonio Inoki of New Japan, a legendary professional wrestler turned politician, wanted to improve relations between Japan and North Korea and came up with the idea of a wrestling event. The new Supreme Leader of North Korea, Kim Jong-il, agreed to the idea and said he would allow some foreign tourists to attend. Inoki met with Eric Bischoff of WCW, and they came up with a *card* (a list of matches on the show). Each night had its own headline match:

- **Night 1:** Scott Norton versus Shinya Hashimoto, which ended in a *time-limit draw* (nobody won before the time limit expired).
- **Night 2:** Antonio Inoki versus Ric Flair, with Inoki winning by using an *enzuigiri kick* (a martial arts kick) to the back of Flair's head.

The Most (Voluntarily) Attended Match

Despite the discrepancy about the number of people who attended the All Elite Wrestling (AEW) *All In London* at Wembley Stadium on August 27, 2023, the fact is it's the show that has verifiably the most tickets sold in pro wrestling history.

The number of tickets sold to this show is verifiable information — 81,035, and one wrestler on the show, Will Ospreay, was so happy to have been a part of the biggest show in wrestling history that he tattooed "81,035" onto his body.

However, a public records request to the Freedom of Information Office at the Brent Civic Centre revealed that the turnstile count for the show was 72,265. That's the actual number of humans who passed through a turnstile that day (although not the total number of humans in the building because many entered not through turnstiles).

For WWE fans angry that AEW had taken the world record attendance from them, this was a life-changing victory. If you go online today, in all the lists of legitimate all-time attendances, AEW is always several slots down from the top, given credit for 72,265 fans at Wembley.

Ospreay was quite disappointed when he heard this news. But luckily for Ospreay, the reality is that *All In* still holds the record.

REMEMBER

The fact is, whether you look at the turnstile count for pro wrestling, boxing, NASCAR, or a Taylor Swift concert, that count is always a good deal lower than the number of tickets sold. Why? Who knows. People buy tickets and something comes up, they can't sell them, they have a family emergency, it's pizza night at school, all sorts of things. No large-scale live event in history has had 100 percent of the people who bought tickets actually show up.

WARNING

So, those all-time lists sort all of the other wrestling events by tickets sold, but only AEW *All In* by the turnstile count. All of those other events would also have lower attendances if the numbers reflected legitimate turnstile counts. And ultimately, it doesn't matter. If 9,000 people didn't show up, fact is they still bought and paid for tickets.

The Most-Attended Show in WWE History

Many fans and pundits believe that the most-attended event in WWE history is *WrestleMania 32* (*WrestleMania XXX* was the last *Mania* that used Roman numerals), held on April 3, 2016, in Arlington Stadium, Arlington, Texas.

Why do we have to base this assessment on belief? Wrestling is an interesting thing. The matches are predetermined (or fake — however you want to phrase it), the characters are larger than life, and even the attendances are, as Vince McMahon once told journalist Dave Meltzer, "part of the entertainment portion of the event."

Yes, the WWE often invents or embellishes attendance numbers. For years, the most-attended show in wrestling history was allegedly *WrestleMania III* in 1987 (which we talk about in the section "The Most-Watched Match in U.S. History" earlier in this chapter). The claimed record attendance was 93,173. The World Wrestling Federation (WWF; the name was changed to WWE in 2002) alleged that *WrestleMania III* even drew more fans than the Pope.

TIP

But, as it turns out, the real number was approximately 78,000, as verified by event promoter Zane Bresloff. But mythology dies hard, and to this day, many fans refuse to believe that their childhood memories of an all-time attendance record weren't on the level.

Interestingly enough, WWF's *SummerSlam* from Wembley Stadium in 1992, which featured Bret Hart versus Davey Boy Smith, was actually the legitimate WWF attendance recordholder for years (78,927), but because the WWF lied about *WrestleMania III's* 93,173, that remained the official record.

WWE claimed 101,763 for Arlington Stadium in 2016, but the actual turnstile count as reported by the Arlington Police was 80,709. WWE basically claimed that more than 20,000 vendors, police, and so on, made up the rest of the number. (Those vendors undoubtedly sold a lot of hot dogs.) But the verified number was 80,709 and given that the verified number of tickets sold for All Elite Wrestling (AEW) *All In London 2023*, in Wembley, was slightly higher (which we discuss in the preceding section), without evidence to the contrary, *WrestleMania 32* still holds only the number-two spot on the all-time wrestling pay-per-view list.

REMEMBER

Some people say that WWE's turnstile count was much higher than AEW's turnstile count, and theoretically that proves that WWE actually sold more tickets to the event. They certainly could have sold more tickets. However, in 2023, when the news broke that AEW set the new all-time attendance record, WWE made no effort to provide any evidence to the contrary, any proof that any of their events (including *WrestleMania 32*) had, in fact, verifiably beaten *All In*. Had the WWE had that information available, they almost certainly would have released it. The fact that they didn't strongly suggests that they don't have it.

The Match That Almost an Entire Nation Watched

On November 7, 1977, in Seoul, South Korea, Giant Baba and Jumbo Tsuruta wrestled Kim Duk and Kintaro Oki in front of 31.8 million viewers. Although this South Korean match doesn't qualify as the most-watched match, it does stand as the match that the highest percentage of a country's population watched.

Professional wrestling was very popular in Korea in the 1960s and 1970s, basically considered to be the national sport (even though it was well-known by the mid-'60s and prior that pro wrestling was a show and amateur wrestling was real), and Koreans gathered in droves to watch televised matches. Oki at the time was considered a national hero, and this tag-team match was the pinnacle of his career.

Hogan versus André in *WrestleMania III* (which we talk about in the section "The Most-Watched Match in U.S. History" earlier in this chapter) drew 26.64 million viewers in 1988, at a time when the U.S. population was 244.5 million. Well, Baba and Tsuruta versus Duk and Oki drew 31.8 million viewers when South Korea's population was 36.4 million. In other words, 88 percent of the entire population of Korea watched this match live on TV, as compared to 11 percent of the U.S. tuning in to watch *WrestleMania III*.

The Most-Watched Match

The most-watched match of all time took place on May 24, 1963, from the Tokyo Gymnasium in Tokyo, Japan. Rikidōzan, also a national hero in Japan, faced "The Destroyer" Dick Beyer, in a match that drew 60 million viewers live on Japanese television.

The population of Japan was approximately 95.9 million at the time. Super Bowl LIX, in 2025, drew 128 million viewers in a country with a population of 340 million, meaning 37 percent of the country watched live. For Rikidōzan versus Lou Thesz, 64 percent of the country watched live. And that was in 1963, not 2025.

Rikidōzan had another record-breaking match several years earlier when he faced Thesz on October 6, 1957. That match actually drew a significantly larger television *share* (the percentage of TVs turned on at the moment that tuned into that broadcast), an 87.0, but because Japanese households had far more televisions in 1963, Rikidōzan versus Destroyer drew more total viewers. (Trivia note: One of the biggest reasons for the explosion of television sales in Japan between 1957 and 1963 was, in fact, consumers buying televisions to watch Rikidōzan matches.) Because of the splintering of television viewership, likely no match can ever come close to drawing a live audience this large ever again.

TIP

Both Rikidōzan matches ended in a 60-minute draw, one of the reasons for the gigantic viewership. Historically, the longer a match goes, the more people tune in to see the outcome. Chapter 10 discusses Rikidōzan in greater detail.

IN THIS CHAPTER

» Winning the crowd

» Breaking barriers (literally and figuratively)

» Moving on to bigger and better

» Sticking it to the man

Chapter 15
Ten Industry-Changing Promos

When two wrestlers meet in the ring, they show off skills that require grit, endurance, and determination. But mastering the physical side of professional wrestling (as far as having in-ring skill and a unique physical presence) represents only half of what it takes to succeed in the business. To truly be considered a star, a wrestler must be able to connect with the audience verbally.

Some of the most memorable names in the history of the business not only gave you the big fight at the big show, but they also could talk fans into the building, (get fans hyped up to see the big fight between two feuding wrestlers) so to speak.

Two vital attributes help ensure that a particular *promo* (the talking part of pro wrestling, often monologues) resonates with an audience:

- The timeliness of the subject matter
- The authenticity of its delivery

Many promos in professional wrestling are iconic, but the ten segments that we talk about in this chapter are ingrained in pro wrestling fandom's collective consciousness, not just for their quality, but also for how they changed the landscape of pro wrestling.

Dusty Rhodes' "Hard Times" Promo

On October 29, 1985, Mid-Atlantic Championship Wrestling welcomed back its premier babyface Dusty Rhodes, who had disappeared from the wrestling world for more than a month after a bad loss to the diabolical heels Arn and Ole Anderson, who acted as enforcers for the World Heavyweight Champion, the iconic "Nature Boy" himself, Ric Flair.

Flair was the personification of 1980s excess, the jet-flying, limousine-riding, Rolex-wearing, filthy rich World Champion. Rhodes played the role of the common man, the working class, jeans-wearing son of a plumber (although, ironically, he also sported a classic 1980s-era solid gold Rolex watch).

Rhodes had a lot to get off his chest following his return, and he delivered a promo that resonated not just with diehard wrestling fans, but also with the general audience. He attacked Flair's hedonistic persona, contrasting it with how the economy affected the poor and working class, focusing on:

- Economic issues
- Employment issues
- Working class struggle

Rhodes vowed to win Flair's World Heavyweight Title for the people.

TIP

When it comes to delivery, very few had the gift of gab that Rhodes possessed. When he decided to shoot from the hip, he did so with an intensity and cadence that made the promo feel truly authentic. Wrestling fans still remember this promo fondly as an all-time great monologue.

Ron Simmons, the First Black World Champion

Former football defensive tackle for the Florida State University Seminoles and the NFL's Cleveland Browns, Ron Simmons, pivoted from professional football to professional wrestling, working for World Championship Wrestling (WCW, which you can read about in Chapter 6) starting in 1987.

In 1992, his opportunity to shine unexpectedly appeared. Jake "The Snake" Roberts put Sting, the original number one contender against the World Heavyweight Champion Big Van Vader, out of action at the same event where Simmons won the title. So WCW held a raffle to pick who would face Vader, and Simmons won that raffle.

Simmons (see Figure 15-1) proceeded to challenge Vader for the most prized championship in all of WCW. On August 2, 1992, the two behemoth athletes faced off at a *house show* (meaning it wasn't televised) in Baltimore, Maryland. The incredibly physical confrontation ended with Simmons lifting the nearly 400-pound Vader, laying Vader out with a powerslam and getting the pinfall victory — and the WCW World Heavyweight Championship Title.

FIGURE 15-1: Ron Simmons (left) with Bruce Reed, the "Doom" tag team.

Photo by Wrealano@aol.com

REMEMBER

In a promo during an episode of *WCW Saturday Night* the following week, Simmons revealed that it was his dream to become the top star and world champion of WCW. What made Simmons's win so momentous was the fact that he was the first Black wrestler to become World Champion of any major televised wrestling promotion. Simmons was a trailblazer and, in that moment, helped pry open a door that seemed closed to non-white athletes in the top pro wrestling promotions.

Shane Douglas Ignites a Revolution

The National Wrestling Alliance (NWA) held a tournament to crown a new World Heavyweight Champion in 1994. Because Eastern Championship Wrestling (ECW) was the strongest promotion in the NWA, the NWA Board of Directors agreed that one of ECW's top wrestlers, Shane Douglas, would win the tournament and become the new champion — which he did on August 27, 1994.

WARNING

Douglas grabbed the microphone and unleashed an unscheduled and scathing indictment of the ECW and the NWA. He stated that he had no interest in a dead organization passing the torch to him.

But this promo was a legitimate double-cross: Douglas grabbed the microphone and began with a few flowery words, but then suddenly changed his tone and said, "They can all kiss my ass." He threw down his newly won NWA Championship belt and declared himself the "new ECW Heavyweight Champion of the world."

The NWA, obviously, was furious, and moved to strip Douglas of the championship. Tod Gordon, the head of ECW, then announced that ECW was being renamed *Extreme Championship Wrestling* and that Douglas was their first World Heavyweight Champion. The birth of the new ECW signaled the real beginning of the 1990s pro wrestling renaissance and eventually spawned World Wrestling Federation (WWF)'s Attitude Era, which you can read about in Chapter 6.

Austin 3:16 Catches Fire

In the 1996 World Wrestling Federation (WWF) *King of the Ring* finals, Steve Austin defeated Jake "The Snake" Roberts. After receiving the crown and scepter, and a microphone, Austin proceeded to mock the born-again Christian Roberts, saying his loss proved Jake just didn't have it anymore. In the middle of his promo, Austin threw in the line, "Talk about your Psalms, talk about your John 3:16. Austin 3:16 says 'I just whipped your ass'!"

The unplanned, off-the-cuff remark resonated with fans. Within a few weeks "Austin 3:16" signs began appearing in the crowd at WWF shows, and the momentum began to grow.

By 1998, the now "Stone Cold" Steve Austin became the single biggest star of the 1990s boom period (refer to Chapter 6), he sold out arena after arena, and moved record amounts of merchandise — much of it "Austin 3:16" T-shirts, of course.

Hulk Hogan: The NWO's Third Man

Two WWF wrestlers, Scott Hall and Kevin Nash, disrupted World Championship Wrestling (WCW) programming in 1996, drawing new TV viewers. Nash and Hall teased that a third member of their faction would soon debut at *Bash at the Beach* on July 7, 1996, with a hostile takeover match featuring Hall, Nash, and the mystery third man versus WCW wrestlers Sting, Lex Luger, and "Macho Man" Randy Savage.

Hall and Nash came out for the match without their third partner to build anticipation for the big debut. Luger was quickly injured and taken out on a stretcher, so the match was now two-on-two.

Hall and Nash were destroying Savage and Sting — and who should run down to allegedly make the save for the babyfaces, Savage and Sting? Hulk Hogan. But it was a *swerve* (not what fans were expecting). Hogan attacked Savage and crushed him with two atomic legdrops. The unthinkable had just occurred: After being the biggest babyface star in both WWF and WCW for almost 15 straight years, Hulk Hogan had turned heel.

REMEMBER

Hogan cut a post-match promo calling his team the New World Order of wrestling. And with that line, the NWO was born, and it catapulted WCW to the number-one position over WWF in the Monday Night Wars (which you can read about in Chapter 6) for 83 straight weeks, riding the wave of the NWO.

The Montreal Screwjob

In 1997, Vince McMahon, the owner of the WWF, told WWF Champion Bret Hart that the WWF was having financial issues. He suggested Hart negotiate with rival WCW to try to get a deal. Hart and WCW came to an agreement, and Hart was slated to leave WWF.

Traditionally, when a WWF Champion leaves for whatever reason, they *put someone over* (meaning lose to them) before they go. McMahon wanted Hart to lose to Shawn Michaels, whom Hart legitimately hated (the feeling was mutual). Because Hart's WWF contract gave him reasonable creative control, he said he would lose to anyone in the company other than Michaels. And he certainly didn't want to lose to Michaels at November's *Survivor Series* because that show was in Montreal, and Hart was a Canadian national hero.

McMahon agreed to do a disqualification (DQ) finish at *Survivor Series,* after which Hart would either lose the title to someone else on a different show before his contract expired or vacate the title the next night on *Monday Night RAW.* But McMahon was, quite frankly, a liar. He wanted Michaels to beat Hart, and under no circumstances did he want Hart to head to WCW without having lost the WWF title.

WARNING

And so, at *Survivor Series,* McMahon told referee Earl Hebner the plan. When Michaels put Hart into a *sharpshooter submission* (Hart's own hold), Hebner rang the bell and declared Michaels the winner via submission — and then sprinted backstage into a waiting getaway car (seriously). They legitimately double-crossed Hart in front of a live PPV audience. Known as The Montreal Screwjob, this event went down as the most famous pro wrestling finish of all time.

McMahon stated that he knew others felt that he screwed Hart over. McMahon then matter-of-factly stated that the only person who screwed over Bret Hart was Bret Hart. Chapter 6 provides more details about the Montreal Screwjob.

Russo Bashes Hogan at the Beach

In 2000, Vince Russo, creative head of WCW, and former WWF creative team member, came up with a crazy idea to try to save the floundering WCW. Russo, who was also an on-screen character for WCW, wanted to use the *Bash at the Beach* PPV event to convince fans of the following storyline:

- Hulk Hogan forces WCW to make him champion.
- Russo then exposes Hogan to the world.
- Hogan quits the company out of anger.

You're probably asking yourself, "How was this storyline going to turn the ship around for the WCW?" That's a great question, and no one (other than maybe Russo) has an answer.

TIP

Russo also wanted to convince the wrestlers that this storyline was real because the other wrestlers didn't like Hogan, and Russo wanted them to see him as a hero if they thought he exposed Hogan and got him to quit. (If you're still wondering how any of this was going to help the WCW improve its business standing, well, join the club.)

WCW Champion Jeff Jarrett, who wasn't in on any of this storyline, did as requested backstage by Russo for the PPV match; he *laid down* (meaning he literally just laid down on his back) for Hogan and let him win. Hogan, who was in on the storyline, acted all angry in the ring and stormed out of the building in front of all the wrestlers backstage. Russo then came out to do his big victory promo. He outlined the storyline he'd come up with, talking up Jarrett and slamming Hogan (something that is typically never done in professional wrestling). Russo explained that he had been going back and forth with Hogan, who had been flaunting the "creative control" clause in his contract. Russo stated that Hogan decided to change the predetermined outcome of the match. After using very colorful language to describe Hogan, he then stated that the real world championship would be decided in an impromptu match that night, between Booker T and Jeff Jarrett, two people that Russo (and fans) felt were deserving of the opportunity.

Well, everything went according to plan until Russo ended his promo by calling Hogan a "big, bald son of a b----." Hogan ended up legitimately angry at this name-calling to the point that he sued Russo for defamation of character. This storyline designed to make Russo a hero and bolster WCW backfired: Hogan, the biggest draw in WCW history, never worked for the company again.

Flair Delivers a Eulogy for WCW

On March 26, 2001, WCW *Monday Nitro* opened in historic fashion. McMahon, owner of the rival WWF, came on screen to announce that he had just purchased WCW. He went on to say that the promotion's fate was in the palm of his hands. Of course, one of the pillars of WCW, Ric Flair, took umbrage with McMahon's comments stating he was going to hold WCW in the palms of his hands. Flair listed several greats from Harley Race to Ric Steamboat, noting that McMahon could never hold greats such as them. He then noted that it was the last time he'd ever be on Turner Broadcasting and called WCW the greatest wrestling organization.

Flair's final match in WCW would be against his longtime rival Sting. Flair didn't want a somber exit, so he got fired up, which reenergized the crowd. Flair followed up by talking about how much blood and sweat they gave to the business. He took jab after jab at McMahon, stating that McMahon never wrestled for an hour or was on the road 40 straight days.

REMEMBER

McMahon effectively destroyed all the WWF's national competition in 2001, with the death of WCW and Elite Championship Wrestling (ECW). But millions of WCW fans didn't switch to WWF when WCW fell; they just quit watching wrestling. WCW's death was the death of not only the company, but the biggest boom period for pro wrestling up to that point in history. It took nearly two decades and the departure of McMahon himself for now-named World Wrestling Entertainment (WWE) to finally explode again.

The Infamous CM Punk Pipe Bomb

By the time pro wrestler CM Punk signed with World Wrestling Entertainment (WWE) at the end of 2005, he had already made an impressive name for himself on the independent wrestling scene in promotions such as Ring of Honor. But the tattooed, sports-jersey-wearing Chicago native didn't fit the WWE look or carry himself in a corporate style. He won the World Heavyweight Championship in 2008, a secondary belt behind the WWE Championship belt, which John Cena held. And he remained in Cena's shadow for years, never able to achieve his dream of headlining *WrestleMania*, the biggest show of the year.

On the June 27, 2011, episode of WWE *Monday Night RAW*, Punk beat down Cena in the middle of the ring and then sat cross-legged at the top of the entrance ramp and delivered a scathing *shoot promo* (allegedly real, not storyline) about Cena, McMahon, and several of the top brass of WWE — on live television.

Punk took glee in how uncomfortable Cena looked. He also proclaimed that he had several things that he wanted to get off of his chest:

- Punk proclaimed himself to be the best in the world. He stated that Cena wasn't better than Punk at anything, with the exception of kissing the ass of Vince McMahon.
- Said that, just like Brock Lesnar, he was going to split after winning the WWE Championship Title.
- Berated the fans for supporting WWE, even though the company treated him so poorly.
- Said because of McMahon's yes men, he was a millionaire instead of a billionaire.
- Disparaged the McMahon family.

His mic then went dead, with the idea that WWE had cut it to prevent him from saying anything worse.

REMEMBER

Of course, the entire promo was storyline, designed to present Punk as a heel and turn audience support behind McMahon, Cena, and WWE. But the promo backfired (much like the Bret Hart storyline, which we talk about in the section "The Montreal Screwjob" earlier in this chapter). Punk became the voice of the disgruntled WWE fans, a babyface speaking out against the evil corporate empire.

The *pipe bomb* (so named because it felt like a conflagration of reality was unleashed in a tightly scripted show) became an all-time legendary promo. Even after Punk quit the WWE in 2014, fans continued to chant his name during live WWE segments that they hated for years.

Becky Lynch Becomes the Man

In 2018, Becky Lynch (see Figure 15-2) went on a winning streak and quietly became one of the most popular women on the WWE roster. McMahon didn't seem to have his finger on the pulse of the WWE audience at all at this time. He heavily supported Charlotte Flair (daughter of all-time great Ric Flair), whom the audience disliked, and he saw Lynch as just a secondary player, even though the fans had gotten very strongly behind her. Vince had the following storyline take place at the WWE Women's Title match at *SummerSlam* between Lynch, Flair, and the wrestler "Carmella":

» Flair wins the planned match.

» Lynch then attacks Flair, turning heel.

In McMahon's mind, the audience would cheer at Flair's win and boo Lynch's turn to a heel.

FIGURE 15-2: Becky Lynch with Roman Reigns.

Photo by `Wrealano@aol.com`

You can probably imagine what actually happened: When Flair won, fans were furious. And when Lynch turned heel on Flair, fans cheered like crazy.

REMEMBER

Still, McMahon tried to push Lynch as a heel. But the harder he pushed, the harder the fans fought it. Lynch finally won the title from Flair at October 2018's *Hell in a Cell* event, then defended it successfully in the first-ever Last Woman Standing Match at the WWE Women's *Evolution* show on October 28th. On *SmackDown* two days later, Becky cut a promo that changed her career. She touted how she bested everyone, including Flair, and stated, "I am the man."

Lynch stated that though she got folded on a stack of chairs, beaten and put through a table, she found the wherewithal to get up again. She stated that at the end of the *Evolution* event, everyone saw who deserved to be in the main event. She ended with stating that defeating Charlotte Flair proved that Becky Lynch was "The Man".

On the November 12, 2018, episode of *RAW*, Nia Jax accidentally punched Lynch in the face during a multi-person scuffle in the ring, which destroyed Lynch's nose and gave her a concussion. But she didn't go down, and with blood streaming down her face, she finished the angle. The bloody images of Lynch fighting through a broken nose shot her to an even higher level of stardom.

TIP

The injury, the title reign, and taking on the tough-guy persona elevated Lynch to elite status. For a time in 2018 and 2019, she was unquestionably the single biggest star (according to merchandise sales and ratings) in all of professional wrestling — male or female. This was the first (and, at the time of writing, only) time in all of U.S. pro wrestling history that a woman has ever held that spot.

IN THIS CHAPTER

» Seeing sports stars try their hand at professional wrestling

» Getting actors to take a different sort of stage

» Mixing music and professional wrestling showmanship

Chapter 16
Top Ten Celebrity Crossovers

Professional wrestling shares a tight-knit relationship with mainstream entertainment that's existed for decades, including Mexican professional wrestler El Santo joining renowned Mexican actors in films or an actor dressed as the movie character RoboCop showing up at the World Championship Wrestling (WCW) 1990 pay-per-view event, *Capital Combat*. Many wrestlers have crossed over into music ("Macho Man" Randy Savage, with his 2003 studio album *Be a Man*), acting (John Cena and "The Rock"), and even voice acting (Mick Foley voiced a character in the animated movie *Avatar: The Last Airbender*). In addition, several prominent mainstream entertainment icons have made appearances for wrestling promotions. This chapter looks at the top ten crossovers.

Muhammad Ali Takes on Antonio Inoki

Billed as *The War of the Worlds*, the Ali versus Inoki match was the first high profile bout between a boxer and a professional wrestler. The *angle* (storyline) started in 1975 at a formal reception, where Ali made a claim to Ichiro Hatta, then-president of the Japanese Amateur Wrestling Association, that he'd offer a million dollars to any Japanese wrestler who could beat him. One of the most astute minds in Japanese pro wrestling, Antonio Inoki, offered Ali $6 million to lose to Inoki in what was planned to be a *worked* (staged) boxer-versus-wrestler match. Inoki wanted to capitalize on a win over Ali and become one of the most famous wrestlers in the world, and Ali, having never made $6 million for a fight in his life, was willing to do it for that kind of money.

But in the days before the match, he got cold feet over concerns about what a "loss" to Inoki might do to his reputation. The match came very close to falling through. In the end, instead of being cancelled, both sides incredibly agreed to just do a legitimate fight instead.

At the last minute, the match organizers set up a unique set of rules, essentially preventing Inoki from

- Doing *suplexes*, throws, tackles, knee strikes, or elbow strikes
- Using kicks unless the fight transitioned to the ground

REMEMBER

These completely one-sided rules favored Ali. However, in those days, nobody used *leg kicks* (striking the legs), and so the rules didn't ban them. Inoki used that to his advantage. For much of the 15 rounds, Inoki laid on his back and delivered hard kicks to Ali's legs. Ali was unwilling to go to the ground with the grappler. The fight ended in a draw. Furious fans threw trash into the ring and chanted, "Money back!"

The entire event did damage to both fighters:

- **Ali:** The repeated kicks to Ali's legs caused damage in the form of blood clots and infection, almost to the point of requiring amputation. Ali never performed at the same level in a boxing ring ever again. On top of that, he got only $2.1 million of the promised $6 million.
- **Inoki:** His reputation took a huge hit for his perceived lack of fighting spirit, but in the ensuing years, he hired several legitimate combat sports athletes to come to New Japan Pro-Wrestling and lose to him in worked mixed matches; he ultimately became an all-time legend in Japanese professional wrestling.

Despite the damage to the men and to the sport on that day, Ali and Inoki, both showmen of the highest order, developed a lasting friendship.

A King Duels with a Jester

How did a Hall of Fame wrestling champion and commentator such as Jerry "The King" Lawler cross paths with comedian and television star Andy Kaufman? Kaufman, a longtime wrestling fan, began appearing on television shows (including *Saturday Night Live*) in 1981, offering a cash prize to any woman who could beat him in a wrestling match.

Jerry Lawler, the top star of the Tennessee-based Continental Wrestling Association (CWA)'s Memphis territory, agreed to put together a storyline with Kaufman:

- **Wrestling the crowd:** Kaufman began by doing his schtick, legitimately beating several women in the crowd until confronting an actual wrestler, Foxy.
- **Wrestling a pro:** Kaufman won that *worked* match by the skin of his teeth. Jerry Lawler then entered the fray and stated that he'd train Foxy to defeat Kaufman in a rematch.
- **Having a pro rematch:** During that rematch, Kaufman kicked Foxy, which generated tremendous heat (got intense boos, which wrestlers who are heels desire). After a staged argument, Lawler challenged Kaufman to an official match, which Kaufman accepted.
- **Facing Lawler:** On April 5, 1982, before 8,000 fans, Lawler gave Kaufman a banned *piledriver* (a move where you drop someone on their head) and supposedly injured Kaufman's neck (it was pretend). Kaufman began showing up on mainstream TV wearing a neck brace.

Lawler and Kaufman worked their act so well that many people believed it was all legitimate, with one promoter sending Lawler a telegram thanking him for "protecting the business" against outsiders.

A few months later, both men appeared on the TV show *Late Night with David Letterman*, where Kaufman started taunting Lawler, Lawler slapped him, and then Kaufman threw water in Lawler's face and exploded into a profanity-laden tirade.

TIP

It turns out this publicity fit into a bigger plan. The previous month, Lawler had a one-on-one cage match with heel manager Jimmy Hart, whom Lawler supposedly beat within an inch of his life. On January 10, 1983, Lawler challenged AWA Champion Nick Bockwinkle, who was now managed by Hart. Hart came down to ringside completely covered in bandages, looking like a mummy. When Lawler was about to get the win, Hart hit the ring to distract Lawler, and Bockwinkle got the pin. But then Hart removed the bandages — and it wasn't Hart after all, it was Andy Kaufman.

Cyndi Lauper Boosts Women in *WrestleMania I*

Deals for celebrities to appear in professional wrestling programs can happen in the strangest places. Cyndi Lauper met "Captain" Lou Albano, a popular manager with the World Wrestling Federation (WWF) on a flight from Puerto Rico, and the two decided to work together. Albano appeared in Lauper's video for the song "Girls Just Want to Have Fun," and the two did a series of cross-promotional appearances.

On March 31, 1985, Lauper accompanied pro wrestler Wendi Richter in a women's championship match against Leilani Kai, who had the Fabulous Moolah (a women's champion managed by Albano) in her corner. Moolah interfered in the bout several times, and so Lauper got involved, to neutralize Moolah. Richter countered an aerial attack and rolled Kai up for the pinfall victory.

We can't overstate the visibility boost that Lauper gave professional wrestling in the mid-1980s. The ratings, live attendance, and mainstream attention that the WWF garnered throughout 1984 and early 1985 helped catapult WWF's success to new heights. Refer to Chapter 6 for more details about Lauper's involvement.

Mr. T Draws Attention to *WrestleMania I*

Whether it was watching him portray former Army Sergeant B.A. Baracus on the hit television series *The A-Team*, Clubber Lang in *Rocky III*, or himself in his self-titled animated series, anyone who was a child in the 1980s can tell you that actor Laurence Tureaud, also known as Mr. T, played a huge part in their childhood. Mr. T also had a significant impact on the first *WrestleMania*.

During the second *War to Settle the Score* event between Hulk Hogan and Roddy Piper in 1985 Mr. T aligned himself with Hogan, the WWF Champion and top babyface star. Soon after, the WWF announced that Hogan and Mr. T would challenge Piper and "Mr. Wonderful" Paul Orndorff to a tag team match in the main event of the first *WrestleMania*.

As if this event hadn't already generated a ton of mainstream press, boxing icon Muhammad Ali served as a guest referee in the match.

The match almost fell through at the last minute because of concerns about reputations:

» Mr. T worried that one of the wrestlers would legitimately beat him up and kill his mainstream aura as one of the toughest men in the world.

» Neither Orndorff nor Piper wanted to lose to Mr. T, an actor, which required Orndorff agreeing to take the pinfall from Hogan.

Ultimately, Hogan convinced Mr. T that everyone in the match would take care of him, and Orndorff agreed to lose, but only to Hogan.

The match wasn't a great technical wrestling bout, but it was a gigantic business success. The show drew more than a million closed circuit buys and sold nearly 20,000 seats at Madison Square Garden, generating more than $5 million in revenue. It also helped catapult Hogan into mainstream superstardom. Flip to Chapter 6 for more details about this match.

When Giants (Proverbial and Literal) Collide

Here's the storyline of how a National Football League (NFL) two-time Super Bowl Champion Lawrence Taylor ended up in a program against one of the toughest people to ever step foot into a WWF ring, Bam Bam Bigelow:

» **Laughing at the *Royal Rumble*:** At the 1995 *Royal Rumble,* the enormous Bigelow lost a match to the much-smaller Shawn Waltman, also known as the 1-2-3 Kid. Taylor, who was in the crowd, was laughing. Bigelow got into Taylor's face about the laughter. Taylor tried to de-escalate the situation, but Bigelow shoved him to the ground, which led to a short-term suspension (all storyline).

» **Issuing a challenge:** Bigelow challenged the NFL linebacker to a wrestling match, which Taylor at first declined. However, Bigelow's taunting over the next few weeks got under Taylor's skin and he agreed to a match at *WrestleMania.*

» **Training publicly:** WWF set up Taylor's training to be a very public spectacle, even to the point of building a ring in Times Square (the perfect place to shoot an angle where the two men got into a brawl).

» **Flopping:** Though the match itself at *WrestleMania XI* wasn't a masterpiece, Bigelow made Taylor look like a million bucks.

Taylor getting involved with the WWF got mainstream press all over the country, but virtually all of the stories were negative. The show flopped.

Feud Moves from the Court to the Ring

Very rarely do athletes who feud in one sport carry over that rivalry into another sport. On March 16, 1997, Chicago Bulls power forward and basketball's resident bad boy, Dennis "The Worm" Rodman, debuted as a member of the New World Order (NWO), a group led by the iconic Hulk Hogan, at the *Uncensored* pay-per-view event from World Championship Wrestling (WCW).

While this storyline unfolded, Rodman was also competing in the National Basketball Association (NBA) Finals, where the Bulls defeated the Utah Jazz four games to two. Fortune shined upon the star player for the Jazz, "The Mailman" Karl Malone, who struck up a friendship with WCW star Diamond Dallas Page (DDP) and ended up his tag team partner.

At the July 1998 *Bash at the Beach* pay-per-view event, Hogan and Rodman faced Page and Malone in a main event that (if you include entrances and extracurriculars) went an astonishing 45 minutes. The match itself was atrocious. Rodman allegedly showed up in no condition to perform, and at one point appeared to put his head down on the top turnbuckle while waiting for a tag and fell asleep. Outside interference allowed Hogan and Rodman to pick up the victory.

As horrible as the match was, from a business standpoint, the program was a success. Along with a blitzkrieg of media attention, the pay-per-view did a whopping 1.5 *buy rate* (percentage of people with PPV access who bought the show), the second highest in the history of WCW. Of all the celebrities that WCW brought in over the years (and they brought in a lot: everyone from the Godfather of Soul James Brown to comedian and late night TV host Jay Leno), Rodman by far generated the most revenue.

Mike Tyson Coronates "Stone Cold" Steve Austin

In the mid-1990s, the WWF began pushing a younger generation of stars. The newest star on the rise was "Stone Cold" Steve Austin. Austin won the 1998 WWF *Royal Rumble*, guaranteeing him a title shot at *WrestleMania XIV*. The story of five-time World Heavyweight Champion and boxing legend "Iron" Mike Tyson and Austin played out in three events:

- ***Monday Night RAW:*** Vince McMahon brought in Tyson as a celebrity guest enforcer on a January 1998 edition of *Monday Night RAW*. When "Stone Cold" walked down to the ring, Tyson tried to shake his hand, but Austin flipped Tyson off, and Tyson began shoving Austin. Dozens of security guards came in to separate the two men.

  REMEMBER

  This clash was one of the most famous angles in the history of pro wrestling, generating mainstream headlines literally all over the world. Every major national network in the United States aired the footage, and every major newspaper worldwide wrote about the event. It gained considerable attention as far away as Japan, where fans considered Tyson an icon.

- **Another *Monday Night RAW:*** In March 1998, Tyson returned to *RAW*, this time confronted by the current champion, the "Heartbreak Kid" Shawn Michaels and the faction Degeneration-X, which included Triple H and Chyna. Just when it looked like a brawl was about to break out, Michaels ripped off Tyson's shirt to reveal that he had a Degeneration-X T-shirt on underneath. It looked like Michaels had the referee, the self-professed "Baddest Man on the Planet," (according to boxing promoters and the media) in his back pocket.

- ***WrestleMania:*** During the main event of *WrestleMania XIV*, Tyson wasn't overtly on the side of D-X, feigning impartiality in the early minutes of the match. However, when Michaels knocked out the referee, Tyson assumed referee duties and delivered a fast three-count to give Austin the victory and the WWF Championship.

  A visibly upset Michaels demanded answers from Tyson. However, Tyson knocked Michaels out and ripped off his own D-X shirt to reveal a Stone Cold T-shirt underneath.

This storyline, and the ascension of Austin to the top of the WWF, acted as the tipping point that thrust WWF back to the top spot over WCW, a position they never lost again.

Battle of the Billionaires

Real-life friends Vince McMahon and Donald Trump worked together in 2006 and 2007 to create a storyline for *WrestleMania XXIII*, the highest-grossing *WrestleMania* up to that point that set the record for worldwide pay-per-view (PPV) buys. Here's how the story went:

- WWE held a mock wrestling match between celebrity lookalikes impersonating Trump and Rosie O'Donnell, who had beef in real life.
- A few weeks later, on *RAW*, while McMahon was delivering a promo, the actual Donald Trump appeared on the Titantron to relay a message that he could run World Wrestling Entertainment (WWE) better than McMahon.
- After weeks of bickering, the two agreed that each could have a representative wrestle on their behalf at *WrestleMania XXIII*, with the "Samoan Bulldozer" Umaga wrestling on behalf of McMahon and the "All Mighty" Bobby Lashley wrestling on behalf of Trump.

They agreed that the person the loser represented would have their head shaved. In a less-than-fair match, which had "Stone Cold" Steve Austin as a guest referee, Lashley was declared the winner. McMahon, who squirmed and cringed, got his head shaved. Though Austin shared beers with Trump at the end of the match, he then delivered a *stunner* (Austin's finishing move) to "The Donald."

The key to the success of this storyline was a combination of factors; an incredible amount of mainstream buzz and a simple storyline where two men with very famous heads of hair were involved in a match where one of them, for the first time in history, would be shaved bald for the world to see.

Floyd Mayweather Delivers Knockouts

What does a man who dominated the world of boxing with 13 championships and an undefeated record do when his schedule in 2008 clears up? For Floyd "Money" Mayweather, the answer was enter the world of professional wrestling:

- ***No Way Out:*** On February 17, 2008, Mayweather appeared in the crowd at WWE's *No Way Out* PPV event, jumped the guardrail, and came to the rescue of one of the company's top babyfaces, Rey Mysterio, who was being attacked by the 7-foot, 400-pound giant, Paul Wight, known as "The Big Show." Because of the enormous size difference, Wight taunted Mayweather, then got down on one knee and let Mayweather have the first punch. Mayweather proceeded to unleash several straight shots to the face of "The Big Show" (resulting in a legitimately broken nose — this ain't ballet, as they say), before Wight chased Mayweather out of the ring.

- ***Monday Night RAW:*** The next evening, "The Big Show" called out Mayweather, challenging him to a *No Disqualification match* (meaning anything goes) at *WrestleMania XXIV.*
- ***WrestleMania XXIV:*** Mayweather and Wight battled each other until Mayweather won with a knockout.

Some outlets claimed that Mayweather netted $20 million for this match, but the real figure was closer to $2 to $5 million. Given that the PPV made more than $50 million in revenue, Mayweather was more than worth the cost.

Shaquille O'Neal Was All Elite

The 7-foot-1-inch multi-time NBA champion and Most Valuable Player Shaquille O'Neal made several non-wrestling appearances for WWE, such as *WrestleMania* 32. O'Neal made his professional wrestling TV debut in All Elite Wrestling (AEW) at the end of 2020, getting involved in an already heated feud between Jade Cargill versus Brandi and Cody Rhodes:

- **Hints:** Cargill hinted at O'Neal's involvement on the November 11, 2020, AEW *Dynamite* event, saying that Cody Rhodes had "awoken the beast" (referring to Shaq).
- **Cameo:** O'Neal appeared on the Young Bucks supplementary YouTube series *Being the Elite.*
- **Interview:** On the December 9 *Dynamite* event, commentator Tony Schiavone moderated an interview with Brandi Rhodes (recovering from an injury at the hands of Jade Cargill) and O'Neal. After terse words were exchanged, Brandi threw water at Shaq and left.
- **Dynamite:** Red Velvet, in the injured Brandi's place, teamed with Cody to take on Cargill and Shaq on the March 3, 2021, episode of *Dynamite.*

REMEMBER

This match took place one year into the COVID-19 pandemic, and so AEW allowed only small crowds into their weekly shows at Daily's Place in Florida. For that reason, they missed out on a gigantic gate. They did, however, draw more than 1 million viewers on TNT, their highest number in over a year.

Index

Numerics

A

B

C

D

E

F

G

H

I

J

K

L

M

N

O

P

Q

R

S

T

U

V

W

X

Y

Z

About the Authors

Bryan Alvarez wanted to do several things growing up — write books, host a radio show, and become a pro wrestler. You can argue that he was too dumb to realize that these goals were foolish, and thus he succeeded in all three. He's the author of *100 Things WWE Fans Should Know and Do Before They Die* (Triumph Books), as well as the co-author with R.D. Reynolds of the award-winning and bestselling *Death of WCW* (ECW Press), originally published in 2004 and remaining in print to this day.

He's the co-owner of news and commentary site *Wrestling Observer/Figure Four Online* (`www.f4wonline.com`), where he hosts more than a dozen podcasts every week. He's also hosted the radio program "Wrestling Observer Live" since 1999, when it debuted on the very first internet streaming radio service, and continues to air on Sports Byline USA terrestrial radio seven days a week. He has produced more than 18,000 audio and video shows, all archived on his website. He lives in Bothell, Washington, with his beloved children Paisley and Hanalei, whose names he put in this book in the hopes that they'll consider him cool for maybe a few more years.

Gene Selassie has had two interests since childhood: comic books and pro wrestling. As an adult, he covered the former at comic news publication Graphic Policy and pop culture platform Geeks Have Game, while covering the latter at news sites `OneOfUs.net` and The Scrum Sports. That background led him to writing his first book, *And How They Rumbled: The 80 Best Pro Wrestling Bouts over the Past 40 Years.* He is no stranger to the *For Dummies* brand because he wrote *Avengers For Dummies* (John Wiley & Sons, Inc.), about the Marvel comic superhero team. His writing has taken him through the worlds of prose, comic books, sports journalism, and even screenwriting, earning him an Eisner Award and a Ringo Award nomination in the process. He resides in Texas with his wife and stepsons, who are all as geeky as he is.

Dedication

Bryan: This time, this one is for me — a dummy.

Gene: This book is dedicated to my family, friends, fellow creators, and every single person who has shown me love and supported each of my creative endeavors. Without you, this wouldn't be possible.

Authors' Acknowledgments

Bryan: I'd like to thank all my friends and family too numerous to mention, but particularly Mom and Dad and Granny, without whom I simply wouldn't be where I am today. As it regards this book, thank you so much to Jennifer Yee, Tim Gallan, Chad Sievers, and Laura Miller at Wiley, and of course my awesome co-author Gene for kicking open the door to make this happen. A huge thank you to Tony Leder and Dave Meltzer, and everyone who works so hard at `f4wonline.com`, and all my friends — yes, friends — who subscribe. And most importantly, in the case of this particular book, thank you a million times over to Lance Storm, "Filthy" Tom Lawlor, and Karl Stern, who advised me on every single chapter as only the best of friends can, by repeatedly telling me how absolutely stupid I was for writing something. I couldn't have done this without their help, and I'm forever grateful. And finally, to Hanalei and Paisley, your daddy loves you so much.

Gene: I thank Jennifer Yee, Tim Gallan, Chad Sievers, and Laura Miller from Wiley Publishing. Their continued faith in me is greatly appreciated. Props to Chris Cox and Wright Sulek at `OneOfUs.net`, along with Trevor Grout at The Scrum Sports for giving Gene the platform to write about the sport that he so dearly loves. I also thank Richard Whittaker for the time devoted to co-hosting and editing the *Thumbtacks & Screwjobs* podcast. Finally, I give a shout-out to every professional wrestler I've ever met, who were nothing but kind and more than gracious with their time: ACH, Angelina Love, Booker T, Jay and Mark Briscoe, Christopher Daniels, Eddie Guerrero, Matt Hardy, Mark Henry, Chris Jericho, Frankie Kazarian, Jay Lethal, Ricky Saints, Ron Simmons, Elix Skipper, Trish Stratus, and the hundreds of others that I don't have the room to list.

Publisher's Acknowledgments

Senior Acquisition Editor: Jennifer Yee

Project Manager and Development Editor: Chad R. Sievers

Copy Editor: Laura K. Miller

Senior Managing Editor: Kristie Pyles

Production Editor: Umeshkumar Rajasekhar

Cover Image: Patricia Marroquin/Getty Images